AF512433

HOUSING IN THE THIRD WORLD

HOUSING
IN
THE THIRD WORLD
Analyses and Solutions

Edited by
LESLIE KILMARTIN
HARJINDER SINGH

CONCEPT PUBLISHING COMPANY, NEW DELHI 110059

ISBN 81-7022-284-2

First Published 1992

© Editors

Published and Printed by
Ashok Kumar Mittal
Concept Publishing Company
A/15-16, Commercial Block, Mohan Garden
NEW DELHI 110059 (India)

Lasertypeset by
Microtech Advance Printing Systems (Pvt.) Ltd.
H-13, Bali Nagar
NEW DELHI 110015

PREFACE

This volume is one of a series of publications to emerge from the activities of the Research Committee on Housing and the Built Environment of the International Sociological Association (ISA). The Former Working Group, elevated to Research Committee status by the ISA at its recent meeting in Madrid, also conducts a vigorous programme of international conferences and seminars for its more than 300 members.

In this collection of readings, we have attempted to compile a source-book which will be of use to both students of housing and to urban policy-makers in Third World countries. The contributors are drawn from a wide range of countries and disciplines. They have provided a set of chapters with contemporary relevance and whose contents and reference material will prove invaluable. It would be a quite futile task to attempt to be comprehensive in coverage of this enormous and complex topic. We have therefore been selective in our choice of contributions and believe we have achieved considerable success in addressing the most important issues.

LESLIE KILMARTIN
HARJINDER SINGH

CONTENTS

Part III: Solutions

LIST OF CONTRIBUTORS

Leslie Kilmartin,
Centre for Urban and Social Research, Swinburne,
Institute of Technology,
Melbourne - Australia.

Carole Rakodi,
Department of Town Planning,
University of Wales,
Cardiff - UK.

Harjinder Singh,
G.R. School of City and Regional Planning,
Guru Nanak Dev University,
Amritsar - India.

Mary Jo Huth,
Department of Sociology and Anthropology,
University of Dayton,
Dayton - Ohio - USA.

Suzana Pasternak Taschner,
School of Architecture and Urbanism,
University of Sao Paulo,
Sao Paulo - Brazil.

Claudio Acioly Jr.,
The Dutch Development Organisation,
Sny - Bissau,
Guinea - Bissau.

Lucia Maria M. Bogus,
Department of Sociology,
University of Sao Paulo,
Sao Paulo - Brazil.

Patricia Klobus Edwards,
Department of Urban Affairs and Planning,
Virginia Polytechnic Institute and State University,
Blacksburg - Virginia - USA.

A Graham Tripple,
Centre for Architectural Research and Development Overseas,
University of Newcastle,
Upontyne - UK.

Kenneth G. Willis,
Department of Town and Country Planning,
University of Newcastle,
Upontyne - UK.

Earl W. Morris,
Department of Design, Housing Apparel,
University of Minnesota
Minnestota - USA.

Mary Winter,
Department of Family Environment,
IOWA State University,
USA.

Arthur D. Murphy,
Department of Anthropology,
Baylor University,
USA.

Charles L. Choguill,
Department of Town and Regional Planning,
Sheffield University,
Sheffield - UK.

Makau Kiamba,
Department of Land Development,
University of Nairobi
Nairobi - Kenya.

Kosta Mathey,
Department of Architecture and Applied Sociology,
University of Kassel,
Kassel - Germany.

Roy Dark,
Department of Town and Regional Planning,
Sheffield University,
Sheffield - UK.

D. Alexander,
Department of Town and Regional Planning,
Sheffield University,
Sheffield - UK.

Jean Darke,
Department of Town and Regional Planning,
Sheffield University,
Sheffield - UK.

A. Manogue,
Department of Town and Regional Planning,
Sheffield University,
Sheffield - UK.

Naomi, Carmon,
Faculty of Architecture and Town Planning,
Israel Institute of Technology,
Haifa - Israel.

Medhat M. Hassan,
College of Environmental Design,
King Fahd University of Petroleum and Minerals,
Dhahran - Saudi Arabia.

LIST OF FIGURES AND TABLES

Figures

Tables

INTRODUCTION:
Analyses, Contexts and Solutions

LESLIE KILMARTIN

It is a sobering experience to contemplate the housing problems of the Third World countries. The sheer scale and complexity of their problems and the enormity of their implications — not only for the people of those countries but for all humankind — are daunting prospects. According to estimates by the United Nations, in thirtyfive years' time, half of the world's 8.4 billion people will live in the cities of the developing world. Moreover, nearly half of those urban dwellers will be in slums and squatter settlements (UNDP, June 1990). Other anlyses suggest that 25 million new households will be added to the urban areas of the developing countries by the end of this century (Rondinelli, 1990). The need for appropriate responses from governments in both the under-developed and developed countries and from private sources could hardly be more obvious or more urgent.

Governments have responded in a variety of ways but rarely adequately. This is due to a complex set of reasons including inadequate resources, lack of commitment, and the inertia of class-based and sometimes corrupt bureaucracies in highly stratified societies. As well, there is a continuing belief identified in a number of the following chapters that government investment should be in the 'productive' sectors of the economy rather than in fields such as housing.

As inventive as the human mind may be, only a small range of types of solutions can be devised. We see in the literature as well as in the following contributions the swing away from direct state provision of housing. Instead, there are programmes to upgrade and legitimise squatter settlements and the provision of residential sites, minimally serviced by government, no which households can construct their own dwellings employing local materials and appropriate technology. All too often, these schemes and others outlined below fail to assist those for whom they are allegedly intended.

These scenarios are not, of course, the inevitable outcomes of some iron law of human development. There are some hopeful signs and some of these are reviewed in the following chapters. It appears, however, that we should not expect rapid progress in housing provision in developing countries. There are too many forces at work to give us much hope for that. For example, as Gulati notes, the housing problems of the Third World must be seen in context. While such problems are highly conspicuous in and around urban settlements, they are merely the most visible manifestation of the pain that accompanies economic and social transformation. Housing cannot, therefore, be considered in isolation from the prevailing social, economic and political climate (Gulati, 1985).

The papers in this collection fall into three broad groups. Allocation to one or other of these is, of course, somewhat arbitrary but is designed to assist the reader by adopting some logical ordering. *Part I* provides papers which give analytical overviews of the topic while *Part II* contains contributions which refer to contexts in which the provision of housing may be usefully set. Finally, *Part III* presents papers which propose solutions to the problems of housing provision in the Third World.

I. ANALYSES

The first reading in this section provides a broad introduction to the topic. Carole Rakodi reviews theoretical and empirical approaches to housing in the Third World and usefully sets the scene for the whole set of readings in this volume. Her fundamental message is as simple as it is profound, namely that the way forward in housing policy research is to consider housing for the urban poor within the context of the housing sector as a whole. Such analyses will then lead to the development of sectoral rather than sectional policies. Specifically, this means that housing analyses must take into account supply and demand, and the production and consumption of housing across all income groups. Moreover, a fuller understanding of housing markets will be achieved through analyses pitched at both city and national levels. In the following set of readings, various authors take up this challenge.

A further important orientation provided by Rakodi relates to theoretical perspectives. By and large, the authors in this volume do not explicitly develop theoretical arguments and Rakodi provides a reminder that a fuller understanding of housing—whether in the developed or the Third World countries—will be well-served by attention to this matter. Nonetheless, Rakodi herself demonstrates the frustrations that researchers encounter in relying on one or other of the major mega-theories: neo-classical economics and the political economy perspective. In her discussion, she outlines the essentials of each as applied to the question of housing in the Third World countries. In the end, however, she demonstrates that each has its strengths and weaknesses. Though she does not make the point herself, it is worth noting that neither is of much use to policy-makers or to scholars attempting to make policy recommendations. The perceived advantage of the political economy perspective, from Rakodi's standpoint, is that is directs the researcher to the economic, political and social contexts of housing.

A second major contribution in Rakodi's paper is her assertion that particular attention should be paid to the producers of housing. This will lead into an account of the central actors in this process, their class affiliation and interests and the important areas of access to land for residential development, the work of service agencies, the structure and capacity of the residential construction sector, the supply of building materials, and the availability of construction skills.

The other three papers included in this first overview section deal with housing in three very different countries, India, China and Brazil. Singh's review of recent housing problems and policies in India reveal that little progress appears to have been made in solving one of that country's most pressing problems. Indeed, he reveals that India's rate of construction of shelter is one of the lowest in the world. This fact needs to be seen in the context of India as a relatively industrialised economy in the developing world.

Singh shows how Indian housing policy has progressed through the familiar stages of housing programmes, slum clearance and relocation schemes, environmental improvement and upgrading of slum schemes, and sites and services schemes. All were found to have serious deficiencies. At base, no matter what policies have been introduced, it is apparent that a high proportion of the Indian population simply cannot afford any form of decent housing. Even a high proportion of households above the poverty line (60%) endure some form of environmental degradation which detracts from their residential quality.

In the end, Singh concludes, the chief factor working against progress in the field of housing in India is the same factor which blocks social progress generally and which maintains the profound wealth and income inequalities, that is, the class structure. Moreover, the Indian State has consistently acted in ways which reinforce that structure and which support the powerful upper and middle classes.

In her review of housing policy in China since 1949, Huth shows that for a majority of that time, public investment in housing was deliberately held down since it was seen to be an unproductive segment of the economy. As a consequence, housing is one of the foremost problems facing China today. As from 1978 and the reforms introduced following the death of Mao Zedong, new attention was devoted to housing as part of an orientation that recognised the city as the motor of development in China.

On the face of it, the situation of housing in China might appear quite satisfactory especially compared with that in India outlined by Singh. Generally, more of the people of China are housed and they are better housed. Their rents are very low indeed as well. However, official policy aimed at gradual increases in the average amount of living space available to urban residents in China has failed. In Huth's view, the current policy to increase average living space to 8 square meters per person by the year 2000 will also fail. Huth goes on to enumerate a set of deficiencies in housing in Chinese cities which have to do with factors such as type of housing (an over-emphasis on high rise apartments), problems of land accessibility and cost, poor building materials, insufficient attention to housing rehabilitation, abuses of power by minor officials and corruption.

Above all, Huth notes the emerging power of the *danwei.* These are industrial enterprises or companies which are responsible for many social service functions in addition to purely business ones. Huth shows how the larger, more powerful *danwei* exercise disproportionate influence in the housing systems of Chinese cities such as Beijing. In effect, the *danwei* appear to act as class fractions in a notionally classless society. Certainly, as far as urban resources are concerned, these enterprises act to secure and maintain privilege.

The theme of social and class inequality at the national level is also taken up by Taschner in her paper on housing in Brazil. She notes by way of introduction that Brazil is a country characterised by strong regional and social differentiation and she goes on to show how these processes are played out with respect to housing. While there have been some objective improvements in housing stock, quality and provision, severe problems remain.

One of the enduring facets of Brazilian housing is the presence of the *favelas* or squatter settlements in and around the major urban settlements. For a long time, government policy regarded these settlements as expendable and various attempts were made to bulldoze them and to relocate their residents to more peripheral locations. These programmes were abject failures and have been officially recognised as such. Now the *favelas* are being upgraded with more appropriate services.

As with the analysis of both India and China, Taschner identifies the class structure as basic to the housing problems of Brazil. There continues to be a maldistribution of the country's wealth and over 34 per cent of Brazilian families live at the poverty level. This fact needs to be set against the analysis provided by the author of the activities of the National Housing Bank over a two-decade period. In effect, the bank relentlessly pursued policies and programmes to promote home-ownership. Apart from promoting the well-being of various sectors of private enterprise through a massive construction programme, the bank's policies resulted in a disproportionately low number of low income households benefiting directly from their actions.

These three papers, then, provide a useful introduction to this collection in that they comply with certain of the guidelines set out by Rakodi in the first paper. In particular, they relate housing policies, programmes and issues to the larger class structure of the society. In all three we see class and stratification systems being played out in the field of housing. As well, the processes of industrialisation, urbanisation and modernisation play their part in setting the scene for the housing problems identified in all three societies. The authors outline for us the failures of official housing policies and bring forcefully to centre stage the complex interplay between policy formulation, ideology and policy evaluation.

II. CONTEXTS

In this section are five papers which are devoted to the contexts in which housing is planned and provided and in which housing policies are developed. Four reveal deficiencies in aspects of planning which have a direct bearing on the provision of housing. The paper by Acioly highlights problems inherent in the land-use planning system of Brazil while that by Bogus on Sao Paulo reviews some of the regressive effects of state intervention in the urban system. Edwards outlines deficiencies in a USAID programme intended to disseminate information about appropriate technology while Tipple and Willis and Morris *et al.* discuss aspects of owner occupation.

Acioly's paper about the development of Brasilia is a telling critique of city planning and its attendant ideologies. In establishing its new national capital, the Government of Brazil wanted to create a grand and dramatic example of contemporary land-use planning. Drawn directly from elitist notions of the French planner Le Corbusier, Brasilia was to be an administrative capital whose bold urban design would render it a symbol of the nation and a city of international significance. It would also act as an engine for regional development. The dream, however, went terribly wrong. Population projections were shown to be hopelessly inadequate as the new city became a magnet for low income residents of the region seeking to improve their lot. Far from being the planners' ideal city with high quality life styles and housing and a middle class population, Brasilia quickly became surrounded by poor squatter settlements and labour camps. The report is a powerful reminder of the flaws endemic in technocratic, elitist, top-down planning.

Employing a political economy perspective, Bogus reports on a case study of urban regeneration in a suburb of Sao Paulo, Brazil. A political decision had been made to construct a major transport terminal in a locality which had a high proportion of residents who had migrated from rural locations. As one expects in a market capitalist system, the mere announcement of the project led to land speculation, land price inflation, increased rents for tenants and, presumably, increased property values for owner occupiers. In a series of 3 resident surveys, Bogus was able to show the regressive impacts of this state project on poor migrant residents. From a metropolitan wide perspective, the case study shows the process of social segregation at work as market forces dictate land-use and therefore social composition of specific metropolitan locations.

In her paper on the diffusion of information about appropriate technology for housing development, Edwards reveals the fate of a programme supported by USAID in the Dominican Republic. She shows how the whole programme was based on false assumptions which eventually led to a lessening of its intended impact. One serious flaw appears to be the relatively small proportion of funds granted to research and development activities as opposed to those devoted to diffusion of information. There were also serious organisational weaknesses, a failure to take into account the economic situation of the nation as a whole and an over-ambitiousness. Edwards concludes this case study of organisational failure with a review of some of the more general deficiencies of the appropriate technology approach.

Although several papers in this collection deal with the question of tenure, two are predominantly devoted to that matter and address slightly unusual aspects, at least as far as housing in developing nations is concerned. Tipple and Willis report the findings of a case study in the town of Kumasi in Ghana. They note that renting in the private market has often been assumed by many analysts to represent a transitional stage before the household enters the more desirable status of owner occupancy. They recall that many scholars and governments favour home-ownership as bestowing greater benefits for both the household and the society than renting. Against this, however, is the view that home-ownership is not necessarily a undisputed good and that renting may be a more desirable tenure form in some circumstances. There is also the important point developed by the World Bank that private landlordism both generates investment in housing and costs government little or nothing.

The authors go on to show with their case study that among the tenure groups in Kumasi, few benefits of a material kind flow to owners over tenants. Much more significant are the differences which derive from differential access to services in the household. A noteworthy feature of this paper is the use of multivariate analyses of survey data. As Gilbert and Varley (1990) found in their study of 2 Mexican settlements, within tenant and owner categories, there is a good deal of variation in terms of income. These observations from such diverse settings should serve to remind us of the dangers of assuming the applicability of models from the more developed societies where owner occupancy is usually an indicator of higher income.

The authors also show that such techniques have a useful role in housing research in the Third World countries and they demonstrate that they can be used not only to order data in meaningful ways but also to derive predictions which may be of use in the policy-making process.

An equally unusual approach is that employed by Morris *et al.* in their survey of resident of Oaxaca in Mexico. Proceeding from a 'housing adjustment model' derived from north American research strategies, the authors survey male and female residents concerning their views of their housing needs and preferences. This represents a type of consumer sovereignty research rarely assumed to be applicable in the study of the poor of the Third World societies. The researchers are guided in this by the assumption that a sound housing policy can only be derived from knowledge of the needs, aspirations, values, intentions, satisfactions and housing conditions of households.

On the matter of tenure, the researchers find an overwhelming preference among Oaxaca residents for owner-occupancy. This finding is confirmed for two other Mexican cities by Gilbert and Varley (1990). As a corollary, private tenure is not preferred and, perhaps not surprisingly, is relatively unavailable. Unlike their American counterparts, new Oaxacan households tend to proceed to home-ownership as quickly as they can, settling for smaller dwellings which can later be extended as funds become available. They are highly independent of both government and family assistance in either buying or building their houses.

III. SOLUTIONS

This section contains a number of papers which discuss solutions to the problems of housing undertaken in several Third World countries. There is no one solution, of course, partly due to the rather different problems facing each country and partly due to the resources and reformist tendencies of different local and national governments. Above all, there is no absolute solution as well because the problems of housing are merely a sub-set of the problems of inequality within and between countries. Nonetheless, most authors assume that some ameliorative measures can be developed.

Choguill provides a useful overview of policy solutions which have been implemented in various countries over recent years. He tends to favour the approach based on the work of Turner and of Mangin who assume that the poor are rational and that, given opportunities and resources, they will achieve their own housing improvements. It is unlikely, however, that the same solutions are appropriate for all situations. He speculates that sites and services and upgrading schemes are more relevant in higher income countries of the Third

World while subsidies might be more appropriate for the poorest. In the former case, Choguill warns against the mindless application of housing and planning standards 'derived from other (wealthier) countries and other times. If it is important — as it certainly appears to be — to reduce housing costs, then standards should be reviewed so that they reflect indigenous conditions.

Urban regeneration in Nairobi, Kenya, is the focus of the contribution by Kiamba. As we see in other countries, rural-urban migration over the past three decades has brought about significant housing and related problems in Kenya. In the mid-1960s, studies showed that up to 70 per cent of households in Nairobi could not afford legal housing. To deal with this problem, the Government of Kenya introduced legislation which adopted a 'realistic' urban housing policy which at the one time acknowledged urban squatting an inevitable fact of modern life, recognised the need to harness both local and international capital to address the problem, and acknowledged the undesirability of imposing high housing and planning standards on squatter settlements.

In line with development elsewhere in the Third World countries, a new role for government was identified, namely to provide the land and to ensure security of tenure and basic services. This meant that government would legitimise and upgrade squatter settlements and that private enterprise would undertake the provision of finance for housing and development.

This new approach, implemented during the 1970s, met with some successes though Kiamba alerts us to two problems, one practical and the other analytical. The practical deficiency of the programme is that in the projects reported, studies reveal that in the end, only three-quarters of the occupations of new housing were those originally provided with financial assistance. As is so often the case, a sizeable proportion of the intended beneficiaries simply were unable to sustain repayments; they were obliged to sell their houses to more affluent persons.

The second analytical of theoretical matter relates to the role of the Kenyan State and its collaboration with national and international capital. Adopting a political economy framework, Kiamba reviews the familiar arguments about the benefits to the capitalist system as a whole and to individual capitalist enterprises of having a well-housed, indebted labour force contributing actively to its own housing construction and therefore to its own oppression and enslavement. In the end, Kiamba seems to acknowledge that even if this analysis is correct, it nevertheless is the case that without bridging the capital gap, there is no possibility of addressing housing problems in developing countries. Of course, the same arguments are equally applicable in the more developed countries.

The next two reports are from the Third World countries which have explicitly rejected the intrusion of and reliance on capitalist enterprises to address their severe housing problems. In both cases, they are countries whose governments are avowedly socialist and who therefore attempt to solve the same housing problems with means derived directly from the socialist perspective. These two papers are concerned with forms of community-based programmes for housing provision. Interestingly, both deal with Latin American societies where the traditions of self-help and community based housing programmes have taken root.

Furthermore, both societies have relatively recent revolutionary experiences which provide valuable reservoirs of national commitment which can be tapped in various forms, including that of the philosophy of voluntary work.

The first of the two papers is by Mathey who reviews the development of the Microbrigadas in the early 1970s in Castro's Cuba. While the experiment was very successful in providing housing aside from that provided by the state and by individual self-build housing, by the end of the decade, certain difficulties had emerged with the Microbrigada's work. In particular, it emerged that the methods employed were not as efficient as those that would derive from more skilled workers producing in a more industrialised system.

A new opportunity for collective self-build housing emerged in the 1980s, however, due to the shortage of housing for the growing population. This time, certain corrections were made to the Microbrigada programme including a more equitable distribution of housing to those in need rather than exclusively to those members of brigades. The chapter concludes with a valuable discussions of the later refinements to the movement and its applicability to other Third World countries.

The potential for self-build practices in the Third World countries is also one of the focuses of the chapter by Darke, *et al.* In reviewing the reforms of the Sandanista government of Nicaragua, these authors show the need that emerged for collective efforts to solve the critical housing shortage in that country post-1979. They warn that self-help is not a panacea and does not remove the need for state involvement in housing provision.

They also confront criticisms of some referred to above that self-help programmes are ploys which socialise the poor into the market economy and which can be used by governments to absolve themselves of responsibilities for housing the poor. In the end, Darke *et al.*, while acknowledging the force of these arguments, remind us that we should beware of losing sight of the potential social, political and ideological benefits of self-help housing in a collective and socialist context which may give powers of democratic decision-making down to the level of the neighbourhood. And, Merrett (1988) argues, self-build housing cannot be viewed as a form of double exploitation, in Marxian terms.

While Israel is not considered to be a Third World country in the sense that other countries in this collection are, Carmon's report on housing upgrading and sales of public housing might provide useful solutions in some Third World countries. Project Renewal was a national programme of housing renewal introduced by the national government in the early 1980s to address the problem of housing rehabilitation in distressed (by Israeli standard) neighbourhoods. Much of the housing in these neighbourhoods had been constructed hastily some forty years earlier and was now in need of major repair.

The most successful solution designed by the government was a programme of what Carmon calls public-individual partnerships whereby the state provided resources to householders to either rehabilitate or to enlarge their dwellings. A perceived advantage of this scheme was the directness of the relationship between the state and the householder with no 'middle-men' extracting their share of the resources.

Ultimately about 50 per cent of the dwellings in the ten study areas benefited from the scheme and this included a range of low and middle income households. Among the positive outcomes were the high proportion of those expressing satisfaction with the result, the objective increase in housing standards in the participating neighbourhoods and the sense of achievement of the participating individuals. Carmon also highlights the benefits to the state of Israel which achieved major improvements in the durability of housing stock through the efforts of its occupants, whether public tenants or owner-occupiers.

The generation of housing finance is the main focus of the chapter by Hassan. Referring to the situation in Egypt over the past four decades, the author shows how the state has devoted a declining proportion of its expenditures to housing. One is not surprised to learn that the declining state funds tend to be disproportionately directed to upper income groups. The problem has been exacerbated by the fact that the state has been receiving less revenue due to certain policy changes. Add to this the problem of increased rural-urban migration and the severity of the situation can be begun to be appreciated.

Hassan proposes a package of solutions to the problem which would have wide applicability if they are feasible. In effect, he outlines a series of steps that could be taken to stimulate private savings and he sets out the arguments in favour of the use of subsidies to low-income households. These, he argues, must be direct to the householder so as to subsidise consumers rather than producers and so as to maximise the ingenuity and enterprise of the householder through self-determined solutions. The remainder of Hassan's solutions are concerned with reducing costs of house construction.

CONCLUSION

In a recent review of programmes designed to provide housing in the Third World nations, Rondinelli (1990) acknowledges, as many of our contributors do, that the old programmes must now be supplemented with new approaches. In particular, he notes that a growing consensus is emerging among urban experts that there must be a heavier reliance on private sector provision. In addition, he suggests number of new approaches which should be considered. The following chapters shed empirical light on these suggestions and add considerably to the body of knowledge on housing provision in Third World countries.

REFERENCES

UNDP (June 1990), *Source* (Special Report: The Urban Challenge), Division of Information, United Nations Development Programme : 5.

Gilbert, Alan and Ann Varley (1990), 'Renting a Home in a Third World City: Choice or Constraint?' *International Journal of Urban and Regional Research*, 14(1).

Gulati, Padmini (1985), 'Introduction to Part III: The Provision of Housing; Self-Help Arrangements in Less-Industrialised Countries', in Willem van Vliet *et al.* (eds.) (1985), *Housing Needs and Policy Approaches: Trends in Thirteen Countries*, Durham, Duke University Press: 203.

Merrett, Stephen (1988), 'Self-Build Housing and the Exploitation of Labour', *Housing Studies*, 3, (4):247-9.

Rondinelli, Dennis A. (1990), 'Housing the Urban Poor in Developing Countries', *The American Journal of Economics and Sociology*, 49(3): 258.

PART I

ANALYSES

1

HOUSING MARKETS IN THIRD WORLD CITIES: Research and Policy into the 1990s[1]

CAROLE RAKODI[2]

INTRODUCTION

For many years, research on housing in the cities of developing countries focused on the most immediate and visible housing problems: those of the urban poor, living in unauthorised housing on pockets of undeveloped, often marginal, land within the built up area or on the urban periphery, or in slum and tenement housing nearer the centre of cities. The emphasis in policy responses, driven by the availability of aid and pressure of influence from outside (especially the World Bank and the UN), as much as by local priorities, was on projects targeted, not always very effectively, at the urban poor.

A common chronological pattern was a progression from the construction of complete dwellings for rent, or, more recently, sale, by the public sector, to the provision of serviced plots, to the upgrading of unauthorised areas. Although in many places one or other of these strategies was tried and abandoned, in others they now proceed simultaneously, although emphasis often shifts between them over time. The solely project-oriented approach to urban housing problems has begun to be questioned in more recent years. Problems of replicability and the 'hijacking' of housing or plots intended for the poor by higher income groups, is leading to a realisation that housing for the urban poor must be considered within the context of the housing sector as a whole. This has led to the initiation of sectoral policies in addition to isolated projects. However, these are by no means universal and the objectives of many housing projects are thwarted by inappropriate sectoral or wider economic policies.

The focus of research on particular segments of housing markets is still strong, but its deficiencies with regard to understanding and explanation of the processes of urban development and as a guide to policy are becoming evident. In this paper, therefore, I argue for housing policy which is based on a consideration of supply and demand, or production and consumption of housing to all income groups, and which may focus public sector resources on sector-wide policies instead of, or in addition to, specific housing projects. To provide a basis for such an approach to policy, research must attempt to understand urban housing markets more generally, both at national and city levels.

Two alternative theoretical frameworks have been used in attempts to understand housing markets: a neo-classical approach to the urban economy and housing economics and a political economy framework. Discussions of the economics of housing traditionally analyse the sector in terms of supply and demand, while in political economy approaches urban housing markets are discussed in terms of the production, consumption and exchange of housing. In this paper, first I will look at supply and production, and then at demand and consumption.

PRODUCTION AND SUPPLY OF HOUSING

Formal and Informal Housing Supply

Early analysis of the housing problem in terms of a shortfall in housing supply was apparently borne out by figures such as those presented in the World Housing Survey in 1974, in which it was clear that in formal sector, public and private, dwellings completed per 1000 population were considerably fewer in low than high income countries. Responses to the apparent deficits in housing supply included arguments put forward to support the allocation of a larger proportion of public resources to housing and services, work designed to obtain recognition for the contribution to housing supply made by the informal sector and policies to increase housing supply. Examples of the first are Grimes (1976), Burns and Grebler (1977) and McAllum and Benjamin (1985).

Early attempts to measure housing supply were criticised. Because housing tended to be defined as authorised, legal housing of an approved standard produced by the formal construction sector, housing supply was underestimated. Since the 1960s, it has been pointed out that a large proportion of housing has been supplied without official approval under land, planning or building regulations, by the so-called informal or unconventional sector. The form and extent of illegality vary both between and within cities, but all such housing suffers, at least initially, from a lack of utilities and services. To ignore this latter component of housing supply is less common today, although it is still often labelled unsatisfactory in terms of particular housing and planning standards and the apparent deficit thereby revealed referred to, misleadingly, as a housing shortage.

Early writing aimed at achieving recognition of the contribution made by unauthorised construction to the supply of housing. Research concentrated on showing that the residents of slum and squatter areas were less marginal than marginalised, while attempts to discourage the most common government reactions of the time (neglect and refusal to provide utilities and services at least and frequently demolition, often without provisions for rehousing) laid emphasis on the positive contribution of the residents of such areas to the urban economy and housing supply, their basically conservative political attitudes and the appropriate nature of the housing solutions adopted. The latter were held to allow for mobility within the city as migrant priorities changed; incremental investment in housing and gradual house consolidation as household finances permit; opportunities for use of household labour as a means of cost saving; opportunities for income earning, including construction of additional rooms to let; and housing designs suited to the supply of local skills and materials and to the needs of particular households (see, for example, Turner, 1967, 1972; Payne, 1977; Perlman, 1980).

Much recent research has continued to be fascinated with the characteristics of low income informal sector housing areas, often, although not always, studying the economic, social and political organisation of such areas and their housing characteristics in isolation from the wider urban system. No attempt is made here to summarise the findings of this research in a comprehensive fashion, but see, for example, Drakakis-Smith (1981), Leeds (1981) and UNCHS (1982). Some studies do, however, reach conclusions which are of wider relevance, such as Ward's (1978) attempt to ascertain the social and economic determinants of differences in house consolidation levels by urban households in similar housing situations in Mexico City; Jimenez' study (1983) of the determinants of value of dwellings in a squatter housing market in Manila; and Benjamin *et al.*'s in-depth analysis (1985) of the nature and amounts of investment in housing in Indonesian *kampungs*. Recently, the focus has shifted from the study of squatter areas to illegal land subdivision (see, for example, Chabbi, 1988, El Kadi, 1988).

Rental housing is significant both for the urban poor in general (Hamer, 1985) and within informal housing areas in some cities, but has been relatively little studied until recently, perhaps because of the pre-occupation of analysts and policy advocates with the positive benefits of self-help and house ownership (but see Gilbert, 1987). A study by Edwards (1982) in Bucaramanga, Colombia found widespread renting, but concluded that "petty landlordism shows no sign of developing into a larger scale, more avowedly capitalist activity". A totally different situation was found by Amis (1984) in Nairobi, where in unauthorised settlements, political backing and access to formal sector credit has enabled larger scale, often outside capital to displace local small-scale petty landlordism.

Informal sector housing is seen as complementary to private conventional housing; which is produced by the formal sector for those who can afford to pay the market price for properly surveyed and authorised land and approved house construction, generally with access to formal sector credit for mortgages. There are amazingly few studies of the private conventional housing sector, although it is, of course, included in those studies which attempt to understand characteristics of city-wide housing markets. The studies of Drakakis-Smith (1977, 1981), Johnstone (1980), Mehta and Mehta (1987) and Barnes (1982) are among the few exceptions in South East Asia and Africa. Some public sector housing is also often provided, generally predominantly for the lower middle income groups. This housing is usually subsidised and so limited in quantity.

Such a twofold division of housing production into conventional and unconventional has been subject to a number of criticisms, of which some reflect criticisms of the wider division of the urban economy into formal and informal sectors and others are specific to the housing sector (see, for example, Moser, 1978, 1984; Santos, 1979). In a dualistic analysis, informal sector housing is seen as a 'temporary dysfunction' of the urban housing market, likely to disappear once the urban economy and environment has been modernised. In the meantime the sector is labelled backward and un-modern, and neglected, or actively discriminated against by government. Criticisms include the descriptive nature of the distinction between formal and informal, concealing the links between the two sectors in terms of their relationship to land allocation processes, infrastructure installation, building materials supply etc. It is also criticised for being a static concept, failing to recognise change in the practical and legal status of areas over time, as they consolidate or deteriorate. Finally, it is criticised for the way in which it divides the urban housing market into two, thereby concealing the segmented nature of housing supply. Increasingly, the accumulating evidence on the prevalence and characteristics of illegal land subdivision emphasises the inappropriateness of such a twofold division.

One reaction to the latter criticism has been to develop more complex categorisations of housing production and supply (Drakakis-Smith, 1979), housing delivery systems (Angel *et al.*, 1977), or of lower income settlement types (Leeds, 1981). Angel *et al.* base their typology on surveys in six Asian cities. Housing for the low income urban population (bottom 40 per cent of the income distribution) alone is produced through seven subsystems (squatter housing, temporary land tenure, private housing, commuter housing, employer housing, public construction and public assistance), each of which contains a variety of arrangements for housing delivery. Leeds (1981), drawing on research from Latin America and Portugal, distinguishes between squatter settlements, government created shack towns, private area squatter settlements, titled plots without services, emergency housing, multi-house projects and inner city slums, the latter subdivided into entrepreneurial rooming houses, temporary space rentals such as hotels, apartment buildings, private separate houses and apartment-house housing projects. Much of interest is also learnt from more general studies, such as Gilbert and Ward's (1985) account of housing, land and the state in three Latin American cities.

Such housing typologies may provide a basis for analysis of the organisation and characteristics of production and supply by each type of housing delivery system (see especially Leeds, 1981), but run the risk of being sterile descriptive tools, degenerating into ever more complex subdivisions of housing supply and delivery without providing explanations of the perceived categories or of processes at work in the housing market. More radical criticisms of the formal/informal sector concept are based on marxist theory.

The mere recognition in the 1960s of the significance of the informal sector and the efforts of authors and consultants to use the characteristics of housing production in that sector to provide guidance

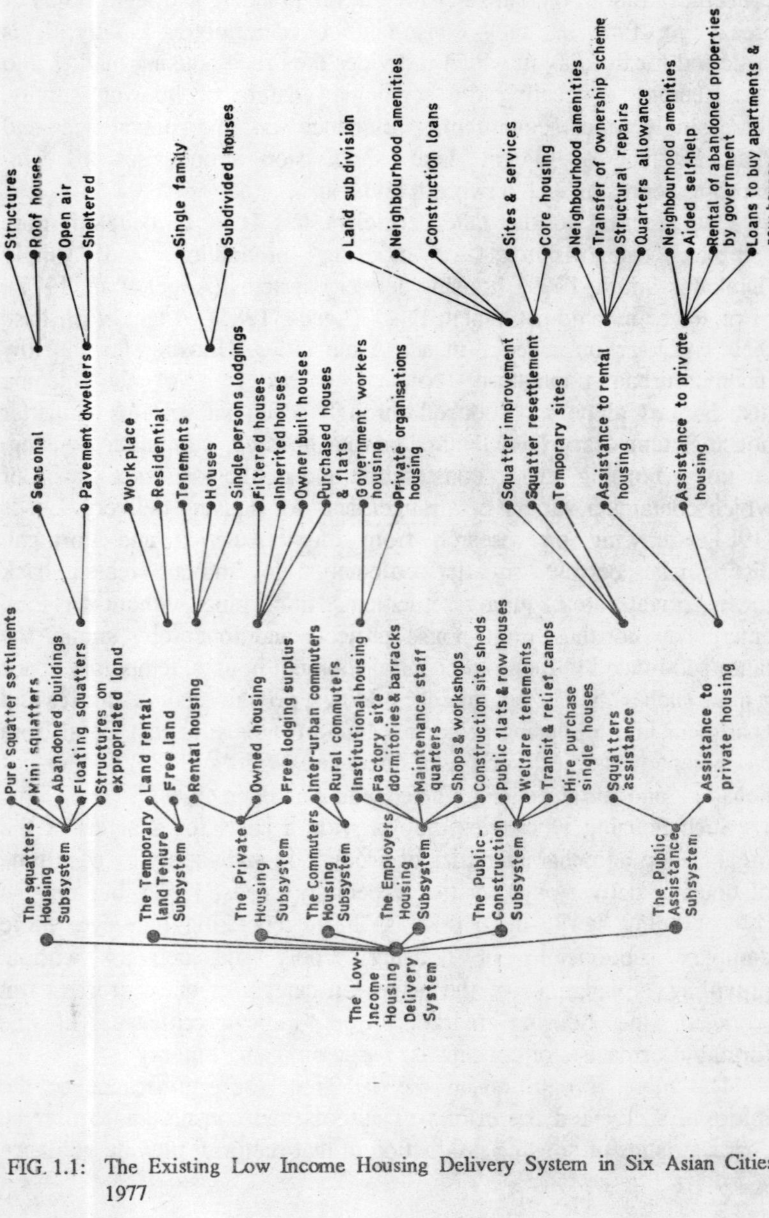

FIG. 1.1: The Existing Low Income Housing Delivery System in Six Asian Cities, 1977

for changes in policy were influential. Wider shifts in development policy, and concern with the formulation of the Redistribution with Growth and basic needs approaches, underlay and reinforced attention paid to informal sector housing production as a research focus and as a basis for the favoured housing policies of the 1970s: serviced plot provision and upgrading of unauthorised areas. However, isolated studies of unauthorised housing areas or of public housing programmes tell us little about other components of housing supply, except by default, while programmes that seek to deal solely with the needs of low income residents are beset by problems of leakage.

There is a need, therefore, both for more holistic analysis of (albeit segmented) housing markets and to identify the factors which affect housing supply.[3] These may include, *inter alia*, land, the supply of which influences the location and cost of housing and may act as a constraint on public housing programmes (see, for example, Dunkerley *et al.*, 1978; Zetter, 1984; McAuslan, 1985); the procedure for obtaining planning and building permission; the availability of utilities and services (Kirke, 1984); accessibility and transport; the availability of finance (UN, 1978a; Wegener, 1982); and the capacity of the construction industry. The latter is in turn influenced by its organisation, the availability of capital and sufficient suitable labour, technology choice and the supply of building materials (Edmonds, 1979; Wells, 1984; Stretton, 1981; Ganesan, 1983; Moavenzadeh, 1987).

These constraints may be seen as market imperfections, or distortions introduced by attempted public intervention. Much of the housing policy debate has concentrated on measures for increasing the supply of accessible serviced land, dwelling units and housing finance and the need to revise standards in order to bring supply costs down has been stressed. Occasionally, attention has also been given to improving the supply of building materials and to increasing the capacity of the construction industry. The outcome of interventions designed to relieve constraints on supply, both actively (construction of public housing for rent or sale, serviced plot programmes, infrastructure provision, building materials development or supply) and passively (ceasing to bulldoze squatter settlements) thus needs to be evaluated.

Modes and Forms of Housing Production

The second main framework which has been utilised in the study of urban housing may be loosely labelled a political economy approach, although in practice these two approaches are not totally distinct and many analysts make use of concepts and theoretical insights from both (for example, Gilbert and Ward, 1985). Developments in housing theory at the end of the 1970s, both in Britain (see for example, Lambert *et al.*, 1978; Bassett and Short, 1980) and developing countries attempt to place the housing question in its economic, political and social context. These approaches regard the analysis of state intervention as inseparable from analysis of the modes of production which give rise to the class interests represented in the state.

The first attempt in the literature related to Third World cities to refer the modes of production debate specifically to housing was that by Burgess (1978), who classified housing by mode and form of production, into the dominant capitalist mode of production, which produces the industrialised form of production, and the dependent petty commodity form of production, which produces manufactured and self-built forms of housing.

The industrialised form of housing production is characterised by Burgess as the dominant form, in which capital is invested according to the laws of capital accumulation, and is directed towards the purchase of industrially elaborated building materials, the acquisition of often sophisticated technology, the payment of an often highly differentiated labour force and the production of a housing object, the characteristics of which are determined through the conditions of the market. The result is an industrialised and standardised product, consumed entirely through the mechanisms of the market. The dominance of this form is established in one or more of these areas: exclusive allocation of national and urban housing budgets to provision of finished housing objects, domination of the industrialised building materials industry based on large foreign or national monopolies, and supply of land by large property companies dominated by state and finance capital. However, as Drakakis-Smith (1979) correctly points out, public housing is not allocated in accordance with market criteria; while production of it is industrialised, consumption is affected by forces other than market values.

The petty commodity mode of production is divided by Burgess into two forms, the manufactured and self-built forms, distinguished according to the degree of differentiation of the workforce, the extent of use of wage labour, the identity of the producer and the consumer,

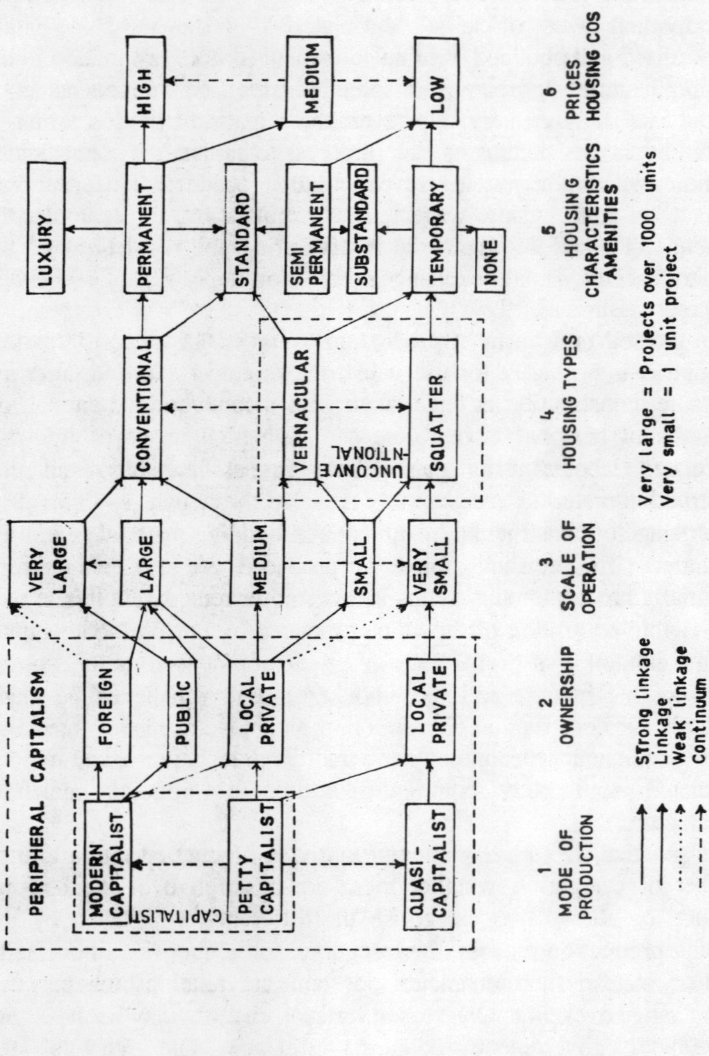

FIG. 1.2: **A Model of Urban Housing in Malaysian Cities**

and the means of production. Thus in the manufactured form, the identity of the producer is different from the consumer, who is generally from the middle and upper income groups; production involves a small number of paid workers often recruited via complex subcontracting arrangements and managed by a builder in the name of an individual owner of capital; and materials used are to some extent standardised and obtained from an equivalent form of production in the building materials industry, with some industrialised components and a limited use of machinery. However, the expansion of this sector is limited by factors such as its lack of access to capital and sophisticated technology and relatively low levels of labour productivity. Its survival is made possible by low wage levels permitted by, for example, the existence of a sizeable industrial reserve army and restrictions on the industrial sector, such as exchange controls on imports of materials and machinery (Burgess, 1978).

In the self-built form of production, Burgess (1978) considers that production is primarily for use value; the producer and consumer are the same; construction is undertaken with income-derived capital, on the basis of personal labour time and with high levels of free and kin-related labour, using paid labour for skilled jobs; and that construction materials are generally recycled throw-aways, although at a later stage of construction, manufactured building materials are often purchased. The housing object is produced for use, although it potentially has commodity status if it is sold or rented, and this in turn may enable realisation of the value produced by unpaid labour inputs and the extraction of profit. Rates of production depend on the amount of disposable income and the amount of time which can be made available for construction. Construction methods are labour intensive, involve rudimentary technology and traditional techniques, and may be associated with petty commodity modes of building materials manufacture.

In practice, as with any attempt to divide production into a limited number of categories, whether these are descriptive of the housing product, or attempts to categorise the different forms taken by the housing production process, the categories are neither fixed nor totally distinct; instead their characteristics and the relationships between them change over time. One reason for such changes may be the extent to which government policies influence and change the interconnections between the various modes and forms of production, and especially, the extent to which upgrading represents the penetration of a capitalist mode of production into housing previously produced within the self-built form of the petty commodity mode of production, as asserted by Burgess (1978).

The assumptions of much housing research and policy with regard to the nature of the state are rarely made explicit. There is a tendency in some cases to assume a neutral state, allocating resources in accordance with technical and rational criteria such as efficiency and equity, or a liberal state, governing in the public interest, but pursuing misguided policies which need to be corrected. Often managerialist explanations are advanced for housing problems and the outcomes of housing policy. These may be relevant where political or economic elites control the shaping of policies, local bureaucratic structures are powerful, there is a high level of public intervention in local housing markets and well-developed professionalised housing management (Bassett and Short, 1980) and are often of use even where not all these conditions apply, in the detailed analysis of institutions, organisations and policy outcomes. However, the explanation they offer may only be partial, while it is suggested that they do not provide an adequate theoretical framework for understanding housing markets or the underlying structural causes of housing problems. In addition, it is necessary to examine the nature of the state, the different interests it represents, the motives of these interests in undertaking particular policy interventions and the changes in each of these over time. State intervention in housing is seen as having a number of purposes; the reproduction of labour power, valorisation of land and capital, legitimation and the maintenance of social order, closely related to the role and functions of the state in general at national and local levels (Burgess, 1978; Peattie, 1979; Rakodi, 1986, 1988). Housing policy is of particular importance to the reproduction of labour, may advance the interests of finance, landed and industrial capital, may facilitate the extension of social control to areas which were previously not integrated into political and administrative systems, and may provide ideal opportunities both to buy or reward political supporters and to defuse demands for radical change.

Self-help and community organisation is often advocated as providing an alternative or complementary form of organisation for the solution of housing problems. However, such a form of organisation, despite its support from both left and right of the political spectrum, is not a self-evident good. The terms need to be unpacked and defined, the potential and limitations of both individual and community self-help explored in some detail (see, for example, Burgess, 1978; Gilbert and Ward, 1984a, 1984b).

Burgess' work has given rise to ongoing debates on the utility of his production categories in understanding housing production (for example, Rakodi, 1983), and the implications of his view of the role of the state in housing for understanding the outcomes of serviced plot and other 'self-help' programmes. With respect to the former, Moser (1982), for example, on the basis of a study of self-help housing production in Indio-Guayas, a squatter area in Guayaquil, concludes that none of the housing produced in the area can be understood outside the process of commodity formation, because, although much of the housing is produced by owners for their own occupation and thus for its use value, building materials used are produced and distributed by capitalist enterprises, varying amounts of paid labour are used in house construction, and, most importantly, most residents have had to pay for land. In Moser's view, therefore, there is little value in distinguishing between manufactured and self-built forms of petty commodity production.

Johnstone (1984), referring to Malaysia, agrees with Burgess that modes of production vary as to their scale of operations, technological arrangements, capitalisation and division of labour, and notes that within peripheral capitalism, pre-capitalist forms of production persist whose character and extent are determined by the nature and expansion of the capitalist sector into the indigenous economy. The precise form of integration and dependence, he suggests, depend on the socio-political framework, the resource base of the country concerned and the extent of local production prior to capitalist contact. In the Malaysian context, he identifies three types of conventional housing (public, private and tenement or slum housing) which are built in a capitalist form of production, associated with foreign, public and local private ownership, the latter being dominant.

Within the pre-capitalist mode of production, he identifies different forms of production, distinguished by the social form of labour, the character of exchange and the generation of surplus. Petty capitalist production of housing differs only from capitalist production in terms of scale; it is primarily aimed at the production of a surplus, and in Malaysia produces vernacular housing in urban areas and is to be found to some extent in squatter areas. The latter, however, are mainly associated with petty commodity, simple commodity and domestic production of housing.

Petty commodity production, it is suggested, is a transitional form, in which housing is produced on a small-scale by an artisan, for its exchange value. Some artisans engaged in building to order or for sale manage to extract surplus value, expand in size, begin to employ wage labour, and make the transition to petty capitalist production. Simple commodity production is also artisanal production of housing, in which the producer is concerned only with the reproduction of his own means of subsistence, and in which the house is produced for a particular individual. Finally, domestic production is used by Johnstone to refer to production in which subsistence requirements are obtained without exchange. In this case he is referring to self-built housing, or auto-construction, as it is sometimes termed, in which the house is built for its use value, although its status may change from a potential to a real commodity if it is placed on the market for sale or rent. However, Johnstone insists that even this form of production is quasi-capitalist, because it is related to the capitalist system by the use made of mass-produced building materials, especially timber. Although domestic production is self-help in the sense that the labour used is own and family labour, specialist stages in the construction process may be subcontracted out to artisans, thus blurring the distinction between this and the simple commodity form of production. Johnstone has related his model to Malaysia, but is well aware of the danger of it being used rigidly. He stresses that production and housing types should be viewed as continua, and the focus should be on the relationships between the capitalist and other sectors and particularly, the way in which the future development of petty and quasi-capitalist forms is dependent on and determined by their relationship with the capitalist mode.

Schlyter (1984) also utilises the concept of domestic production to characterise squatter housing and both she and Johnstone, therefore, criticise the inclusion by Burgess of self-built housing for a household's own use in the petty commodity form of production, in which housing is built for exchange. All three authors are in agreement that there is in fact a continuum of forms of production, even within squatter areas, and that no one form of production is associated exclusively with a particular type of residential area. The latter point is recognised by Burgess himself in more recent work, in which he admits the difficulty of categorising areas by the mode or form of production of the housing within them and opts instead for a classification based on legal status (Burgess, 1985a). This point is also illustrated by attempts to apply the analysis to serviced plot schemes, in which infrastructure installation and wet core or core house construction by large-scale contractors form part of the industrialised form of production, while housing production may be petty capitalist, petty commodity, simple commodity or domestic production, depending on local circumstances (see, for example, Ghana, 1984; UNCHS, 1987; Nimpuno-Parente, 1987 and Gore, 1985).

The outcomes of policy interventions designed to influence the nature of housing production are analysed in the light of current thinking on the form and functions of the state[4] and the political interests and social groups whose interests are, directly or indirectly, served by particular policies. The debate on Burgess' own views has been carried forward by Gilbert and Van der Linden (Burgess, 1985; Van de Linden, 1986; Gilbert and Van der Linden, 1986; Burgess, 1987).

Any analysis of the production of housing in a city or urban sector must first identify the housing producers. Merely describing the types of housing constructed by different producers is, however, insufficient, and an explanation of the observed housing stock must be sought in the organisation and financing of the construction process, examining the nature and volume of house production by large- and medium-scale capitalist enterprises, public authorities, small-scale or artisanal enterprises and individual households. Of interest to policy-makers are, in each case, the availability of spare capacity, the capacity to expand production, the conditions necessary for such expansion to occur, and the potential constraints on housing supply:

(a) access to land, which is determined by tenure and the land administration system, the distribution of ownership, responsibility for subdivision, systems for regulating use and construction and eligibility criteria for access to the formal land market;
(b) the ability of service agencies to keep pace with demand for physical infrastructure and utilities, which is related both to their administrative and financial structure and to the supply standards adopted;
(c) the structure and capacity of the residential construction sector, including the locus of control, sources of capital and profits and perceived constraints on producing the volume of different types of residential construction required;

(d) the supply of building materials, including questions of cost, distribution and shortages;
(e) the availability of construction skills, both within construction firms and households, the latter being important especially where self-help construction is advocated.

DEMAND FOR HOUSING

Typically in a Third World country a mismatch is identified between the supply of what is defined as adequate housing and the demand. While clear economic definitions exist for the latter, housing has always been a problematic area of study for economists because of its special characteristics. Housing markets and the economics of housing in the cities of Third World has, in particular, been a field of study which has, until recently, largely been neglected by economists (McAllum and Benjamin, 1985). In practice, most of the analyses of housing problems have been carried out by planners and policy-makers concerned to satisfy housing needs. Some of the problems with this approach are discussed below. In recent project planning and research, attention has centred on assessing effective demand for housing. Methodological and policy aspects of the concept of effective demand are explored in this section. The final subsection introduces some of the concepts utilised in a political economy approach to understanding the consumption of housing.

Housing Need

Housing need is defined in the 1974 UN Housing Survey to include demographic, replacement and vacancy elements (UN, 1976). Estimates of housing need produced on this basis (see UN, 1976; Yeh and Laquian, 1977) show, of course, a massive shortfall in supply. Policy recommendations for increased supply follow, often accompanied by arguments for devoting a larger share of national resources to construction, in particular housing. Invariably, the definition of an 'adequate' house is based on standards which represent an aspiration rather than a realisable goal. The result is to produce estimates of housing need which are clearly beyond the capacity of a country with limited financial resources, low income people and an underdeveloped construction industry to supply. While the planners' aim in the exercise may have been to ensure the provision of housing of a suitable standard, and the allocation of additional resources to investment in housing in order to achieve the aim, the end result may well be a feeling of helplessness in face of the scale of the problem.

The main deficiency in the use of simple estimates of housing need in housing policy formulation is that they do not take into account resource availability at either national or individual level. The resources available to both government and the construction industry nationally, and to the great majority of urban families, are clearly limited. In most cases, therefore, to define housing need in terms of normative planning standards unrelated to the cost of housing, means that at both the national and city level the supply of acceptable units can never be sufficient in volume to satisfy total estimated need, while at the individual level many urban households cannot afford to pay for the housing units provided. This, of course, has long been recognised. Responses have included acknowledgement of the importance of housing supplied outside the formal enumerated construction sector; policies to reduce the supply price of housing and its components (Grimes, 1976; World Bank, 1972, 1975); and a shift of analytical emphasis to the demand, rather than the need, for housing.

The latter has taken two forms. First has been the concern of policy-makers and project planners to ensure that governments, and especially intended beneficiaries, can afford the solutions proposed. Second has been a recent research programme by the World Bank into the characteristics of effective housing demand in the cities of Third World countries. In the following section, assumptions on effective demand and alternative methods of assessing ability to afford housing options will be reviewed, together with their implications for housing policy formulation.

Effective Demand and Affordability

At the national or city wide level, if public agencies are committed to providing adequate housing and services to the entire urban population, it is inevitable that in order to achieve such improvements for lower income residents, public expenditure will be required. The difference between the cost per unit of a dwelling to an 'adequate' standard of construction and servicing and the ability to pay of urban residents may be met by public subsidy. In Third World countries such public subsidies may be substantial, although often confined to civil servants and public officials and often highly regressive (Winpenny, 1982;

Sanyal, 1981).

The problem is that given the limited availability of public resources, such levels of subsidy cannot be maintained alongside a policy goal of meeting the housing needs of the whole urban population. The World Bank, especially, feels strongly that governments cannot and should not sustain subsidies on a large-scale and that housing policies need to be designed, therefore, on the basis of full, or nearly full, cost recovery, so that they are replicable on a scale sufficient to improve housing conditions for the entire urban population (see also Lee, 1985). In addition, the World Bank emphasises the need to shift the financial burden of paying for housing from the public sector onto the urban population, by judicious use of pricing policies, mobilisation of the energies and resources of the community via self-help, and progressive development, which is assumed to have a cost reducing effect (Nientied and Van der Linden, 1985).

As important an influence on housing policy formulation as the elimination of large-scale public subsidies has been the change of emphasis from housing need to effective demand and the ability of 'target' populations to afford the housing strategies proposed. The earliest and still the most common estimates of effective demand are based on 'rule of thumb' methods in which it is assumed that urban households can afford to pay a certain proportion of their income for housing (Grimes, 1976; Johnstone, 1980). Grimes based his calculation on an assumption that 15 per cent of monthly income would be available for housing. More often, it has been assumed that urban households can spend up to 25 per cent of their monthly income on housing. Gradually, the deficiencies in this method of analysis have been recognised (World Bank, 1985; Mayo and Gross, 1987; Malpezzi and Mayo, 1987) and attempts made to modify it accordingly, by improving estimates of housing costs and taking into account differing household characteristics. Thus it has been recognised that monthly economic rental (for tenants) or loan repayments (for owner occupiers) do not constitute the full cost of housing and estimates of the monthly cost of housing have been refined to include recurrent payments (for utilities, house maintenance, property taxes etc.) in addition to capital repayment (including the initial capital cost of shelter, land and perhaps infrastructure provision, depending on the pricing policies of agencies providing utilities) (see, Roberts, 1980; Lee, 1985).

It has also been noted that the 25 per cent figure has been taken as a benchmark rather than a ceiling, and recognised that it may not be valid to assume that all urban households can afford to pay the same proportion of their income for housing (UN, 1984). Although in practice low income households may have to pay a higher proportion than high income households, expenditure on food is relatively income inelastic and constitutes a higher proportion of total household expenditure for low than for middle or high income households. It may, therefore, be more realistic to assume that a smaller proportion of household income is available for expenditure on housing by low than by high income households (Davidson, 1981) and even by large than by small households (Strassman, 1982; Follain and Jimenez, 1983a). The latter has not, to my knowledge, been taken into account in any analyses of ability to afford a particular housing project to date, although Winpenny (1982) notes that the National Housing Bank of Brazil relates maximum housing payments to family size as well as income.

Two alternative approaches may be envisaged to overcome some of the difficulties of the 'rule of thumb' method. Assumptions on availability of income for housing purposes may be based on actual payments for housing or on residual income available after other basic needs have been satisfied.

Effective Demand based on Actual Payments for Housing[5]

Following recognition, some years after implementation of low income upgrading and sites and services projects by the World Bank began, that "The old rules of thumb turn out to be inadequate" (Mayo, quoted in World Bank, 1985). The World Bank have adopted this approach in a major research project on "Housing Demand and Finance in Developing Countries" which began in 1981. The first phase of this project (1981-84) was concerned with patterns of effective demand for housing and findings were based on analysis of 16 cities in eight countries (Colombia, Egypt, El Salvador, Ghana, India, Philippines and South Korea). Using city-wide household sample survey data, patterns of housing expenditure were related to household income, household size and tenure. Even where city-wide data are available, problems with using actual expenditure on housing occur, leading the World Bank to prefer data for tenants for calculating ability and willingness to pay (Mayo, 1985); although results for owners are similar, the level of expenditure on housing by owners is generally greater than by tenants because of a desire to hedge against future rent increases by buying, to generate income and future capital gains, and as a safe refuge for surplus capital in countries with few investment alternatives (Mayo and Malpezzi, 1984).

In other contexts, care would need to be taken in using returns which may have recorded self-help incremental construction as zero monthly expenditure or may include households paying subsidised rents. The main findings of the World Bank study, using average proportion of income spent on housing, were that low income households generally spend higher fractions of their income for shelter than do high income households and that the proportion of income spent on shelter for all households increases with the level of economic development (Mayo, 1985). In this first stage of analysis, housing was treated as a composite good. A second element in the research was to examine the demand for housing characteristics, such as space, location and quality.

A review of procedures used in a number of studies to estimate the household demand for housing characteristics and their results concludes that while the theoretical basis of econometric approaches is sound, difficulties in operationalising procedures have led to a variety of empirical findings (Follain and Jimenez, 1983b). A refined model was estimated using data from five cities in three Third World countries (Davao, Bogota, Cali, Seoul and Busan). Findings were that household willingness to pay for living space increases with income, but at a less than proportionate rate; willingness to pay for living space declines as household size increases; and willingness to pay for several quality measures is quite responsive to income (Follain and Jimenez, 1983a).

Later analyses reinforce the initial findings that effective demand is influenced primarily by income level, although also by tenure and general level of economic development (Malpezzi and Mayo,1987) as well as by access to credit. The approach adopted by the World Bank study places it squarely in the tradition of econometric modelling of housing supply and demand. It overcomes the criticism made by Lee (1985) of analyses which base estimates of the propensity to pay for housing on surveys of single communities, often with more or less homogeneous types and standards of housing, by using city-wide data. Its findings demonstrate some general principles with regard to effective demand for housing and reinforce the criticisms of the adoption of a single 'rule of thumb' with respect to the proportion of income which can be assumed to be available for housing. However, although the research results may be expected to yield background information of value to policy-makers, they do not yet give sufficient guidance as to what proportion of income may be assumed to be available for expenditure on housing and services, partly because of the use of average rent-to-income ratios, and partly because the approach fails to recognise the problems of absolute poverty and ability to pay for housing, as well as the failure of existing market mechanisms to satisfy even basic minimum housing needs.

Affordability, Poverty and Basic Needs

The second approach to overcoming deficiencies in earlier estimates of affordability is to assess the income necessary for basic needs satisfaction and to regard the remaining income as available for expenditure on housing (England and Alnwick, 1982; Rakodi, 1987). Lee (1985) criticises the assumptions underlying this method, although not its particular application by England and Alnwick, including the assumption that minimum expenditure to satisfy basic needs, especially food, is assumed to be similar for every household, irrespective of its income and thus that there is a direct relationship between per capita expenditure and average household income regardless of household composition. While there are some grounds for his criticism, it does not appear to be inherent in this method, and although estimates of poverty lines (or minimum income necessary to satisfy basic needs) are as problematic as estimates of household income, the methodology nevertheless has advantages over arbitrary assumptions of the proportion of income available for housing related expenditure.

It also enables approaches based on goals of satisfying basic needs, which ostensibly underly World Bank approaches to policy formulation (World Bank, 1980a, 1980b, 1980c), but are apparently neglected in the housing demand studies reported above, to inform housing policy and project design. Finally, it takes seriously the problem of absolute poverty, and the inability of many low income urban households to meet even minimum expenditure needs, irrespective of any necessary expenditure on housing (England and Alnwick, 1982; Mohan *et al*., 1981). Policy based on a research finding that low income households have a rent-to-income ratio which is greater than high income households is likely to lead to the very problems of affordability that the World Bank is aiming to avoid.

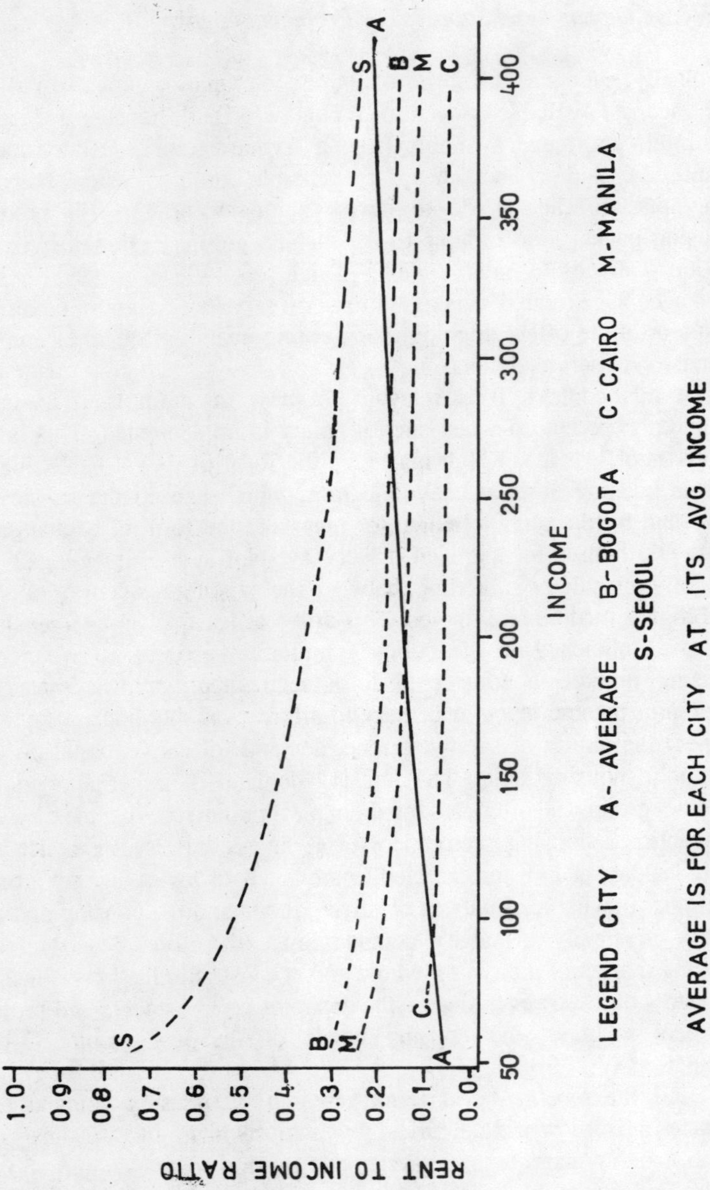

FIG. 1.3: Rent-to-Income Ratios by Income for Renters

Effective Demand and Supply: The Problem of Leakage

Typically, estimates are made of the income level necessary to afford the cheapest available conventional contractor-built housing and/or the minimum mortgage available from a formal sector housing finance institution and/or the cheapest available public sector housing. Attempts are then made to devise strategies which will produce housing packages affordable to the income groups excluded from the options already available (e.g., Davidson, 1981). Such housing packages have tended to take the form of very low cost public housing units, or, more often, upgrading of existing unauthorised areas and the provision of serviced plots.

In this context, it is relevant to draw attention to a common problem experienced when such a policy is implemented. This is the problem of leakage, which may take the form of illegal subletting of public housing units at economic rents which exceed the subsidised rent paid by the eligible tenant, or may take the form of exchange of plots and houses in upgraded or serviced plot areas, either legally or illegally, by sale or subletting, between the existing resident or allottee and higher income households. This arises at least partly as a result of a basic deficiency in the policy formulation process, in which the housing market is considered in a segmented way. Estimates of minimum income levels necessary to afford available housing options neglect the ability of supply to meet demand for conventional private or public housing units. The housing demand of upper and middle income groups is often assumed unquestioningly to be met by the conventional housing sector. However, unless this is in practice the case, leakage of housing targeted to the needs of lower income groups is almost inevitable. Analysis of effective demand for housing and the ability of supply to satisfy demand must, therefore, deal with the housing market of a city as a whole and not just with the lower income segments of it, however sincere the desire of policy-makers and project planners to meet the housing needs of the low income urban population.

Until the recent World Bank research on housing demand and finance in Third World countries, few analysts had, however, analysed urban housing markets in the systematic fashion advocated here. Some of the findings of the World Bank city-wide household sample surveys have been presented above. Handbooks on planning and analysing an urban housing survey, produced originally for the Kenyan government, have also been published as part of the research programme (Malpezzi *et al.*, 1982; Malpezzi, 1984). A slightly earlier research project was carried out by Strassman, who was commissioned by the World Bank in 1978 to carry out a survey of the housing market of Cartagena in Colombia (Strassman, 1982) and who presented such an analytical framework for a hypothetical city using a stock-user matrix (Strassman, 1978).

Usually, Strassman hypothesises, lack of land and finance for housing combined with population growth, result in households being able to obtain less housing than they would willingly pay for, resulting in shortages of housing in the upper price ranges and upward pressure on house prices. The policy implications of such an analysis are that public intervention to ensure that the effective demand of those able to afford private sector conventional housing is met, by ensuring availability of land, services, finance, building materials etc., is as important as policies aimed at providing affordable options to the lower income groups. Strassman recognised the problem of diverting scarce resources into luxury housing if demand exists; this may be particularly problematic in countries with little indigenous building materials production and limited foreign exchange. He also notes that, however realistic the standards for housing and utilities which are adopted, there is a certain cost below which minimum basic needs are not satisfied. Some households would be unable to afford even this minimum. Some subsidy may, therefore, in his view be necessary, but would, he concludes, at least for his hypothetical case, represent only a very small proportion of the city's gross product and would, therefore, be sustainable (Strassman, 1978).

Demand for Housing: Ability or Willingness to Pay?

Much of the foregoing discussion has concentrated on recent thinking about estimating demand for housing and ability to pay. While effective demand should form an important focus of analysis, this does not mean that all analysis of housing need is inappropriate (UN, 1984a). It is also necessary to collect information and provide inputs to housing policy formulation on housing preferences; housing standards, both actual housing conditions and targeted minimum standards; and housing requirements and needs (Merrett, 1984). Recognition of the need for complementary analysis of housing need and effective demand converges here with some critiques of current methods of assessing affordability, in which, it is felt, there is too much emphasis on so-called objective assessments of ability to afford housing packages, and not enough on urban residents' expression of "users' experience, attitudes and choices" (Merrett, 1984).

Thus willingness to pay is related to ability to pay, but also to perceived use value of housing and the residential environment, and household expenditure priorities. This in turn has implications for policy formulation and implementation and also for research. The implication for housing policy is that greater flexibility is required (Kioe-Sheng, 1988). Although minimum cost alternatives must be provided in order to ensure maximum access to improved living conditions by low income people, a choice of housing and service packages should also be made available, to enable households to retain control over expenditure of their own resources. Greater choice and flexibility in housing policy would gain considerable sympathy from many authors, especially Turner (1972), who explains housing policy failures to a great extent in terms of the inflexible responses produced by over-centralised, bureaucratic organisational control of the housing process, and the lack of user control over housing. In addition, if a range of options is made available, access to the poorest may be increased by cross subsidisation. Willingness to pay may also be determined in practice by means of schemes which involve saving in advance, to provide a downpayment or blocked balance, as well as evidence of ability and willingness to pay. The need for information on willingness to pay also has implications for research. It provides an argument for asking respondents in different income groups directly what they are (a) able and (b) willing to pay, both occasionally and regularly, for housing and services in general and for particular residential packages.

Housing Finance[6]

Recognition that finance for house construction and purchase is in very limited supply in Third World and that formal sector housing finance is only available to a small proportion of the (higher income) urban population has led to increasing attention to the housing finance system, including surveys of international literature and experience (Renaud, 1984, 1987; Boleat, 1987; UNCHS, 1987), accounts of non-conventional methods of financing housing and suggestions for their promotion (UNCHS, 1984a, 1984b), and recommendations for mobilising large-scale private sector institutions and resources to increase the supply of credit (World Bank, 1986, 1988).

The Consumption of Housing

In the introduction, it was noted that there have been two major approaches to the study of urban housing markets; that of neo-classical economics and that of political economy. The barest outline of relevant concepts used in the latter is given here, as there has been little research work on the consumption of housing in Third World cities within this theoretical framework.

The terms on which households are integrated into the urban economy vary: the urban poor may be integrated as wage workers in capitalist enterprises in which, because of the nature of peripheral capitalism, relatively low wages can be paid. Wage levels in the public sector are linked to those available to workers in the private sector, subject to institutional rigidities. Access to wage employment is available only to some workers, the proportion varying from city to city; the remainder are relegated to eking out a living in non-capitalist or petty capitalist economic activities. Subsistence activities shade into the reproductive activities of households, especially women, and include, for example, agricultural production. Self-provisioning may, in turn, be periodically or permanently extended to yield an income in kind or cash. For women, in particular, such activities as laundering, beer brewing and child minding, are extensions of their domestic roles. In the petty capitalist sector, a high degree of competition and dependent, exploitative relationship with the dominant capitalist sector prevent the accumulation of surplus. The result of this economic system is that the urban poor lack the means necessary to consume the housing available on the market.

Housing and infrastructure are seen as items of private and collective consumption, access to which is determined not just by individual household resources, but also by public policy, and by structural factors which influence the operation of the housing and land markets, financial institutions and the availability of building materials. The resources available to individual households are seen as a function of their role in the urban economy, although social relationships and the extent of their political influence are also important. The conclusion is reached that because of the structural constraints on employment and income available to the poor majority, the housing problem cannot be solved while a capitalist economic system persists. No housing policy, therefore, however carefully tailored to the effective demand for housing, can satisfy the housing needs of the urban poor (Burgess, 1978).

This outline of the political economy approach to analysing housing demand is brief and, admittedly, crude. I have omitted much of the more recent and more sophisticated analysis of the form which the capitalist economic system takes in the cities of Third World (Armstrong and McGee, 1985). However, there has been relatively little attention paid specifically to consumption to date in marxist theoretical contributions to the housing question in the cities of Third World. There has, however, recently been more specific attention to gender issues in the housing context, as women draw attention to their particular needs and disadvantages with respect to housing. This has taken the form, for example, of the National Swedish Institute for Building Research's research programme on women householders and housing strategies in Tanzania, Zambia, Zimbabwe and Botswana (Schlyter, 1988; Larsson, 1988); workshops, organised by MATCH in Canada (Sholzberg-Gray *et al.* (eds.), 1985), as part of the IYSH in Harare (Governments of Zimbabwe and Sweden, 1987), and during the NGO Forum at the UN Decade for Women Conference in Nairobi (Lee-Smith, 1985); work commissioned by aid agencies (UNCHS, 1985; Lycette and Jaramillo, 1984, for USAID; Muller with Vos, 1985, for the Netherlands Women's Council); and work produced for teaching purposes (Moser and Peake (eds.), 1987).

CONCLUSIONS

Neo-classical economic analysis tends to assume a perfectly competitive housing market in which supply will respond to demand unless there are particular constraints (Arnott, 1987; Mayo *et al.*, 1986). The recent interest of economists in the housing markets of Third World cities is largely confined to the large-scale World Bank research project which is attempting to understand the economics of demand, a focus which is typical of the housing economics literature (Olsen, 1987). Some analysis has also focused on identifying constraints on housing supply, and policy, sometimes, on alleviating them.

The discussion noted that application of marxist analyses to housing is a particular manifestation of wider trends in development and theory, and in particular of the urban economy. Earlier dichotomous classifications have increasingly given way to analyses of the forms of economic activity which occur within the urban economy, the relationship of the non-capitalist forms of production to the dominant capitalist mode, and particularly, the way in which this relationship influences and limits the development of petty commodity production, distribution and exchange. There have been remarkably few attempts to apply the initial formulation of the theoretical framework put forward by Burgess (1978) to understanding housing markets in Third World cities.[7]

Marxist approaches have been subject to a number of criticisms. It has been noted that urban characteristics and policy outcomes cannot simply be read off from structural inputs, especially when political and ideological aspects are neglected in favour of economic determinism. Marxist analysts have also been criticised for their failure to give any indication of solutions to problems, such as the housing problem, which do not depend on the destruction of the capitalist system, or , at least, to provide practical guidelines on the achievement of transition from a current state to some preferred future state.

Reference is made in the literature to the desirability of increasing dialogue between proponents of the main approaches to analysis of urban housing markets. This is perhaps a reaction to the way in which the debate was initiated (by Burgess representing his and Turner's views as antithetical) and continued (in the references by Burgess, Gilbert and Van der Linden cited above and in the World Bank economists' disregard for the potential contribution of Marxist theory). Although some doubt is cast on the potential for dialogue between the two approaches by Nientied and Van der Linden (1985), because of their different starting points, questions and methodology, the analyses presented in this paper show that the two main approaches to analysing urban housing markets both have something to offer in terms of increasing our understanding of the underlying processes and of the characteristics of housing producers and consumers, provided these are applied to understanding housing markets on a city-wide basis and the housing sector and its sub-divisions in urban and national terms.

Thus future research must focus both on the process by which housing is produced, and on its consumption. Each group of actors involved in housing development, intervenes at one or more points in the process; the nature of its intervention and the responses by others to that intervention, are the determinants of provision, and the social relations between the actors involved are crucial to understanding the nature of housing markets (Ball, 1983). In addition, research must focus not just on household units as individual economic agents, as does neo-classical economic theory, but also on which groups in the population are able to consume housing made available through different production processes, how the observed consumption patterns can be explained with reference to the insertion of households in different class positions into the political, economic and social system and how these both determine the housing they are able to consume and its characteristics in terms of tenure, quality and cost. In addition, the differences in needs and access to housing by gender, themselves related to the household forms which are the products of societies in which they exist, must be made explicit.

To strengthen policy formulation, an assessment of housing need must be attempted, recognising the pitfalls and limitations of any such calculation; and effective demand for housing analysed, by methods which are further developed to overcome some of the drawbacks of the crude analysis generally used to date. Information is required on the resources available to individual households, including the structure of household income and the likely availability of savings, the income of household members other than the head, and inter-household transfers. Credit for house construction or purchase is essential, and this must be backed by an institutional system which can make capital available for large-scale public sector investment, primarily in infrastructure, as well as for individual house purchasers or builders. The revenue generating capacity of taxes on land and property is important here, although the availability of information on the conventional formal sector system should not lead to an assumption that informal mechanisms for obtaining access to credit are absent. Within this system, the overall incidence of subsidies should be assessed. Thus concern should shift from housing output targets to provision of essential inputs of land, construction capacity and materials, and finance (Van Huyck, 1986). A neglected segment of the market is rental housing, including the effect on the supply of accommodation of government attempts to control rents.[8]

Although in the early stages of urbanisation, it is perhaps justifiable to place a major emphasis on the production and consumption of housing, exchange increases in importance as the housing stock ages. Even within the neo-classical paradigm, which may treat the exchange process as a black box, its smooth functioning is essential for market mechanisms to produce smooth adjustments to changes in demand or supply. In developed countries, considerable emphasis has been given to the study of filtering in the housing market, but comparable studies are rare in Third World countries.[9] The system of exchange is usually organised through a series of intermediaries, who may include estate agents, valuers, surveyors, housing finance institutions, solicitors and land deed registries. The nature of the system may be important in determining which groups consume particular types of housing, while each of the actors involved is likely to be pursuing their own interests, which in turn may have an impact on the supply of housing. The system (or systems, for some may be much more informal than implied above) has not been studied in this way for any of Third World cities. Such an analysis would need to assess the impact of such systems on housing markets, whose interests they serve and who benefits from the profits and fees generated.

NOTES

1. This chapter is a version of a paper which is to be published in *World Development*, in January 1992.
2. © Dr. Carole Rakodi.
3. See Dowall (1988) for an outline of the method for assessing the supply of land and housing which was used in the Bangkok Land Management Study, and Drakakis-Smith (1988) for a brief overview of the components of housing production.
4. Kitay (1987) examines some of the constraints on private sector production of housing, as part of USAID's recent promotion of public-private co-operation on shelter development.
5. Other attempts to analyse effective demand have been made in Tunis (Landeau, 1987) and Bandung (Benjamin *et al.*, 1987).
6. See also Mayo and Gross (1987) who, in noting the substantial subsidies which have characterised most World Bank funded sites and services programmes, and made them accessible to relatively low-income people, stress the potential limitations on replicability imposed by such subsidies which are necessary partly because of the adoption of inappropriate design standards.
7. Although see Mehta and Mehta (1987) on Ahmedabad and Rakodi (1990) on Harare.
8. See Mayo *et al.* (1986) The World Bank has carried out research into the effects of rent control and the need and possibilities for decontrol.
9. In studies of filtering in Quito and Bangkok it was found that residential mobility was primarily explained by a response to the desire for home ownership. Secondary reasons for mobility related to residential satisfaction. In the Quito case (Miller and Romsa, 1982) vacancy chains were analysed, finding that construction of high cost detached housing units helped to absorb middle-income demand, but generated no improvement in housing conditions for lower income

groups as a result. In Bangkok (Savasdisara *et al.*, 1988) current residents of private low-cost estates were more likely to move in response to opportunities for ownership, specially younger renters, compared to residential dissatisfaction, and particularly to dissatisfaction with the dwelling. Further, a case study of upward filtering as a result of upgrading in Tunis, using a stock user matrix, distinguishes between voluntary and involuntary filtering, and discusses potential policy implications and interventions to control such filtering (Johnson, 1987).

REFERENCES

Amis, P. (1984), 'Squatters or Tenants: the Commercialisation of Unauthorised Housing in Nairobi', *World Development*, 12(1):105-114.

Angel, S. *et al.*, (1977). 'The low Income Housing Delivery System in Asia', in R.P. Pama and J.H. DeGoede (eds.) *Low-income Housing — Technology and Policy*, Oxford, Pergamon, III: 1177-1218.

Armstrong, W. and McGee, T.G. (1985), *Theatres of Accumulation: Studies in Asian and Latin American Urbanisation*, London, Methuen.

Arnott, R. (1987), 'Economic Theory and Housing', in E.S. Mills (ed.), *Handbook of Regional and Urban Economics*, II, *Urban Economics*, Amsterdam, North-Holland : 959-988.

Ball, M. (1983), *Housing Policy and Economic Power: the Political Economy of Owner Occupation*, London, Methuen.

Barnes, S.T. (1982), 'Public and Private Housing in Urban West Africa: the Social Implications', in M.K.C. Morrison and P.C.W. Gutkind (eds.) *Housing the Urban Poor in Africa*, Syracuse, Maxwell School of Citizenship and Public Affairs : 5-32.

Bassett, K. and Short, J. (1980), *Housing and Residential Structure: Alternative Approaches*, London, Routledge and Kegan Paul.

Benjamin, S., *et al.* (1985), 'The Housing Costs of low-Income Kampung Dwellers', *Habitat International*, 9(1):91-110.

—— (1987), 'Stretching the People's Housing Resources', *Habitat International*, 11(2): 147-159.

Boleat, M. (1987), 'Housing Finance Institutions', in L. Rodwin (ed.) *Shelter, Settlement and Development*, Winchester, Mass., Allen and Unwin: 151-178.

Burgess, R. (1978), 'Petty Commodity Housing or Dweller Control? A Critique of John Turner's views on Housing Policy', *World Development*, 6(9-10): 1105-1133.

—— (1985a), 'Problems in the Classification of low Income Urban Neighbourhoods in Latin America', *Third World Planning Review*, 7(4): 287-306.

—— (1985b), 'The limits of State Self-help Housing Programmes', *Development and Change*, 16:271-312.

—— (1987), 'A lot of Noise and no Nuts', *Development and Change*, 18(1): 137-146.

Burns, L.S. and Grebler, L. (1977), *The Housing of Nations*, London: Macmillan.

Chabbi, M. (1988), 'The Pirate Subdeveloper: a New form of Land Developer in Tunis', *International Journal for Urban and Regional Research*, 12(1):8-21.

Chana, T.S. (1984), 'Nairobi: Dandora and other Projects', in G.K. Payne (ed.) *Low-Income Housing in the Developing World*, Chichester, Wiley: 17-36.

Davidson, F. (1981), 'Affordable Urban Development', *Planning and Transportation Research and Computation Summer Annual Meeting*, Seminar F:119-126.

Dowall, D.E. (1988), 'The Land and Housing Market Assessment: an Important Tool for Increasing Housing Delivery in Third World Cities', *Habitat International*, 12(4):135-149.

Drakakis-Smith, D.W. (1977), 'Housing the Urban Poor in West Malaysia: the Role of the Private Sector', *Habitat International*, 2 (5/6):571-584.

—— (1979), 'Low Cost Housing Provision in the Third World: Some Theoretical and Practical Alternatives', in M.S. Murison and J.P. Lea (eds) *Housing in Third World Countries*, London, Macmillan: 22-30.

—— (1981), *Urbanisation, Housing and the Development Process*, London, Croom Helm.

—— (1988), 'Housing', in M. Pacione (ed.) *The Geography of the Third World: Progress and Prospects*, London, Croom Helm: 148-197.

Dunkerley, H. *et al.* (1978), *Urban Policy Issues and Opportunities*, Washington, World Bank Staff Working Paper No. 263, I and II.

Edmonds, G.A. (1979), 'The construction Industry in Developing Country', *International Labour Review*, 118(3): 355-369.

Edwards, M.A. (1982), 'Cities of Tenants: Renting among the Urban Poor in Latin America" in A.G. Gilbert, J.E. Hardy and R. Ramirez (eds.) *Urbanization in Contemporary Latin America*, Chichester, Wiley: 129-159.

El Kadi, G. (1988), 'Market Machanisms and Spontaneous Urbanization in Egypt: The Cairo Case', *International Journal of Urban and Regional Research*, 12(1):22-37.

England, R. and Alnwick, D. (1982), 'What can Low Income Families Afford for Housing?" *Habitat International* 6 (4):461-470.

Follain, J.R. and Jimenez, E. (1983a), *The Demand for Housing Characteristics in Developing Countries*, Washington, D.C., World Bank Water Supply and Urban Development Department, Discussion Paper WUDD 43.

—— (1983b), *Estimating the Demand for Housing Characteristics: a Survey and Critique*, Washington, D.C., World Bank Water Supply and Development Department Discussion Paper UDD-42.

Genesan, S. (1983), 'Housing and Construction: Major Constraints and Development Measures', *Habitat International*, 7(5/6):173-194.

Gilbert, A. (1987), 'Latin America's Urban Poor: Shanty Dwellers or Renters of Rooms?" *Cities*, February, 43-51.

Gilbert, A. and Van der Linden, J. (1986), 'The Limits of a Marxist Theoretical Framework for Explaining State Self-help Housing', *Development and Change*, 18 (1):129-136.

Gilbert, A. and Ward, P. (1984a), 'Community Action by the Urban Poor: Democratic Involvement, Community Self-Help or a Means of Social Contro?" *World Development*, 12(8):769-782.

—— (1984b), 'Community Participation in Upgrading Irregular Settlements: The Community Response" *World Development*, 12(9):913-922.

—— (1985), *Housing, the State and the Poor: Policy and Practice in Three Latin American Cities*, Cambridge, Cambridge University Press.

Gore, C. *et al.* (1985), 'Small Scale Informal Construction Sector at Kuwadzana Low-Income Housing Project', Harare (memeo).

Governments of Zimbabwe and Sweden (1987), *IYSH Women and Shelter Seminar*, Harare.

Grimes, O. (1976), *Housing for Low-Income Urban Families*, Baltimore, Johns Hopkins University Press.

Hamer, A.M. (1985), *Bogota's Unregulated Subdivisions: The Myths and Realities of Incremental Housing Construction*, Washington, D.C., World Bank Staff Working Paper No. 734.

Jimenez, E. (1983), 'The Value of Squatter Dwellings in Developing Countries', *Economic Development and Cultural Change*: 739-752.

Johnson, T.E. (1987), 'Upward Filtering the Housing Stock: A Study of Upward Filtering of Housing Stock as a Consequence of Informal Settlement Urgrading in Developing Countries', *Habitat International*, 11(1):173-190.

Johnstone, M. (1980), 'Conventional Housing Provision in Peninsular Malaysia: Spatial Distortions in a Developing Economy', *Habitat International*, 5 (3/4):337-359.

—— (1984), 'Urban Housing and Housing Policy in Peninsular Malaysia', *International Journal of Urban and Regional Research*, 8(4):497-529.

Kioe-Sheng, Y. (1988), 'Housing Priorities, Expenditure atterns and Plot Development in Third World Countries', Paper presented to the International Sociological Association Built Environment Study Group Conference on Housing Policy and Urban Innovation, Amsterdam.

Kirke, J. (1984), 'The Provision of Infrastructure and Utility Services', in G.K. Payne (ed.) *Low-income Housing in the Developing World*, Chichester, Wiley : 233-248.

Kitay, M. (1987), 'Public-Private Co-operation for the Development of low-Income shelter', *Habitat International*, 11(1):29-36.

Landeau, J.F. (1987), 'Tunisia: a Case Study in Analysing the Affordability of Mortgage Loans', *African Urban Quarterly*, 2(3):223-233.

Lambert, J. *et al.* (1978), *Housing Policy and the State: Allocation, Access and Control*, London, Macmillan.

Larsson, A. (1988), 'The Housing Situation of Urban Female-Headed Households in Botswana', *Habitat International*, 12(3):17-27.

Lee, M. (1985), 'Myths of Affordability', *Third World Planning Review*, 7 (2):131-142.

Lee-Smith, D. (1985), 'Women and Habitat at Forum 85', *Settlements Information Network Africa Newsletter*, 9:5-12.

Leeds, A. (1981), 'Lower Iincome Settlement Types: Processes, Structures, Policies', in UNCHS (ed.) *The Residential Circumstances of the Urban Poor in Developing Countries*, New York, Praeger : 21-61.

Lycette, M.A. and Jaramillo, C. (1984), 'Low-Income Housing: a Women's Perspective', Washington: International Centre for Research on Women, report for USAID (mimeo).

Malpezzi, S. (1984), *Analysing an Urban Housing Survey: Economic Models and Statistical Techniques*, Washington, D.C., World Bank, Urban Development Department, Discussion Paper UDD-44.

—— *et al.* (1982), *Planning an Urban Housing Survey: Key Issues for Researchers and Programme Managers in Developing Countries*, Washington, D.C., World Bank Urban Development Department, Discussion Paper UDD-44.

—— and Mayo, S.K. (1987), 'User Cost and Housing Tenure in Developing Countries', *Journal of Development Economics*, 25:197-220.

Mayo, S., (1985). 'How Much Will Households Spend for Shelter?' *Urban Edge*, 9(10):4-5.

Mayo S.K. and Gross, D.J. (1987), 'Sites and Services — and Subsidies: the Economics of Low-Cost Housing in Developing Countries', *The World Bank Economic Review*, 1(2):301-335.

—— and Malpezzi, S. (1984), *A Comparative Analysis of Housing Demand in Developing Countries*, Washington, D.C., World Bank Water Supply and Urban Development Department, UDD-41.

—— *et al.* (1986), 'Shelter Strategies for the Urban Poor in Developing Countries', Paper to the American Real Estate and Urban Economics Association, New York.

McAllum, D. and Benjamin, S. (1985), 'Low-Income Housing in the Third World: Broadening the Economic Perspective', *Urban Studies*, 22:277-287.

McAuslan, P. (1985), *Urban Land and Shelter for the Poor*, London, Earthscan.

Mehta, M. and Mehta, D. (1987), 'Metropolitan Housing Markets: Ahmedabad', *Economic and Political Weekly*, 22(40):1701-1710.

Merrett, S. (1984), 'The Assessment of Housing Consumption Requirements in Developing Countries', *Third World Planning Review*, 6, (4):319-329.

Miller, F. and Romsa, G. (1982), 'Residential Mobility, Vacancy Chains and Perceived Benefits Arising From New Detached Housing in Quito, Ecuador', *TESG*, 73(3):162-172.

Moavenzadeh, F. (1987), 'The Construction Industry', in L. Rodwin, (ed.) *Shelter, Settlement and Development*, Winchester, Mass, Allen and Unwin : 73-109.

Mohan, R. *et al.* (1981), *Measuring Urban Malnutrition and Poverty: A Case Study of Bogota and Cali, Colombia*, Washington, D.C., World Bank Staff Working Paper No. 447.

Moser, C.O.N. (1978), 'Informal Sector or Petty Commodity Production: Dualism or Dependence in Urban Development', *World Development*, 6 (9/10):1041-1064.

—— (1982), 'A Home of One's Own: Squatter Housing Strategies in Guayaquil, Ecuador' in A. Gilbert, (ed.) *Urbanisation in Contemporary Latin America: Critical Approaches to the Analysis of Urban Issues*, Chichester: Wiley: 159-190.

—— (1984), 'The Informal Sector Reworked: Viability and Vulnerability in Urban Development', *Regional Development Dialogue*, 5 (2):135-178.

—— and Peake, L. (eds.) (1987), *Women, Human Settlements and Housing*, London, Tavistock.

Muller, M.S. with Vos, M. (1985), 'Women and Habitat in the Third World: the Urban and Rural Situation', Netherlands Womens Council (mimeo).

Nientied, P. and Van der Linden, J. (1985), 'Approaches to low-Income Housing in the Third World: Some Comments', *International Journal of Urban and Regional Research*, 9(3):311-329.

Nimpuno-Parente, P. (1987), 'The Struggle for Shelter: Women in a Sites and Services Project in Nairobi, Kenya', in C.O.N. Moser and L. Peake (eds.) *Women, Human Settlements and Housing*, London, Tavistock : 70-87.

Olsen, E.O. (1987), 'The Demand and Supply of Housing Service: a Critical Survey of the Empirical Literature' in E.S. Mills (ed.) *Handbook of Regional and Urban Economics, II Urban Economics*, Amsterdam, North-Holland : 989-1022.

Payne, G.K. (1977), *Urban Housing in the Third World*, London, Leonard Hill.

Peattie, L. (1979), 'Housing Policy in Developing Countries: Two Puzzles', *World Development*, 7:1017-1022.

Perlman, J. (1980), 'The Failure of Influence: Squatter Eradication in Brazil', in M.S. Grindle (ed.) *Politics and Policy Implementation in the Third World*, Princeton, Princeton University Press : 250-278.

Rakodi, C. (1983), 'La Politique Du logement Pour Les Bas Revenus a Lusaka, Zambie' (Trans. A. Durand-Lasserve), in *Le logement, L'Etat et les Pauvres dans les villes du Tiers-monde*, Practique Urbaines 2, Talence, Centre d'Etudes de Geographie

Tropicale and Centre National de la Recherche Scientifique : 155-172.

—— (1986), 'State and Class in Africa: a Case for Extending Analyses of the Form and Functions of the National State to the Urban Local State', *Society and Space*, (4):419-446.

—— (1987), 'Upgrading in Chawama, Lusaka: Displacement or Differentiation?' *Urban Studies*, 25(4):197-318.

—— (1988), 'The Local State and Urban Local Government in Zambia', *Public Administration and Development*, (8):27-46.

—— (1990), 'Housing Production and Housing Policy in Harare, Zimbabwe', *Journal of Urban Affairs*. 12(2):135-156.

Renaud, B. (1984), *Housing and Financial Institutions in Developing Countries*, Chicago, International Union of Building Societies and Savings Associations.

—— (1987), 'Financing Shelter' in L. Rodwin (ed.) *Shelter, Settlement and Development*, Winchester, Mass., Allen and Unwin : 179-205.

Roberts, B.W.G. (1980), 'The Capital Costs of Urban Development', *Third World Planning Review*, 2(1):26-44.

Santos, M. (1979), *The Shared Space: The Two Circuits of the Urban Economy in Underdeveloped Countries*, London, Methuen.

Sanyal, B. (1981), 'Who Gets What, Where, Why and How: a Critical Look at Housing Subsidies in Zambia', *Development and Change*, 12:409-440.

Savisdara, T. *et al.* (1988), 'Residential Mobility in Private Lower-Cost Housing in Bangkok', *Housing Studies*, 3(4):250-258.

Schlyter, A. (1984), *Upgrading Reconsidered — the George Studies in Retrospect*, Gavle, The National Swedish Institute for Building Research.

—— (1988), *Women Householders and Housing Strategies. The Case of George, Lusaka*, Gavle, The National Swedish Institute for Building Research.

Sholzberg-Gray, S. *et al.* (eds.) (1985), *Women in Human Settlements, Management for Change*, Ottawa, MATCH International Centre.

Strassman, W.P. (1978), *Housing and Building Technology in Developing Countries*, E. Lansing, Michigan State University.

—— (1982), *The Transformation of Urban Housing: The Experience of Upgrading in Cartagena, Colombia*, Washington, Johns Hopkins University Press.

Stretton, A.W. (1981), 'The Building Industry and Urbanisation in Third World countries: A Philippine Case Study', *Economic Development and Cultural Change*, 29:325-339.

Turner, J. (1967), 'Barriers and Channels for Housing Development in Modernising countries', *Journal of the American Institute of Planners*, XXXIII: 3.

—— (1972), 'Housing as a Verb" in J. Turner and R. Fichter (eds.), *Freedom to Build*, New York, Macmillan : 148-175.

UN (1976), *World Housing Survey, 1974*, New York: UN.

—— (1978), *Non-Conventional Financing of Housing for Low-Income Households*, New York, UN.

—— (1984), *Guidelines for the Preparation of Shelter Programmes*, New York: UN.

UNCHS (1982), *Survey of Slums and Squatter Settlements*, Dublin, Tycooly International Publications.

—— (1984a), *The Promotion of Non-Conventional Approaches to Housing Finance for Low Income Groups*, Nairobi, UNCHS.

—— (1984b), *Community-based Finance Institutions*, Nairobi, UNCHS.

—— (1985), *Women and Human Settlements*, Nairobi, UNCHS.

—— (1987), *Global Report on Human Settlements, 1986*, Oxford, Oxford University Press.

—— (1987), *Case Study of Site and Service Schemes in Kenya: Lessons from Dandora and Thika*, Nairobi, UNCHS.

Van der Linden, J. (1986), *The Sites and Services Approach Reviewed*, Aldershot, Gower.

Van Huyck, A. (1986), 'New Directions in Asian Housing Policies', *Habitat International* 10 (1/2):5-10.

Ward, P. (1978), 'Self-help Housing in Mexico City: Social and Economic Determinants of success', *Town Planning Review*, 49(1):218-249.

Wegener, R.H. (1982), 'Low-income Housing Finance: an Integrated Approach', *Habitat International*, 6(4):425-439.

Wells, J. (1984), 'The Construction Industry in the Context of Development', *Habitat International*, 8 (3/4):9-28.

Winpenny, J. (1982), 'Housing the Poor', in P.J. Richards and M.D. Leonor (eds.), *Target Setting for Basic Needs*, Geneva, ILO : 71-104.

World Bank (1972), *Urbanization*, Washington, D.C., World Bank, Sector Working Paper.

—— (1975), *Housing Sector Policy Paper*, Washington, D.C., World Bank.

—— (1980a), *Poverty and Basic Needs*, Washington, D.C., World Bank.

—— (1980b), *Shelter*, Washington, D.C., World Bank, Poverty and Basic Needs Series.

—— (1980c), *Water Supply and Waste Disposal*, Washington, D.C., World Bank, Poverty and Basic Needs Series.

—— (1985), 'Making Shelter Projects Replicable', *Urban Edge*, 9(10):1-4.

—— (1986),. 'Financing Shelter: the Economic Dimension', *Urban Edge*, 10:1-6.

—— (1988), *The Emerging Role of Housing Finance*, Washington, D.C., World Bank, Infrastructure Urban Development Department.

Yeh, S.M.K. and Laquian, A.A. (1977), *Housing Asia's Millions*, Ottawa, International Development Research Centre.

Zetter, R. (1984), 'Land Issues in Low-Income Housing', in G.K. Payne (ed.) *Low-income Housing in the Development World*, Chichester, Wiley.

2

URBAN HOUSING POLICY IN INDIA: Context, Shifts and Implications

HARJINDER SINGH

CONTEXT

(a) Housing Situation

The Housing sector continues to remain as a marginal sector of the economy for purposes of resource allocation. Like other Third World economies, investment in housing in terms of annual flows ranges between 2 to 4 per cent of Gross Domestic Product (GDP) (Government of India, 1988a). In 1984-85 this percentage was 3.22 (Munjee, 1988). Housing stock in the country was estimated in 1981 at 28 million units which consisted of 18 million *pucca* (made of bricks and cement), 6.8 million semi-*pucca* (bricks and mud) and 3.2 million *kutcha* (mud and thatch) units. The share of urban housing was 24.27 per cent. This number was far less than of the urban households indicating shortage of 5.9 million dwelling units (National Building Organisation, 1985).

According to NBO in 1981, two million households were roofless, 1.7 million were staying in over-crowded houses and 3.1 million houses were below minimum acceptable standard of housing. Another disturbing aspect of the situation is that the gap between need and supply is widening very fast. The shortage has increased from 3.0 million in 1971 to 5.9 million dwelling units in 1981 (Table 2.1). In 1990, it is estimated to be at 9.7 million units.

According to the National Commission on Urbanisation (Government of India, 1988) in 1981, 6 to 8 million households were living in slums alone. The annual rate of household formation is also likely to increase from one million in 1981 to 1.7 million in 1991 and

2.2 million in 2001 with an average household size of five persons. Added to this is the old and dilapidated housing stock which needs to be replaced. Of this stock, 21 per cent is 40-year old, and 10 per cent is more than 60-year old, 37 per cent of urban households were without electricity and 66 per cent were without latrine facilities. What concerns most is the rate of construction of shelter (per capita) in the country which is one of the lowest in the world (UNCHS, 1987). Even in comparison to many Third World countries this also holds true (Table 2.2). Cuba, a far smaller country produces half as many houses every year as does India.

TABLE 2.1: Shortfall of Urban Housing Units

Components	Number (in million)
1. Shelterless households	0.2
2. Over crowding and congestion	
(a) Excess of households over available housing units	1.1
(b) Number of married couples requiring separate room/house	0.3
3. Replacement of *kutcha* units	3.1
4. Obsolescence/Replacement of old housing units (over 80-year old)	1.2
5. Total	5.9

Source: National Building Organisation.

TABLE 2.2: Annual Growth Rates of Construction (1975-80)

Country	Construction	Construction per capita	Produce in physical units	
			Plywood	Cement
Argentina	6.8	5.4	-2.8	6.3
Egypt*	28.0	6.9	6.9	0.4
India	1.8	-0.2	7.2	1.8
Kenya*	4.4	0.2	3.4	7.4
South Korea	12.2	10.5	4.4	9.1
Malaysia	12.6	10.0	3.9	10.2
Mexico	12.6	10.0	3.9	10.2
South Arabia	11.4	8.3	—	23.8
Thailand	11.6	8.3	11.8	6.2

Note: * Refers to Annual Growth Rate for 1975-79.
Source: UNCHS (1987).

The low level of income of the vast majority of the households and very high housing costs make even a modest dwelling beyond their reach. According to the Housing and Urban Development Corporation (HUDCO), three out of four families cannot afford a house costing more than Rs. 6600 (Jayaram, 1988). The World Bank Survey (1975) reveals that 64 per cent of households in Ahmedabad and 63 per cent in Madras were unable to afford the cheapest dwellings available at that time (Jayaram, 1988). Most of the households (52.9%) in the country had rental accommodation (India: 1980). In the major metropolitan cities their proportion was higher i.e. Ahmedabad (76.3 per cent), Bangalore (74.2 per cent), Bombay (85.2 per cent), Calcutta (81.3 per cent), Delhi (83.8 per cent), Hyderabad (78.3 per cent) and Kanpur (91.3 per cent) (Gupta, 1985). Table 2.3 reflects the position of current rental housing. It gives percentage distribution of households by monthly rent groups along with the area occupied by them.

TABLE 2.3: Rental Accommodation in Urban Area

Monthly rent group (Rs.)	Percentage of households	Average no. of persons per household	Average total area in sq m per household
0 — 10	19.58	3.29	16.86
10 — 20	26.14	4.08	18.67
20 — 50	29.77	5.80	25.99
50 — 100	9.75	5.26	29.28
100 — 150	2.34	5.51	53.83
150 — 250	1.47	5.53	71.26
250 — above	0.56	5.36	82.49
Not recorded	10.39	3.11	25.84
All	100.00	4.17	25.14

Source: Sarvekshana, October 1977, p. 232. 28th Round of N.S.S.

Nearly one-fifth and one-half of them pay rent less than Rs. 10 and Rs. 20 per month respectively. Over 75 per cent pay rent less than Rs. 50. The accommodation occupied by nearly half of them was less than 19 sq metres. Of the total households, 86 per cent occupied accommodation less than 26 sq m, an equivalent to the area, i.e. 25 sq m, recommended by the Ministry of Urban Development (Government of India, 1988) for the urban poor. The results of 28th Round of National Sample Survey (Table 2.4) also indicate the overall housing situation i.e. type and nature of accommodation in terms of rooms and space in possession of all sample households. More than half of them lived just in one room satisfying the specifications laid down by the NBO, four persons were living in a room with an average living area of 13.77 sq m indicating extreme over-crowding. Three-fourths of households had living space up to two rooms. Only 14.22 per cent households had three or more living rooms with 51.84 sq m area. More than 7 per cent of households had no living area at all. They were mainly squatters or pavement dwellers. On an average, the living room area per household with 5 members was just 21.24 sq m and the total living area including 'other available area' was just 27.76 sq metres.

TABLE 2.4: Housing Accommodation in Possession of Urban Households

Type	Percentage of households	Average no. of persons per house	Average living room area sq m per household	Other area available in sq m
1. No living room	7.23	1.25	—	14.15
2. One living room below NBO specifications	2.15	3.38	7.09	1.17
3. Two or more living rooms below NBO specifications	0.29	5.52	17.00	4.32
4. One living room satisfying NBO specifications	51.05	4.17	13.77	3.22
5. Two living rooms as per NBO specifications	25.03	5.74	26.14	7.17
6. Three or more living rooms as per NBO specifications	14.22	6.96	51.84	14.19
7. No response	0.03	1.99	—	—
Total	100.00	4.74	21.24	6.52

Source: *Sarvekshana*, 1977, p. 232.

(b) Magnitude of Poverty

The magnitude and growth of urban poverty is reflected by the growing number of slums and squatter settlements. Slums are growing at an average rate of 10.7 per cent per annum (Gupta, 1988). The Task Force on Housing and Urban Development (Government of India, 1983), estimated that in 1981, 20.88 to 26.33 per cent of total urban households were living in slums. The lowest estimate of households in this range was six million. Distribution of slum population by size –

class-wise in urban centres reveals its concentration in metropolitan cities (Table 2.5).

TABLE 2.5: Distribution of Slum Population by Size/Class — 1981

Size/Class of Cities/Towns	Percentage of slum population	
	Low estimate	High estimate
One million plus	33.00	38.00
0.10 — 1.0 million	17.91	24.59
Less than 0.10 million	15.04	19.72
All Classes	20.88	26.33

Source: Government of India, Planning Commission, Task Force on Housing and Urban Development, 1983.

The figures of the table indicate that the problems of poverty and accommodation are positively linked with the size of the city. The metropolitan cities (12) alone account for 38 per cent of the slum population. Almost three-fourths of this population was concentrated in the four largest cities: Calcutta, Bombay, Delhi and Madras. Projection by the Task Force for the year 2001 also assume the continuation of the present magnitude of the problem with 62 to 78 million out of 310 million people living in slums. The share of metropolitan cities (20 by that time) is expected to be higher than 32 to 36 million slum dwellers. The estimates of the Task Force are considered on the lower side as an index to indicate the urban poverty. The estimates of Task Force have great limitations because of the conceptual difficulties arising out of the varying definitions of 'slums' used in different surveys. In many cases only 'declared slums' or slums within municipal limits have been included. Undeclared slums, slums outside the municipal limits as well as squatters and pavement dwellers from a significant proportion of the urban poor. Thus it is not difficult to conclude that incidence of poverty, is quite higher than the estimated by the Task Force.

(c) Occupation, Income and Expenditure of Urban Poor

The present housing situation is attributed largely to the very low income level of households (Table 2.6). The distribution of households by monthly income reveals that at 1986-87 prices, 45.67 per cent of them have a monthly income up to Rs. 800, an amount which is just enough to survive in urban areas. Households with monthly incomes higher than Rs. 2,000 constitute 14.68 per cent, of which 3.37 per cent belong to higher income group. Table 2.6 also reflects the incidence of urban poverty prevalent in the country as well as the low paying capacity of a large section of the population.

TABLE 2.6: Distribution of Urban Households by Monthly Income — 1988

Sl. No.	Monthly income (in Rs.)	Percentage of households	Cumulative percentage
1.	Up to 400	12.33	12.33
2.	401 – 600	17.32	29.65
3.	601 – 800	16.02	45.67
4.	801 – 1000	13.68	59.35
5.	1001 – 1250	10.47	69.62
6.	1251 – 1500	7.07	76.89
7.	1501 – 2000	8.43	85.32
8.	2001 – 3000	7.84	93.16
9.	3001 – 4000	3.47	96.63
10.	4001 and above	3.37	100.00

Note: Rupees 25 are approximately equal to 1 US dollar.
Source: Report of the National Commission on Urbanisation, Vol. II, 1988.

The employment pattern of the urban poor is revealed by a number of studies. According to a survey conducted by National Institute of Urban Affairs (Raghupathi, 1989) in 1988, more than half i.e. 55.1 per cent of the urban poor were employed as production and related workers, transport, equipment operators and labourers (Table 2.7). The employment pattern of the urban poor also reveals that the percentage of self-employed workers was highest (41.7 per cent) closely followed by casual workers (38.4 per cent). The remaining (19.9 per cent) were in wage employment. The Survey also reveals that the average daily earnings of wage employment earned the highest i.e. Rs. 27.80 while casual employment earned the lowest i.e. Rs. 12.27. Those who were self-employed, were earning Rs. 16.23. The table also provides more detailed information about each category of occupation. Highest concentration of poor workers was found in the least productive occupations while the most productive occupation had the least of them. It shows the negative relationship between the productivity of an occupation and the concentration of the poor workers.

TABLE 2.7: Occupational Classification and Monthly Income of Urban Poor Workers, 1988

Division	Occupation	Percentage of workers	Monthly income (Rs.)
0 – 1	Professional, technical and related workers	2.2	724
2	Administrative, Executive and Managerial workers	0.1	1720
3	Clerical and Related Workers	6.0	954
4	Sales Workers	12.1	557
5	Service Workers	8.4	524
6	Farmers, Fishermen, Hunters, Loggers and Related Workers	5.9	448
7-8-9	Production and Related Workers Transport, Equipment Operators, Labourers	55.1	424
–	Workers not classified by occupations	10.2	710
	Total	100.00	514

Note: The National Institute of Urban Affairs (NIUA) had conducted a survey of the urban poor in 1988 covering 686 slums in 79 cities and towns spread over 14 states and 2 union territories. The number of households surveyed was 23263.

A study of squatters' resettlement colonies of Delhi (Sharma, 1983) also points out that they were engaged in the informal sector mainly in its industrial, trade and commercial and service sectors. Some other surveys and studies of the urban poor also reveal that largely they were employed in the informal sector. The income level of 9.4 per cent households was up to Rs. 300 per month, 45.5 per cent had incomes in the range of Rs. 300-600 and 32.0 per cent were in the range of Rs. 601-1000. Only 14 per cent of households had incomes higher than Rs. 1000. A study conducted by the Society for the Promotion of Area Resource Centres (SPARC) in 1985 (Sharma, 1988) of Bombay pavement dwellers revealed that in 1985, 74 per cent of them were self-employed and earned less than Rs. 540 per month. Of them, only 14 per cent were earning over Rs. 750 per month. A study of pavement dwellers of Calcutta (Jagannathan and Halder, 1988) indicates that they were largely employed in the informal sector earning between Rs. 320 to Rs. 440 on a daily wage basis. Their occupational distribution shows that 44 per cent of them were employed in transport sector as porters, cart-pullers and rickshaw-pullers, 20.7 per cent were self-employed as vegetable vendors, hawkers etc. Others were shop assistants (8.4 per cent), daily labourers (9.7 per cent) and domestic servants (3.2 per cent). The study further reveals that willingness to pay was uniformly low among them. They were willing to pay up to 5.5 per cent of their total earning for purposes of accommodation. The study attributes poor income — shelter linkages to three sets of factors. Firstly, in order to maintain access to earning opportunities most of the pavement dwellers perforce required residence close to their place of work. Secondly, at least 36 per cent of them preferred to remit earnings of their native villages where their other family members were living. Thirdly, 10 per cent of them were unable to think of shelter because of intense poverty. Not only the willingness to pay was very low among the urban poor, their capacity to pay for shelter was even lower than that. An indication is available from the 28th Round of the National Sample Survey. The Survey points out that average per capita monthly expenditure on food items was 67.73 per cent, while non-food items and rental accommodation were left with 28.77 per cent and 3.5 per cent respectively. The low rent paying capacity of the urban poor, besides meagre earnings, was because food items alone consume more than two-thirds of their total earnings.

HOUSING PROGRAMMES FOR THE URBAN POOR: SHIFTS IN APPROACH

The main programmes undertaken by the government to mitigate the housing problem of the urban poor were:

- Slum Clearance and Relocation Schemes (SCRS).
- Environmental Improvement and Upgradation of Slums Schemes (EIUSS).
- Site and Services Schemes (S & S).

Under the slum clearance and relocation schemes (1956), the strategy was to get the existing slum areas cleared off and settle the slum dwellers at alternative sites. They were given highly subsidised tenements. These schemes did not succeed in the sense that (a) these could provide shelter only to a marginal segment of slum dwellers. For instance in Delhi where these programmes were implemented vigorously only 20.66 per cent of the target population could be settled up to 1977, (b) the programmes did not benefit the target groups. The majority of those who were settled in the resettlement colonies were replaced by comparatively higher income groups. The failure may be explained in terms of (i) The resettlement colonies were brought up in the peripheral areas of the cities which were quite distant from their earlier place of living and working. This not only disturbed their social fabric but also threatened their source of income. Because, for the poor, employment is more important than shelter, that is why in order to maintain access to earning opportunities most of them perforce require residence close to their place of work (Jagannathan and Halder, 1988). (ii) Resettlement colonies being far from work places raise the transport cost and reduce the working hours which in turn further depletes their income. This acted as a stimulus to sell whatever shelter they had and to move closer to their work places. In Delhi a Survey of resettlement colonies (Sharma, 1983) reveals that before the relocation, 46.27 per cent of them were doing their jobs within a distance of 2 km. Those working within 4 km radius were 70.21 per cent. Of them 9 per cent had to travel a distance beyond 11 km. After the resettlement, 38.74 per cent could find work within the distance of 4 km and 42.44 had to cover more than 11 km distance. (iii) Shortage of supply of dwelling units meant for low and low-middle income groups pushes these groups to get accommodation in areas which are otherwise meant for the urban poor. They appropriate the highly subsidised shelter either by registering themselves as poor or by offering handsome amounts to the intended beneficiaries.

In the light of the experience of Slum Clearance and Relocation Schemes, the approach was changed. In 1972, the Environmental Improvement and Upgradation of Slums Scheme was implemented under which utilities like water supply, electricity etc. were provided at the existing sites. The aim was to improve the environment with less social and financial cost. However, the element of subsidy was reduced. Shelter norms were also lowered down on the plea, that since the affordability of the poor has not improved, a greater element of subsidy would mean the transfer of home ownership to higher income groups. Instead of lowering the norms, the better course to confront the problem would have been to raise the affordability level of the target groups. Per capita investment to provide the basic amenities was too low i.e. Rs. 151. Security of tenure was also not granted. The improvements made proved to be of a temporary nature.

Again, there was one more experiment in this regard. Under Site and Services Schemes (S&S), the poor were provided small plots

(25 m^2) along with necessary infrastructure. They were supposed to construct the structures later on depending upon their affordability. The cost of infrastructure was borne by the government. The element of subsidy was again reduced. The SCRS also suffered from the location and siting considerations. The shifting of the responsibility of the government to provide subsidised shelter to the poor, in each successive programme, is the hallmark of the policy. Consequently the shelter programmes became more and more demand based instead of need.

In 1970 the Housing and Urban Development Corporation (HUDCO) was set up to provide loans to the agencies engaged in housing production. The approach adopted by these agencies has been of commercial nature. Resource mobilisation became the major consideration for investment. First of all, far fewer dwellings were constructed or sites developed for the economically displaced segments of the population. Secondly, because no subsidy was to be provided, the recovery of full dwelling costs has made the shelter programmes less affordable. The involvement of the World Bank in Housing Development reinforced the shift (Wadhwa, 1988). The projects financed by the bank were based on full cost recovery approach. Affordability became the basis of housing provision. To make housing accessible for the poor the cost was reduced by further lowering standards. Even that did not succeed because affordability of the poor was assumed to be four to five times higher than actual. The outcome was that despite reducing the cost, shelter remained out of reach of a large proportion of the poor.

The shifting in the approach of the government can also be traced in its Five-Year Plans. Until the Fifth Plan, the approach had been to provide subsidised housing to certain weaker sections of the community. Since the Sixth Plan, a change has been noticed regarding subsidised housing. The public sector housing schemes for the economically weaker sections which were highly subsidised, were formulated taking their paying capacity as the basis. In the Seventh Plan the same approach was continued. During the Plan, the government came out with a housing policy in 1988 which envisaged further shifting of the burden of housing provision to the individual households.

HOUSINE POLICY, 1988

The policy aimed to help all people and in particular the houseless and the inadequately housed to secure for themselves affordable shelter through access to land, materials, technology and finance and to encourage investment in housing for the growth of conservation and upgrading of housing stock (Government of India, 1988a). The policy indicated the following major changes:

Firstly, it assigned major role to the private sector for housing development by:

- making credit facilities available to the private and household sector;
- amending Urban Land and Ceiling Act (ULCRA) – 1976 to release the supply of residential land for the private sector;
- inducing entrepreneurs to take up the production of building materials;
- giving budgetary rebate in income-tax on investment in housing;
- amending the Rent Control Act to induce private investment.

Secondly, 'affordability' instead of the 'need' of the target groups was made the basis for housing provision. Social housing had been sought to be replaced by affordable housing.

Thirdly, instead of acting as promoter of housing development, the state confined its role to that of a facilitator. Instead of taking up housing projects by itself as in the past, it will now facilitate housing production by inducing the private and the household sectors to take up housing projects by themselves.

Fourthly, to make housing more accessible to the economically weaker sections, without raising their affordability either through subsidies or raising their income level, following measures were proposed:

- further lowering housing standards;
- provision of building materials in adequate quantity by increasing their production;
- extension of loan facilities;
- promotion of research in low cost housing.

However, the disparities between higher and lower income groups were not sought to be minimised. The gap between plot sizes meant the poor and the rich was allowed to remain. The shift in the housing programmes as noted above had started in the seventies. The state had transferred its burden of providing shelter to the weaker sections of the society. Thus housing policy (1988) only provided an *ex post rationale* for the recent directions in the policy (Wadhwa, 1988).

DRAFT HOUSING POLICY – 1990

With the change in the Federal Government in 1989, the Janata Dal (a left of centre party) government came out with a new Draft Housing Policy in 1990. The policy (Government of India, 1990) for the first time recognises the role of housing activity in the large context of economic development, as a part of strategy for augmenting employment. The policy aims to (a) prevent luxury housing (b) facilitate self-help housing (c) make provision of housing for the poor as a direct responsibility of the State and (d) democratise the housing programmes.

The strategies to achieve the respective objectives have been outlined more clearly than in the previous Policy (1988), though most of the things are the same. To control urban luxury housing the upper limit of plot sizes has been lowered to 120 sq m from 2000 sq m (500 sq m in metropolitan cities). To facilitate the self-help housing for high and middle income groups, the policy envisages the orientation of fiscal and monetary policy, increased investment in housing, greater role for the private and co-operative sectors, and amendment of Urban Land Ceiling and Regulation Act — 1976 for facilitating the supply of residential land. The policy also provides for strengthening of formal and informal financial sources and promotion of rental housing. The major shift in the policy document concerns with the provisions of shelter for the poor. The state has owned the responsibility of shelter provision and seeks to fulfil it by:

- linking the provision of shelter with programmes such as (a) urban and rural poverty and employment promotion (b) shelter upgradation with provision of urban basic services;
- lowering the shelter standards;
- creation of shelter fund by imposing high incidence of taxes on vacant land;
- Direct Acquisition of land;
- Cross-subsidisation under the integrated housing projects;
- Security of tenure.

Peoples' participation in housing development programmes is sought to be encouraged by making the development process more decentralised and entrusting the task to the local municipal bodies.

Though the latest Policy (1990) is not radically different from the Policy (1988) and have many similarities in approach and objectives yet it can be safely stated that in Policy (1990) more concern has been shown for the weaker sections of the society for purposes of shelter provision.

IMPLICATIONS

The later shifts in housing policy documents (1988, 1990) have different implications for each income group. The private sector has been assigned a greater role in housing production. Greater involvement of the private sector, it is expected, would increase the supply of housing for higher, middle and to certain extent lower income groups. It is also hoped that through increased supply it would be able to minimise the rate of increase of house prices. However, care has to be taken that private developers may not be able to form cartels and indulge in speculation and price increasing.

Unfortunately, also the performance of the State agencies is depressing on this account. The phenomenon of price rise and speculation has been witnessed in all the major cities where State agencies had the monopoly in the housing supply. Price rises have made housing more inaccessible not only for lower but also for the middle income groups. This happened as the State agencies themselves indulged in profit-making and speculation. They did this by acquiring peripheral urban land from small and marginal farmers at a price much lower than market value and later on selling it in small quantities at a price many times higher than the development cost (Singh, 1988 and Jha, 1987). At times these agencies notified large amounts of land for acquisition for residential use but which could not be acquired due to inadequacy of financing resources. Thus they kept the notified land out of the market for years. The Urban Land Ceiling and Regulation Act also froze the supply of land for the market. The fundamental reason for the regressive performance was the lack of will of the government, which had its roots in class structure of the society. The dilemma of the situation is that direct State intervention has not succeeded, given its structure, the land market is unlikely to become a better alternative. However, a combination of both the sectors with clearly demarcated areas of operation may ease out the situation. While the private sector may take up 'demand-based' and the State sector may concentrate on need-based projects.

Access to shelter is linked to the income of the household and to the price of shelter. Since the income levels of large segments of the urban population are very low and house prices are rising at a fast rate, it implies that the economically weaker sections and the poor would be unable to have any access to shelter if the State does not come to their assistance. Moreover, there is no rationale for government intervention if it does not take up subsidised housing for the urban poor. Amendments in the Urban Land Ceiling Act to augment the land supply for the private sector, provision of institutional finance through the National Housing Bank, inducement of the private sector to take up production of building materials on a large-scale, income tax rebates for investments in housing; and suitable amendments in Rent Control Act to encourage investment in rental housing will certainly increase the supply of housing stock meant for higher and middle income groups. However, the fate of low income households and the poor will remain sealed till State does not come in a big way to provide shelter to these segments of the population. As things stand, programmes to make shelter accessible to the poor by lowering housing standards i.e. reducing the plot size to 25 sq m and using low quality building materials and extending the loan facilities, will not succeed. Even the reduced plot size and the low quality building materials are beyond the reach of the poor. The rate of interest charged on the loan advanced to these sections is quite high and is beyond their repaying capacity.

Land scarcity and financial constraints, reasons advanced by the State till the recent past for shifting its responsibility for providing shelter to the economically displaced segments were not based soundly. First of all, by fixing the upper limit of large residential plots at 2000 sq m which was quite lavish by any standard, the government kept the bulk of the land as under-utilised. This land could have recycled for the lower income groups by reducing the plot size substantially. Fortunately the latest policy has taken note of this fact and has reduced the plot size to 120 sq m. Secondly, the scarcity of urban land is usually in relative terms; i.e. at particular site(s) and not in absolute terms (Kumar, 1988). Shelter Programmes for the poor along with their employment projects could have been taken up in peripheral areas where land is available at low prices or on their existing living areas. Thirdly, of the total residential land developed by

State agencies, only a marginal proportion of it was allocated to the low income groups, while higher and middle income groups got the major share (Singh, 1988 and Jha,1987). Fourthly, real estate has been one of the most profitable enterprises particularly in larger urban centres. The demand for public housing has always remained many times higher than its supply. The spinning of money by Delhi Development Authority (DDA) and other State agencies from the sales of residential areas indicates that the problem was not so much of scarcity of funds for shelter programmes but of the priorities of different income groups which became responsible for the shift in the policy. The shifts in Housing Policy (1988) were aimed at to promote the interests of higher and middle income groups. The policy also did not address itself to the basic issue of the problem i.e. extreme poverty prevalent among the large segments of urban population on the one hand and the rising costs of shelter on the other. However, the Policy (1990) is aimed to link shelter provision with the economic improvement of the poor. It has also made the provision of shelter as a direct responsibility of the State. The policy also seems to be more serious to curb luxury housing. Though it is too early to pass judgement on the policy programme yet given the political instability and lack of administrative will in the country, it becomes doubtful that the policy measures would succeed in achieving the policy goals in the foreseeable future.

REFERENCES

Government of India, (1983), *Report of the Task Force IV: Shelter for the Urban Poor and Slum Improvement*, New Delhi, Planning Commission: 5-16.

—— (1988), *Report of the National Commission on Urbanisation*, Vol. II. New Delhi, Ministry of Urban Development: 208.

—— (1988a), *National Housing Policy*, New Delhi, Ministry of Urban Development: 1-22.

—— (1990), *Draft Housing Policy*, New Delhi, Ministry of Urban Development: 1-25.

Gupta, D.B. (1985), *Urban Housing in India*, World Bank Staff Working Paper No. 730, Washington, D.C., The World Bank.

Gupta, R.C. (1988), 'Shelter Policies and Programmes in India — Issues and Prospects' (mimeo.).

Jagannathan, N. Vijay and Animesh Halder (1988), 'Income-housing Linkages: A Case Study of Pavement Dwellers in Calcutta', *Economic and Political Weekly*, XXIII, 23(4):1175-78.

Jayaram, N. (1988), 'Housing Problem in Urban India: A Critical Assessment', in *Housing in India — Problem, Policy and Perspectives*, N. Jayaram and R.S. Sandhu (eds.), Delhi, B.R. Publishers: 32.

Jha, Ganga Dhar (1987), 'Urban Land Management: A Case Study of Delhi, (mimeo.).

Kumar, Arun (1989), 'National Housing Policy: The Implications', *Economic and Political Weekly*, XXIV: 1285-94.

Munjee, Nasser M. (1988), *Housing in Economy: Some General Perspectives and the Indian Case*, (mimeo) : 6.

Raghupathi, Usha P. (1989), 'Occupation and the Income of the Urban Poor', *Urban India*, IX, (2):26-35.

Sharma, Neelam (1983), 'Resettlement Colonies in Delhi', (Dissertation), Amritsar, School of Planning, G.N.D. University.

Sharma, Kalpana (1980), 'Housing the Houseless', *Indian Express*, June 24, Delhi.

Singh, Harjinder (1988), 'Politics of Urban Development', *Punjab Journal of Politics*, XI, (1):35-50.

UNCHS (1987), *Global Report on Human Settlements, 1986*: 72.

Wadhwa, Kiran (1988), 'Housing Programmes for Urban Poor: Shifting Priorities', *Economic and Political Weekly*, XXIII, (33):1762-67.

3

URBAN HOUSING IN THE PEOPLE'S REPUBLIC OF CHINA

MARY JO HUTH

INTRODUCTION

During China's Sixth Five-Year Plan (1981-85), 648 million square metres of housing were completed in China's cities, and the Ministry of Urban and Rural Construction and Environmental Protection plans to complete 750 million more under the Seventh Five-Year Plan (1986-90) (Rieser, 1987). Even these impressive achievements, however, pale before the magnitude of the task confronting China's urban planners. Indeed, one of the foremost problems facing China today is housing, and nowhere is this more apparent than in Beijing, the national capital, one-third of whose residents still suffer from inadequate housing (*China Daily*, 1985a).

Most of the increase in Beijing's housing space has occurred during the past twelve years, for per capita urban living space *declined* across the country from approximately 4.5 sq m in 1949 when the Communists took over to about 3.6 sq m in 1978 (Huang, 1985). In the latter year, a change in economic policies led to massive increases in government expenditures for new urban housing. China's current goal is to increase the average urban living space nationally to 8 sq m per person by the year 2000 (Rieser, 1986). However, China's urban housing stock is so poor and its urban population density so high that this goal will be extremely difficult to achieve. For example, Beijing's population grew from an estimated 1.7 million in 1949 to about 7 million in 1958, to 8 million in 1974, and to 10 million in 1990. And it will undoubtedly continue to grow during the last decade of this century, consistent with the national trend in China toward huge increases in the proportion of urbanised population – from about 11.2

per cent in 1950 to 17.4 per cent in 1970, and to 25 per cent in 1990. Moreover, China's population experts predict that by the year 2000, 45 to 50 per cent of the Chinese people will be living in cities (State Statistical Bureau, 1990). Thus, given China's post-1978 reform period emphasis on the city as the catalyst for economic development, its housing problem assumes special importance.

HISTORY OF THE HOUSING PROBLEM

The Period 1949-78

During the 30-year period after the founding of the People's Republic of China in 1949, the Chinese State followed the Soviet model of economic development, stressing investment in heavy industry or in what they called the "productive" primary and secondary economic sectors. Housing and its associated amenities, such as utilities, transportation, communications, and waste disposal facilities, were classified in the "unproductive"; tertiary economic sector, planners making as little investment as possible in their provision and improvement. Thus, between 1957 and 1978, the proportion of the non-agricultural labour force engaged in urban public utilities work decreased by 15 per cent; the proportion engaged in transportation, postal service, and telecommunications decreased by 35 per cent; and the proportion engaged in trade, restaurant service, and insurance decreased by 65 per cent (Whyte, 1[illegible]). The de-emphasis of the tertiary economic sector was also reflected in the decline of Beijing's commercial and service units from 21,290 units in 1957 to 6,450 units in 1977 (Chang, 1983).

Poor economic conditions in China served to further reduce what little government funding was available for the construction of new housing. With the failure of the 1958 Great Leap Forward, the Chinese economy was left in chaos and a two-year period of famine ensued from 1961-62. This was the result of peasants being required to produce backyard steel, making it difficult or impossible for them to harvest their crops and causing serious food shortages. After a short period of recovery, the Great Proletarian Cultural Revolution was launched by Mao-Zedong and his supporters with the purpose of reducing dependence on cities and increasing egalitarianism. Industry, education, medicine and other urban facilities were decentralised and tens of millions of adults, mainly party cadres and members of the intelligentsia, as well as about 17 million young middle school graduates, were "sent down" from cities to villages and small towns (Kirkby, 1985). The ten years of the Cultural Revolution (1966-76) were also the low point of government investment in urban housing. And despite the forced dispersion of many urban residents, cities continued to experience population growth, further exacerbating China's housing problem. As a result, shortly after the Cultural Revolution it was reported that in the largest 192 cities the average floor space per person was only 3.6 sq m (about 40 sq feet), or slightly less than the space of a king-sized bed, per person (Whyte and Parish, 1984).

The Period 1978-85

With the economic reforms instituted by Deng Xiaoping following Mao Zedong's death in 1976, the city was emphasised as the "motor of development" and urban housing was recognised as an area requiring special attention by the State. However, even with huge government investments in new housing, by 1985 the average living space for each urban resident in China had risen to only 5 sq m – an infinitesimal improvement over the figure for 1949 (4.5 sq m) (*China Daily*, 1986a). One of the principal explanations is the failure of central government efforts to control population flow into Beijing, Shanghai, Tianjin, and other large cities, putting further pressure on China's already limited housing stock. Moreover, the State has not received enough revenue from public housing to adequately finance its maintenance, rendering many older structures uninhabitable and causing newer units to quickly deteriorate. Recent estimates suggest that rents are covering only about 24 per cent of the government's rental costs in terms of depreciation, maintenance, and management (Zhang, 1986). Since 1949, rent for public housing in China has averaged only about 5 per cent of a worker's income; indeed, in proportion to total family income, rents have actually decreased. For example, in 1978, the average family in Beijing spent about 2.3 per cent of its total income on housing, but in 1985, the proportion was only 1.25 per cent (*China Daily*, 1987a).

The Seventh Five-Year Plan Period – 1986-90

Because of its status as the national capital, Beijing has been considered a test case for experimentation in public housing under

China's Seventh Five-Year Plan covering the period 1986 to 1990. Consequently, in discussing the current urban housing situation in China, this paper will focus on Beijing. Moreover, only one type of housing – multi-unit public housing – will be considered, for an analysis of urban housing construction in China over the past ten years, as well as current State policy, indicate that apartment buildings have been and will continue to be the focus of housing investment. Also, the overwhelming majority of housing in Chinese cities is either State- or *danwei*-owned; no more than 10 per cent remains under private control (Whyte and Parish, 1984). A *danwei* refers to an industrial enterprise or company, sometimes referred to by the Chinese as a "unit", which is responsible for many functions beyond what would be considered "normal" business activities in the West – namely, the provision of housing, food, health care, education, child care, and other services for their employees. Many *danwei* are, in fact, the size of American suburban communities. Increasingly, the State has allowed more responsibility for housing construction to be taken over by *danwei*, amounting to 60 per cent of the total investment in 1985 – an increase of 12 per cent over 1980 (*China Daily Business Weekly*, 1987).

THE PLANNING AND CONSTRUCTION OF HOUSING IN BEIJING

Each year, *danwei* apply to their appropriate ministries for permission to build a certain number of sq m of housing. Currently there are 32 ministries in China, ranging from Aeronautics, to Foreign Affairs, to Radio, Cinema, and Television, to Water Resources and Electric Power (United States Department of State, 1987). The ministries, in turn, consider the applications submitted to them from all the *danwei* under their jurisdiction and then make recommendations to the State Council, the chief administrative organ of government in China. While the State Council usually approves the ministries' housing construction recommendations, the number of sq m allowed is generally lower than what the individual *danwei* requested. After being notified by its ministry regarding the number of sq m of housing it has been authorised by the State Council to build, the *danwei* takes its notice to the Beijing Bureau of City Planning and Management, which has already received copies of all construction approvals from the Beijing Municipal Government.

The Beijing Bureau of City Planning and Management then

appoints an officer to check the *danwei*'s proposed construction site for any possible conflict with the city's own construction plans. If the site is acceptable, the Bureau issues the *danwei* a permit to begin construction, one copy of which is retained by the Bureau, while another goes to the construction company selected by the *danwei* to perform the work. When the construction company receives its copy of the permit, it may then obtain construction materials from the State and/or the free market.

Danwei which has approval from their respective ministries for new housing, but which do not have their own land, must rely on the Beijing Municipal Development Company to build their apartments, the Beijing Bureau of City Planning and Management deciding how many units will be allocated for each *danwei* and providing the land for the project. In these cases, several *danwei* must usually share housing in an apartment complex, but each one is consulted before the project begins by the Beijing Bureau of City Planning and Management and the Beijing Municipal Development Company regarding the convenience of the proposed site and the suitability of the proposed apartment units. Apartment complexes are especially favoured by smaller *danwei* which not only cannot afford land for housing, but the related costs for utilities, schools, and police protection which the Beijing Municipality finances in these situations. The Beijing Municipal Development Corporation also constructs a small number of "transfer housing units" each year for families whose homes are targeted for destruction by the municipality to make room for new construction of all kinds. This usually involves lengthy negotiations, as residents frequently refuse to move unless they are promised more rooms in the transfer housing than they have in their present soon-to-be-demolished dwellings.

MAJOR PROBLEM AREAS IN BEIJING'S HOUSING SITUATION

Land Accessibility and Cost

As indicated earlier in this paper, *danwei* have become the driving force behind increases in China's urban housing stock, a trend which can be explained by two factors: (1) factories are typically responsible for housing at least two-thirds of their employees (Rieser, 1987), and (2) *danwei* are the organisations which control land use, although, technically, China is a socialist State where the government owns all the land. However, the State's practice of not charging rent for the use of land has had the effect of altering its ownership; that is, state-owned city land has, in fact, become the property of the largest and most powerful *danwei* (*China Daily*, 1985b). As a result, land costs in Beijing have been steadily rising; between 1980 and 1986, the cost of acquiring one sq m of land more than doubled and has continued to increase (Rieser, 1987). Moreover, land-rich *danwei* are not prone to "sell" such an important asset for cash alone. In addition, they require a trade of land or building materials, so that a real estate market of sorts *does* exist in China. Therefore, *danwei* without land or building materials to trade often find it difficult or impossible to build housing for their members. The consequences of this situation can be truly devastating on the human level, as indicated by the following story in a recent issue of *China Daily* (1986b):

> When Lu, an office worker in the *Postal Ministry*, got married in 1981, she and her husband had nowhere to put their wedding bed. In order to let the couple have a private honeymoon, her 60-year old father-in-law gave them his 12-sq m "home" and he moved to a makeshift hut nearby. Three years later, Lu had a baby, but when the child developed arthritis in her father-in-law's tiny, damp accommodation, she and the child moved to her own father's overcrowded house. Lu and her husband have lived separately ever since. They call this life 'a guerrilla war' – a constant moving around to find places to meet.

Similarly, the Beijing Dance Academy, having nothing of value to trade with other *danwei* for land, found it impossible to build housing for its staff until the municipal government allocated a plot of land for the school. In the meantime, several teachers and their families lived in the student dormitories and one lived in a converted utility room.

By contrast, certain powerful *danwei*, by acquiring land wherever and whenever they could, have effectively built "land banks". For example, the People's Liberation Army (PLA) is probably the largest landowner in Beijing because, in the latter stages of the Cultural Revolution (1966-76), it was frequently called upon to maintain order, its soldiers being billeted in temples, parks, and schools. The PLA used this opportunity to acquire vast amounts of land, much of which, notably temples and the large grounds surrounding them, it continues to hold. Recently, it acquired more valuable land in a northern suburb of Beijing when it decided to build a hotel complex to take advantage of the influx of tourists expected as a by-product of the Summer Olympics in Korea, and improved its own site by adding an adjacent piece of land controlled by another *danwei*.

Overemphasis on High-rise Apartments

A major problem deriving from the scarcity and costliness of urban land in Beijing is that after a *danwei* acquires a piece of land, it has a tendency to build as many high rises as possible upon it. Yet, Chinese architects contend that the per unit investment for high-rise apartments is 70 to 80 per cent greater than for medium-rise (5-7 stories) buildings, that the construction of high rises takes 40 to 50 per cent longer, and that their management and maintenance are more than twice as costly (*Beijing Ribao*, 1985a). Medium-rise construction combines brick-bearing walls with reinforced-concrete floor panels, stairs, and balconies – a type of construction which is cheap, fast, and can be performed by even minimally-trained labourers. By contrast, high-rise construction involves the use of expensive mechanised equipment, such as cranes and construction elevators; the provision of expensive elevators for the residents, which increases the demand on an already overburdened electrical generation system; and continued high maintenance costs. In addition, the Beijing Bureau of City Planning and Management feels that the continued proliferation of high-rise apartment buildings would have an undesirable effect on city life in general, destroying the charm of much of the surrounding low, traditional architecture, increasing transportation and utility problems, and militating against the development of a sense of community among the residents. As a result, the Bureau is trying to restrict high-rise apartments to certain sections of Beijing and to limit their density, and within the past few years it has begun to demolish or confiscate illegally-built high rises. However, many *danwei* perceive the costs of building a high rise to be less than those of not having sufficient housing for their employees, and feel that even if they are penalised for some illegal structures, they will have reaped the advantage of using them for several years.

Monotonous Architecture

An unfortunate cosmetic housing problem in Beijing has resulted from the tendency for smaller *danwei* to economise on architectural plans for their apartment buildings by choosing standardised ones already drawn up by one of the municipal design institutes which compensate their architects on the basis of the number of sq m of plans they sell. Under this policy, it is to an architect's financial advantage to produce as many easily-reproducible plans as possible. The result, however, is a "sea" of identically boxy, grey, and boring high rises, the Beijing press frequently publishing articles and cartoons about the difficulty residents and visitors often experience in finding a particular apartment and/or building. Cases of "mistaken identity" are especially common after dark when the small, unlit signs on the sides of the buildings are obscured. While it is possible for a *danwei* to secure more distinctive or individualised designs for its housing projects by conducting competitions among various design offices, offering monetary prizes to the winners, or by hiring free-lance government or university architects, both of these options are much more expensive than going through a municipal design institute.

The Inequitable Distribution and Substandard Quality of Construction Materials

Another serious housing-related problem in Beijing, as well as in other Chinese cities, is poor quality construction materials. While materials such as steel, timber, cement, and glass that were formerly entirely subject to state control can now be purchased by buyers from all parts of China in organised markets that have been set up in major cities such as Chongqing, Shanghai, Shijiazhuang, Suzhou, Tianjin, and Wuhan (Rieser, 1986), as in the matter of land acquisition, smaller and less powerful *danwei* are usually at a disadvantage in acquiring them. Since 1984, such *danwei* may also legally purchase construction materials from factories which exceed their production quotas and sell the surplus on the open market, but such materials are expensive and their quality varies considerably. In 1985, an investigation of Beijing's 93 building materials' factories resulted in 29 of them being forced to close because of substandard production (*China Daily*, 1985c). On the other hand, larger, powerful *danwei*, which always have several construction projects pending, can inflate their requests for State-allocated materials and hoard the surplus for future use or trade it with other large *danwei* for construction needs they lack – land or other building materials. And when they resort to the open market for building supplies, they are usually able to secure the first-quality output, leaving less-well-connected *danwei* with the warped window frames, cracked bricks, defective steel fastenings and prefabricated panels, and dubious-quality cement. But even when up-to-standard materials are used, many *danwei* are tempted to stretch them over as many apartments as possible, leaving essential utility systems out of some buildings entirely. During 1985, an expose in *Beijing Wanbao* revealed that one apartment building in Beijing's Chaoyang District had been without water, gas, and electricity for eight years (1985).

Contractor-related Difficulties

As with access to land and building materials, large, powerful *danwei* have a distinct advantage in securing a contractor for their housing projects. Indeed, many have an in-house contractor. Smaller and weaker *danwei*, however, must choose an "outside" contractor from among the urban development and construction companies which the State now allows to develop and proliferate. But because these contractors are very busy, with large backlogs of jobs to perform, relatively small *danwei* may have to wait several years to get their apartment-building projects undertaken. Moreover, realising their power over the *danwei* requesting their services, contractors often demand apartment units in the new buildings they construct. During December, 1985, the *Beijing Daily* highlighted the widespread nature of this problem in several articles which cited three construction companies that had extorted apartments from a variety of *danwei* all over the city. The worst case was that of the Chinese Academy of Sciences which had a total of 78 apartments extorted from it by one construction company (Lu, 1985).

Municipal Utility Bureau Abuses

Unless an apartment building is part of a larger complex, arrangements for utility hookups are generally made *after* construction has started. The problems resulting from this practice range from serious inconveniences, such as high-rise buildings with elevators that work only sporadically, to buildings which are unsafe and/or unusable because they have no electricity for lighting, no cooking gas, no heat, or no sewerage connections. Some apartment buildings stand vacant for years because they lack utility connections. In Beijing, as in other

Chinese cities, there is not only a shortage of water, gas, and electricity, but municipal utility bureaus are often reluctant to provide the scarce utilities under their control unless a *danwei* gives them a bribe – typically, apartment units in its building or complex. Thus, for smaller *danwei*, with few apartments to offer, utilities may *never* be provided, but these units are in a weak position to complain to higher authorities. How deeply entrenched such abuses have become was revealed recently by the following statement in *China Daily* (1986c):

> Ma Shusheng, Vice-Director of the Beijing Municipal Power Supply Bureau, and three other veteran Party cadres were reported to have been arrested pending trial on charges of embezzling public funds and taking bribes. On the strength of his control over electricity distribution, Ma was found to have extorted thousands of yuan from his company's clientele. Earlier in the year, Ma Xueliang, former Director of the Municipal Public Utility Bureau, and Huang Yugian, former Party Secretary of the Beijing Gas Company's pipeline agency, were sentenced to prison . . . for similar corrupt practices – seeking personal profit by abusing their power over gas supply.

Insufficient Attention to Housing Rehabilitation

Little housing rehabilitation work has been done in Beijing for two main reasons: (1) as indicated earlier in this paper, rents have been too low to cover maintenance and repair costs, and (2) the housing most in need of rehabilitation – the traditional courtyard type – has too many physical limitations to warrant rehabilitation efforts. Courtyard houses, originally occupied by one extended family, are still home for a large proportion of Beijing residents, but, since 1949, most of them are occupied by several different families, each having one, or at most two, room(s). Such houses have no bathing or toilet facilities; neighbourhood bath houses and privies provide for these needs. Residents have typically installed makeshift kitchens for cooking and small sheds in the center of the courtyard for storing personal belongings, food, and coal. If modern bathrooms and kitchens were installed in these courtyard houses, total living space would be reduced so that some residents would have to move out. And because the type of *danwei* whose employees live in courtyard houses are not large, industrial enterprises which can afford to build new housing facilities, the displaced residents would be hard pressed for shelter. Moreover, most enterprises which rely upon courtyard housing are located in the old central section of Beijing which has strict building-height regulations. Consequently, even those which could afford to finance the construction of high-rise apartment buildings to house their employees displaced by the rehabilitation of courtyard houses could not get a permit to do so. Hence, the principal residential units recently targeted for rehabilitation in Beijing are the older State-owned apartment estates, some experts suggesting that they be sold at discount prices to the residents who would then be responsible for renovating the housing at their own expense. Others have suggested that *new* apartment buildings constructed in one older residential area could be sold and the proceeds used to renovate another older quarter of the city (*China Daily*, 1985d).

FUTURE PROSPECTS FOR URBAN HOUSING

In 1985, China's central government announced its goal to provide 12 sq m of housing space per person by the year 2000 (*China Daily*, 1985d). Although, as indicated earlier in this paper, the national goal was recently reduced to 8 sq m of residential space per person, to accomplish this goal and provide everyone with an apartment having indoor plumbing and a private kitchen will necessitate the construction of approximately 150 million sq m of housing and the expenditure of about 45 billion yuan each year over the next ten years (*China Daily*, 1987a). Thus, China faces a mammoth task over the next decade. Without major changes in the mode of urban housing construction and the financing of that construction, progress toward the year 2000 housing goal will be slow.

One reform which was instituted around 1982 in several Chinese cities and which was extended to Beijing in 1985 is the commercialised housing experiment. Under this plan, *danwei* were ordered to *sell* 20 per cent of their apartment units to their employees – especially those without private dwellings or with overcrowded housing. Each buyer is expected to pay about one-third of the cost of the apartment, the remainder of the purchase price being subsidised by the *danwei* or work unit and the State (*Beijing Ribao*, 1985b). Unfortunately, however, there are several problems inherent in the commercialised housing experiment. First, as indicated throughout this paper, smaller, less powerful *danwei* find it difficult to build large apartment buildings, so that the government's edict to offer 20 per cent of their residential units for sale has little practical significance. Secondly, *danwei* are reluctant to "waste" their best apartments on underprivileged buyers; they would rather reserve them as rewards for employees of high rank or with seniority in their organisation. For this reason, Beijing officials claim that most *danwei* fail to comply with the 20 per cent for sale rule and that it is usually the least desirable apartments that are offered for sale – that is, units on the top floors, units with less sun exposure, and units near elevators. Thirdly, even the one-third-of-cost purchase price is staggering for the average Chinese family, the price of an average-size apartment of 50 sq m being about 5,000 yuan or more than five years of the average employee's wages. And if an employee chose to purchase an apartment on the instalment plan, the monthly payments would be about three times the rent for a State-allocated apartment (Rieser, 1986).

Another recent housing reform instituted in 1987 was the separation of housing construction from the State's fixed assets' investment and construction plan. Previously, investment for housing construction had been treated as a subsidiary of investment for the construction of production facilities. By having a separate account category for housing construction, the State hopes to encourage new housing to enter the market directly as a commodity. That this expectation has been reaalised is indicated by the fact that the Ministry of Urban and Rural Construction and Environmental Protection (MURCEP) sold about 200,000 apartments to Chinese citizens within a year after the reform was introduced (*China Daily*, 1987b).

Chinese officials have also begun to propose that the existing State monopoly over construction funds should be terminated. Yang Peixin, a researcher in the State Council's Economic Research Centre, recently suggested that money for urban housing construction should come primarily from the urban banking system and that structural reforms should be undertaken to attract more private savings into the system (*China Daily*, 1986d). Indeed, the consensus of opinion among Chinese officials today is that more emphasis on the private funding of housing construction is the most promising means of achieving China's national housing goals for the year 2000. While raising rents would provide the State with more funds for the maintenance and repair of older housing, the low salaries of Chinese urban workers limit the possibility of raising more money for new housing by this means. Moreover, urban consumer backlash over recent price hikes in previously-subsidised agricultural commodities has created a political climate in which it would be difficult for the government to raise rents significantly. Thus, barring a full-scale attack on the economic reforms begun by Deng Xiaoping, the strong State commitment to increased private home ownership in the People's Republic of China assures the growth of the commercialised housing sector for the foreseeable future.

REFERENCES

Beijing Ribao (Daily) (1985a), December 6:1.

——, (1985b), January 18:1.

Beijing Wanbao (Evening News), 1985 March 13:1.

Chang, Sen-Dou (1983), 'Urbanisation and Economic Readjustment in China.' In Chi-Keung Leung and Steve S.K. Chen (eds.), *China in Readjustment*. Hong Kong: University of Hong Kong Press.

China Daily (1985a), 'Survey on Housing Starts in Beijing.' January 10:3.

—— (1985b), 'Experts Urge New Land Rent System.' November 11:4.

—— (1985c), 'Factories Close.' November 9:3.

—— (1985d), 'Shortage of Housing Yet to be Eased.' May 27:4.

—— (1986a), 'Courtyard Houses Fine But. . . .' June 12:4.

—— (1986b), 'Apartments for 'Young Marrieds.' July 2:6.

—— (1986c), 'Beijing Disciplines 50 Party Members.' July 28:3.

—— (1986d), 'Tangle of Problems Plague Cities.' July 22:4.

—— (1987a), 'Too Low Rents Cause Housing Shortage.' March 21:4.

—— (1987b), 'Plan Will Spur Sales of Housing.' April 22:3.

China Daily Business Weekly (1987), 'Beijing on Private Homes Buying Spree.' March 11:1.

Huang, Tian (1985), 'Urban Housing in China.' Paper presented at the International Conference on Asian Urbanisation, Centre for Urban Studies, University of Akron, Akron, Ohio.

Kirkby, R.J.R. (1985), *Urbanisation in China: Town and Country in a Developing Economy 1949-2000 A.D.* New York, Columbia University Press.

Lu, Jun-hua (1985), 'The Housing Situation in the People's Republic of China.' *International Journal for Development Technology*, 1:257.

Rieser, Ellen (1986), 'Urban Housing in the People's Republic of China: Beijing.' Briefing paper prepared for the Office of International Affairs, U.S. Department of Housing and Urban Development. Ann Arbor, Michigan, The University of Michigan.

—— (1987), 'Current Trends and Policies in Housing and Urban Development in China.' Paper presented at the Annual Meeting of the American Planning Association, New York.

State Statistical Bureau (1990), *Statistical Yearbook of China 1990*. Hong Kong: State Statistical Bureau.

United States Department of State, Bureau of Public Affairs (1987), *Background Notes: China*. Washington, D.C., U.S. Government Printing Office.

Whyte, Martin K. (1983), 'Urbanism as a Chinese Way of Life.' *International Journal of Comparative Sociology*, 24(1-2):71-83.

Whyte, Martin K. and Wiliam L. Parish (1984), *Urban Life in Contemporary China*. Chicago, Illinois, University of Chicago Press.

Zhang, X.Q. (1986), 'On Urban Housing Problems.' *China City Planning Review*, 3(2):3-13.

4

HOUSING IN BRAZIL: Diagnosis and Challenges

SUZANA PASTERNAK TASCHNER

BRAZILIAN HOUSING CONDITIONS

Background

Brazil is a country characterised by strong regional and social differences. The income and housing indicators vary according to the region and to society segments. The low wages for manual work, in contrast with the earnings of technical-managerial services and capital gains have resulted in an uneven distribution of income among different groups. In 1983 the low income groups (50 per cent) of population got only 13.6 per cent of the total national income, while the higher income groups (10 per cent) received 46.2 per cent of the national income (Jaguaribe *et al.*, 1986). According to PNAD (Pesquisa National Por Amostragem de Domicilions — National Survey by House Sampling) data (1984), 66 per cent of the economically active population earned up to 2 minimum wages (In May 1984 minimum wage was equivalent to US$ 66.00 and in the beginning of March 1988 it was equivalent to US$ 60.00). Household income distribution in 1984 showed that 34.04 per cent of Brazilian families earn less than 2 minimum wages (poverty line).

Regional disparity follows the social disparity. In 1982 the Southeast region, 53 per cent of the economically active population earned less than 2 minimum wages, while in the Northeast the proportion amounts to 76.6 per cent. This is reflected in life expectancy and children mortality ratios – 64.4 years of age and 71.6 children per thousand born alive in the Southeast, compared to 51.0 years and 124.4 children per thousand born alive in the Northeast.

The regional disparity has led to the concentration of population in the Southeast region. In 1984, 44 per cent of 131 million Brazilians lived in Southeast region which forms 11 per cent of the Brazilian area. In the Southeast region are located metropolitan areas of Sao Paulo and Rio de Janeiro. The two metropolitan regions held in 1975, approximately, 49 per cent of the Brazilian industrial processing amount (Geiger, 1985).

The growth rate of housing units up to the seventies, was lower than of the demographic growth, thereby increasing the scarcity of houses, especially in cities (the urban population increased from 45.0 per cent in 1960 to 67.6 per cent in 1980 and is estimated to have reached 72.2 per cent in 1984 — PNAD). However, in the seventies, the population growth rate increased and the growth of housing units was above the demographic growth, especially in urban areas, reflecting a strong investment in house building during 1970-84 (Table 4.1). The stepped up activity had resulted from the establishment of the National Housing Bank (BNH) in 1964.

TABLE 4.1: Demographic and Housing Growth Rates (Percentage)

Years	Demographic			Houses		
	Urban	Rural	Total	Urban	Rural	Total
1940-50	3.80	1.60	2.39	4.04	1.60	2.44
1950-60	5.50	1.60	2.99	5.46	1.24	3.00
1960-70	5.16	0.69	2.89	4.93	0.23	2.71
1970-80	4.44	-0.62	2.48	5.62	0.12	3.63
1980-84	4.30	-1.77	2.45	6.59	-0.06	4.74

Source: IBGE Demographic and Building Census 1940, 1950, 1960, 1970 and 1980. IBGE-PNAD — 1984 — (National Survey by Domicile Sampling, 1984).

Tenure

Basically, tenure alternatives in Brazil are either private rental or private ownership. Although there are houses built by public promotion, the state sells them as a private agency. There are neither rented public housing units, nor co-operative or collective properties.

Table 4.2 shows the growing rate of home ownership for Brazil as a whole as well as for the wealthiest (Southeast) and for the poorest (Northeast) regions. The percentage of home ownership was above 70 per cent in 1984. Many specialists are used to associate home ownership with higher income levels. However, in Brazil, where the trilogy periphery/irregular settlements/self-help housing accounts for large part of the housing stock, home ownership and social classes are often inversely related. For the poor population, it is more accessible to purchase a plot of land in cheaper places and self-help construction than do buy houses in the free market.

TABLE 4.2: Private Homes — Rates by Region in Brazil, 1940-84

(Percentage)

Year	Brazil	Region	
		Southeast	Northeast
1940	43.68	34.15	47.57
1950	52.12	40.55	58.65
1960	57.08	46.70	64.01
1970	60.31	54.42	66.47
1980	61.75	55.25	66.67
1984	63.40	58.25	70.23

Source: IBGE — Building Census (1940, 1950, 1960, 1970 and 1980) — PNAD (1984).

In Sao Paulo, the proportion of rental houses was lower in the Periphery Ring — the poorest area (35.2 per cent in 1980) — than in the Central and Intermediate Rings (56.6 per cent and 40.3 per cent (Pasternak Taschner, 1987). The percentage of rental houses in Urban Brazil has decreased from 49.0 per cent in 1940 to 28.5 per cent in 1984. This is the result of both of the National Housing Bank (BNH) performance, stimulating the access to tenure and of continuous government interventions in the Tenancy Law, freezing rents and discouraging the investment in rental buildings.

Also the ideology that only home ownership could provide economic and social security, representing an insurance against an uncertain future in a country where inflation was usually high and unemployment cycles frequent (unemployment insurance was established only in 1985), was spread. Brazilian housing policy was entirely oriented towards increasing private ownership. Diffusion of home ownership, especially amongst less favoured classes was one of the main explicit objectives for the creation of the National Housing Bank.

Nowadays the importance of home ownership is far from being

only ideological. Home ownership provides status, opens doors for loans and for mortgage credit. It is not only a safe investment but also an efficient defence against inflation and arbitrary state intervention in the real estate market.

Housing Quality

(a) Material Quality

The census considers the housing units as durable or inadequate. Durable housing units are those built mainly with permanent materials for the floor, walls and roof.

TABLE 4.3: Proportion of Durable Houses in Brazil, 1940-84

Year	Brazil	Region	
		Southeast	Northeast
1940	32.94	60.38	19.94
1970	73.79	85.13	59.30
1980	88.27	96.16	69.80
1984	91.85		

Source: IBGE — Building Census (1940, 1970, 1980) and PNAD (1984).

A strong trend of improvement in housing quality can be noticed, even in the less developed Northeastern area. However, the indicators are rather deficient. Mud houses, covered with straw and with dirt floors are certainly not fit for living. Neither the house's maintenance status nor the quality of materials or installation, nor age of any other element except for the type of construction material, are taken into account. Additionally, quality does not include security in relation to tenure. During recent years, the old shacks in squatter settlement of the wealthier cities have started to be replaced by masonry units. However, this does not mean that these houses are suitable, considering the insecurity of performance in invaded sites.

There are no reliable statistics on squatters. Even in the major cities, the figures are very often conflicting. According to the Secretary of City Planning, Rio de Janeiro there are over 1.7 million "cariocas" living in squatter settlements, forming 32 per cent of the city's population. These figures contrast strongly with IBGE statistics for the same year, i.e. 628,170 squatters. In Sao Paulo, the squatter population was around 7 per cent or 630,000 people in 1985 (Pasternak Taschner, 1986).

(b) Housing Density

The number of people per house has been declining, for Brazil as a whole between 1940 and 1984. There was a drop of 17.0 per cent – urban housing density declined by 18.9 per cent and rural housing density declined by 7.6 per cent. The rise in index in 1970 is a result of trends during the 1960s, when increases in housing stock were clearly lower than demographic growth (Table 4.1). There are also regional differences. In 1940 housing density was lower in the Northeast (4.95) than in the Southeast (5.23). In 1984, the situation was reversed. In the Southeast it was 4.34 (a reduction by 2.42 per cent in 44 years); in the Northern region, including the Amazon where population has increased in the past 30 years, it was 5.12. This rate is similar to that of 1940 but it is a considerable decrease compared to the figures of 6.0 in 1960 (6.03 persons per domicile). Brazil's North and Central-Western regions have experienced high demographic growth rates (5.02 per cent and 4.05 per cent per year, in the 1970-80 decade), resulting from a national policy that promoted human settlements in those areas. However, the population increase in the North region in the 1970s resulting in this huge growth rate, was only a little over 2.2 million inhabitants, lower than the growth recorded in Sao Paulo.

In any event, the migration to the North was translated into a higher housing density than for the rest of Brazil.

Since a dwelling's square floor area is not included in the census, the average number of persons per room has been utilised as an indicator, and more than one person per room is defined as unacceptable. The number of persons per room considered acceptable varies greatly according to social groups, cultures and countries (UN, 1967).

However, the way this indicator is collected in Brazil shows a serious underestimation. The UN recommendation that the minimum size of a room should be sufficient to contain an adult's bed (at least 4 sq m) is not followed (UN, 1964). Also, the UN advised the exclusion of the bathroom from the total number of rooms. Data from the Census and PNADS do not allow for this exclusion, because there is no information on the use of rooms, (except for the bedroom) and even the bathroom and the kitchen are classified as bedrooms, when they are used as places to sleep.

Bearing these limitations in mind, one sees in Table 4.4 a decrease in average room density, which is strongest in the Southeast region. In the border regions, with a more recent colonisation, the indicator is higher than the national average and it increases until 1970, reflecting a densification of the already precarious housing situation, that resulted from the differential between the growth of the housing stock and the population in the area.

TABLE 4.4. People per Room and People per Dormitory

Year	People per room			People per dormitory		
	Brazil	Southeast	North	Brazil	Southeast	North
1940	1.15	1.10	1.41	—	—	—
1950	1.13	1.01	1.41	2.50	2.33	3.10
1960	1.10	1.03	1.62	2.51	2.43	3.31
1970	1.08	1.00	1.72	2.48	2.42	3.35
1980	0.90	0.85	1.41	2.29	2.25	2.96
1984	0.82	—	—	2.12	—	—

Source: IBGE — Demographic and Building Census (1940, 1950, 1960, 1970, 1980) and PNAD (1984).

Data for 1984 shows, that 27.12 per cent of the housing units in Brazil were having an average of more than one person per room. Overcrowding is more critical in the rural areas, where 36.03 per cent of the houses have an average of more than one person per room and 6.48 per cent have even more than two persons. However, also in the urban areas the situation is less serious, with respective figures of 24.25 per cent and 4.26 per cent.

The situation is even more serious with respect to the average number of persons per bedroom, especially considering what qualifies as bedroom. In spite of this deficient definition, the number of persons per bedroom, even in the wealthier region, is more than two. The long term trend shows a slow but steady decrease. However, it is alarming that in 1984, 39.15 per cent of all Brazilian housing units contained over two persons per bedroom and 13.23 per cent more than 3 persons per bedroom. Overcrowding was still worse in rural areas, where 46.42 per cent of the units had more than two persons per bedroom and 15.93 per cent more than three. In urban areas the proportion of units with more than two and more than three persons per bedroom was, respectively, 36.81 per cent and 12.35 per cent.

(c) Public Services

Table 4.5 shows the improvement, both for the country as a whole and for its two more heterogeneous regions, of water supply conditions. There was an increase by almost 300 per cent in the number of domiciles connected to public water services between 1960 and 1984. There was an annual increase of 4.61 per cent, which was lower in the Southeast (3.47 per cent per year) than in the Northeast (9.12 per cent per year). In spite of this effort, the regional differential increased by almost 10 per cent.

TABLE 4.5: Public Services by Regions: 1940-1984

Year	Percentage of domiciles connected to								
	Public water syst.			Sewers/sceptic tank			Electric power		
	Br	SE	NE	Br	SE	NE	Br	SE	NE
1950	-	-	-	13.09	23.55	3.57	24.56	40.43	8.41
1960	21.09	36.05	5.25	23.79	40.42	6.07	38.54	58.24	49.79
1970	33.26	51.56	12.38	26.57	43.82	7.96	47.56	68.75	23.33
1980	54.91	72.57	31.59	39.60	57.97	16.99	68.28	85.15	43.46
1984	62.20	81.70	42.60	47.86	68.73	16.04	79.39	91.50	56.80

Br = Brazil; SE = Southeast and NE = Northeast

Source: IBGE Building Census (1950, 1960, 1970, 1980) and PNAD (1984).

Sanitary improvement also appeared in relation to the destination of dejecta, since almost 50 per cent of Brazilian domiciles in 1984 presented correct destination for domestic waste — public sewers systems or sceptic tank. The annual increase of domiciles with correct destination for dejecta between 1950 and 1984 was 3.89 per cent per year for the country as a whole. Similarly, Table 4.5 shows not only the alarming sanitary situation in the Northeast but also the increasing differential between this region and the Southeast.

Electrical power is the public utility service with the best performance, as shown in the last columns of Table 4.5. Almost 80 per cent of Brazilian houses enjoy electrical connections.

In 1984 almost 60 per cent of the houses enjoyed public garbage collection services 20.48 per cent disposed of the garbage either in unused lots or threw it into rivers, especially in the rural regions.

A Brief Conclusion

The indicators, somehow, permit the measurement of housing quality. However, to use them with the purpose of sizing the rate of unsuitable housings is rather dangerous. The concept of adequacy is relative and the concrete characteristics of a "healthy house" vary from country to country, from region to region, amongst social groups and above all, with time (Marcuse, 1970; Havel, 1968; Pasternak Taschner, 1983).

Following the minimum requirements established by the United Nations (1962), we will see that the 8.15 per cent of housing units built with rough materials (non-finished wood boards, mud, straw) are unsuitable, as well as 13.23 per cent of houses with more than 3 persons per bedroom, and 34.05 per cent houses without piped water (approximately 10 million units in 1984). Some estimates state that around 30 per cent of the houses in the country are "sub-standard". A special tabulation for the metropolitan area of Rio de Janeiro in 1970 has shown that over 480,000 units had unsuitable water and sewers conditions, representing 31.6 per cent of the total of houses (Vetter and Simoes, 1980).

HOUSING ALTERNATIVES IN BRAZIL

Urban housing markets in Brazil can roughly be divided into three large segments:

1. *The illegal market* — It groups the various sub-markets covering invaded land. These invaded lands can contain invaded rented houses, self-help houses and houses built upon order. The invasion can be either individual or resulting from an organised social movement. In Brazil, houses built on invaded sites are called "favelas" (squatter settlements). At least the two million urban households with less than minimum wage (9.13 per cent of all urban households) are part of this market. Very probably also the almost 4 million households with monthly incomes between 1 and 2 minimum wages (16.50 per cent of the urban households in 1984) cannot afford a house outside this market, which, covers about 25.63 per cent of all urban households.

2. *The private commercial market* — It consists of private rented housing and private home ownership units controlled by private landlords and private industry, either with their own, or with BNH transferred capital. The 8.8 million urban households with more than 5 minimum wages (38.43 per cent of the Brazilian urban households) can buy or rent any type of housing within this market. Most of S.F.H. financings were targeted for the medium income households (above 6 minimum wages). This market is operated mainly by private agents making up the Brazilian Savings and Loan System (Property Credit Societies, Savings and Loan Associations). The private commercial market also serves lower strata, since public housing is not sufficient. Dwellings in this market segment are located in the "periphery" of urban centres, built by house owners (self-help) or by a small builder. When home ownership is out of reach, these people become part of the slum population or live in backyard rooms (the so-called periphery slums). People in these income groups would certainly be qualified for units built by public housing if there were enough of them. They form part of the 7.9 million urban households with incomes between 2 and 5 minimum wages (34.52 per cent of the total of urban families in 1984) who could not afford to buy a public house.
3. *The public market* – It consists of the units built by public promotion (COHAB). Generally, construction is done by private contractors. Approximately 1.2 million units averaging 40 sq m, were targeted for families with 2 to 5 minimum wages.

INTERVENTION POLICY

For analysis purposes, one can study simultaneously two different lines of public intervention policy in Brazilian housing:

(a) Policies related to the "illegal market" that is, the policies that handle squatter settlement problems.
(b) Policies related to private and public commercial submarkets, that stimulate home ownership, and govern rents (Tenancy Law).

Intervention Policy in the "Illegal Market"

The first basic form of state intervention in housing, following the international trend, was the removal and relocation of the "favela". This policy, in force during the 1960s, saw squatter settlements as a focus of disease, crime, social disorders and marginality. This pathology would be extinguished with the extirpation of the settlement from the urban fabric and the relocation of the squatters at suitable units. In Rio de Janeiro, between 1962 and 1974, 26,193 shanty houses and 139,218 people were removed (Valladares, 1978).

However, since the seventies it has become clear the failure in relocating the squatters at traditional housing estates. This failure was evidenced by the abandon and sale of the apartments and return to squatter settlements, Valladares (1978), Rush (1974), Blank (1980), Bank (1986). Nowadays the removal is only used in emergency situations. Therefore, instead of putting squatters in final housing units, there was an attempt to locate them in so-called Temporary Housing Villages (V.H.P.) in Sao Paulo and in the Proletarian Parks in Rio de Janeiro. The theories that mediated this form of intervention held the idea that the squatter settlements were the first housing alternative for the migrants, a "spring board" to the city, a required first stage for integration into the city. At V.H.P. the basic concern was to shorten the "compulsory time" spent by the migrants in the squatter settlements. Therefore, the local state supplied certain basic infrastructure elements such as piped water and sewers systems, collective bathrooms and laundries. Government social assistance also helped people to get jobs and provided occupational training. It was excepted that after one year families would be able to find housing from the private commercial market or from public market. Criticisms of this project were many. In addition to the implicit assumption of social integration, empirical data soon showed that many squatters were not at all recent migrants and the squatter settlements were not always their first living locations. In Sao Paulo, for instance, in 1980, approximately 41 per cent of the family heads had lived in other places in the city, before living in the squatter settlements, and there, they had paid rent or even been owners. (Pasternak Taschner, 1978). The growth of squatter settlements is due to pauperisation rather than to migration. Many migrants living in squatter settlements did not come first to the shanty house where they were interviewed. They had moved in the urban space, following a logical path in the process of increasing prices of urban land and of pauperisation of the working class, from central areas to the periphery, from masonry houses to shanty houses. (Pasternak Taschner, 1986).

By the end of the 1970s, it had become clear that the squatter settlements would remain and that the repressive bulldozer policies had failed. It had also become clear that the squatter settlements did not represent a malfunction of the economic and social system but the physical expression of its contradictions. The large increase of squatter population and their growing political pressures demanded new solutions. Paradoxically, public authorities started looking for legal norms and suitable standards for illegal settlements.

Thus, sanitary infrastructure (water and sewers), electrical power and garbage collection projects were implemented for the illegal settlements. Site regularisation was still an unknown but the implementation of infrastructure in most of the squatter settlements in the major Brazilian cities seemed to indicate the acceptance of the invaders permanence. By the end of 1979 the PRO AGUA programme was started in Sao Paulo. It proposed the extension of the water network to the squatter settlements. Until 1986, 12,000 shanty houses had piped water, in addition to a high number of collective taps installed in the settlements. In the same year, the PRO LUZ (supply of electrical power to "favelas" ,) was created, and in 1987 electrical power had been installed in practically all the shanty houses of Sao Paulo. Additionally, during the first more "progressive" government of Sao Paulo (between March 1983 and December 1985) more ambitious projects of upgrading squatter settlements have been started although at a small-scale. Over 15,000 families benefited from the upgrading programme, almost 12 per cent of the total squatter families in Sao paulo.

Another project, PRO MORAR, implemented in June 1979, proposed the eradication of squatter settlements replacing the shanty houses with masonry houses in the same location and the legalisation of the site ownership. In Sao Paulo, until 1986, eleven PRO MORAR housing estates were built, where 3,142 units were delivered and 2,380 units were under construction. PRO MORAR offered to each family a core-unit (room and bathroom) with the possibility of extension by the dweller. The sites, services and community equipment were supplied by the local government.

The 1980s witnessed the eruption of social movements on housing. These popular movements claimed, in addition to regularisation of site ownership, government support for self-help and mutual-help housing. After collective projects are not specific for squatter population, this is the submarket that used the most the Joao de Barro Programme, created in 1984 by B.N.H. This programme foresees the utilisation of the dweller's own labour. In Sao Paulo, the housing provision programme (specific for squatters) is included in the supply of sites-and-service, financing of construction material for the basic unit, along with technical assistance for self-help housing. In January 1986, the first city government elected by the people took office. Its ideology was entirely different from the previous government. Supported by conservative classes and sections of low middle-class, the government once more talked about squatter settlements eradication, building of popular housing estates (built with the support of private initiative), for middle classes. This policy favouring the private construction industry in two ways: by building periphery estates (since collective construction was no longer permitted) and by building middle-class buildings.

Intervention Policies in "Legal" Sub-markets

(a) Intervention in Rental Housing Market

Until 1920, living in rental housing was a common practice. In Sao, Paulo, in 1940, the percentage of rented houses in the total of housing units was 48.95 per cent; which decreased to 28.46 per cent in 1984. This was basically due to the joining of two approaches – the incentive to home ownership, through the creation of S.F.H. (Housing Finance System) in 1964 and the successive state interventions in the rental housing market, for almost 50 years. In the 1940s, considering the high differential between the population growth and housing stock, especially in urban regions (Table 4.1), rents were increased and reached very high levels. In 1942 the first Tenancy Law was promulgated, freezing rents and making difficult for the landlord to take the repossession of his property.

This state intervention contributed to discourage the building of rental houses. On the other hand, the home ownership ideology, that only home ownership could provide economic and social safety against high inflation, was encouraged. Further after the military coup in 1964, the housing policy was entirely directed in this direction.

In 1969 a second tenancy cycle began. This cycle was the economic reflex of the less populistic policy developed in the beginning of the military government, which modernised the economy and favoured accumulation, by lowering wages of and withdrawing some protection measures extended to the workers. During the second cycle the tenant was protected and civil construction industry was stimulated, since it was the government's hope that it would maintain employment rates. Rent adjustment was released and the draconian laws that governed the repossession of property since 1942 were abolished.

However, in 1977, social pressures were already felt and once more the state intervened in the market, protecting the tenant, assuring the extension of occupancy up to two years after the rental agreement expiration, and in 1981, rental adjustments were made below the inflation rate (90 per cent of the inflation rate). In 1983 the adjustment rate dropped to 80 per cent and the rents were flattened below inflation until 1985. As a consequence, the supply of rental housing was decreased. In February 1986, the "Cruzado" plan froze rents and discontinued repossession of property. The cycle was completed. In thesis, it should have benefited tenants, but it ended up affecting them adversely by reducing dramatically the supply of rental houses. In 1987, with the huge supply crisis, both rents and repossession were released. However, fear and disquiet had taken over the rental sector. The landlords avoid renting, and prefer to sell or to keep their property vacant. The few cases in the market show unbelievable price increases, with landlords trying to make up for the losses accrued since 1982. In June 1987, the government submitted to the Congress a new Tenancy Law and once more property repossession was suspended for 90 days. The new law intended to release rent for high income houses and link the rents for medium and low-income houses to salary readjustments. Panic struck the investors and by mid-1987 the rental housing market was entirely paralysed. "The rental housing market tends to disappear if there is no sensible policy for the sector" (Magazine VEJA, June 30/87).

(b) Intervention in Housing Production

Until 1937, both production and distribution of the housing units were left to the discretion of private initiative. By the end of the 1930s the pressure exercised by the sudden urban population growth was added to the scarcity of housing. That led workers to claim for housing provisions from the state. The Retirement and Pension Institutes (IAPs), were created in the decade and organised in accordance with occupational categories (industrial workers, bank workers, etc.). Between 1937-64, 279 housing estates were built in the country, totalling 47,789 dwellings. In addition to direct construction, IAPs have financed the purchasing or building of additional 76,236 units (Farah, 1985).

In 1946 the Federal Government created an other agency i.e Popular Housing Foundation, to build houses for all income groups with funds arising from the one per cent interest tax on the sale of property. Until December, 1960, it had built 143 housing estates, containing around 17,000 units, each with floor area between 60 and 70 sq m.

In 1960-64 the Brazilian economy was in serious crisis. Inflation was 100 per cent per year. GNP growth rate was 10.3 per cent in 1960 and 5.3 per cent in 1962 and dropped to 1.5 per cent in 1963 and 2.4 per cent in 1964. By stimulating the construction industry through public financing housing construction programme, it was expected that the economy would improve since the construction industry absorbs mostly unskilled labour, especially rural migrants. It also had important multiplier effects, stimulating indirect employment and the construction materials industry.

In addition, in Brazil, the construction industry does not depend on imports, making it a privileged instrument in the conjunctural economic policy. The implementation of the Housing Financing System, five months after the military takeover, followed a class strategy of the authoritarian state, striving to find in housing an instrument to legitimatise itself, using the "dream of home ownership". Above all, it was a form to supply employment to unskilled manpower, stimulating civil construction, making civil construction attractive to the domestic capital and acting as a buffer to the economic recession (Bolaffi, 1977 and 1983; Azevedo and Gama de Andrade, 1982; Valladares, 1983 and 1985; Veras and Bonduki, 1986; Maricato, 1987).

One can notice that the generation of employment by civil construction was significant. The sector was responsible for 13 per cent of new jobs in the 1960s and 10 per cent between 1970-80. In 1980 the construction industry employed 7.2 per cent of the economically active population of the country. The total of people employed by the industry was 24.4 per cent of the EAP during the same year.

S.F.H. and B.N.H. have been discussed at numerous places. The Housing Financial System, financed 4.4 million housing units, – 24 per cent of the total increase of housing stock in Brazil between 1964 and

1986, (when the system was discontinued, due to its bankruptcy). Out of these 4.4 million houses, a little over 1.2 were addressed to low income families (up to 5 minimum wages, which were 66.86 per cent of the total Brazilian families in 1984).

S.F.H. is often cited as an example of ingenious institution for channelling an important part of national savings towards the execution of construction programmes with high financial autonomy. Its funds came from three different sources.

Compulsory Savings – represented by the payment of the Service Time Guarantee Fund (F.G.T.S.) managed by B.N.H. F.G.T.S. represents the deposit by the employer of 8 per cent of the payroll in an account in the name of the employee, yielding quarterly interest.

Free Savings – Collection of sources voluntarily deposited in a savings account. These savings yield 6 per cent interest per year and monthly monetary correction. It is called the "Sistema Brasileiro de Poupanca Emprestimo" (Brazilian Savings and Loans System).

Induced Savings – government savings funds given to financial agents or to borrowers.

Between 1967 and 1984 the composition of B.N.Hs. resources was deeply changed. In 1967, 93.4 per cent of its funds arose from the compulsory savings (F.G.T.S.) – less costly money that allowed the investment of resources in low-income housing (partially subsidised). In 1984 F.G.T.S. participation in the funds of S.F.H. had dropped to 30.90 per cent. The most important part of the money arose from the free savings (62.1 per cent), more expensive money, which was expected to be provided for prompt liquidity.

The housing market became segmented by the division of work among the various public and private agents, under B.N.H.'s control, each one of them serving one of the segments. For example, the popular market (for families earning up to three minimum wages and later on up to 5 minimum wages) would be served by the COHABSs (Housing Companies at local or state level). The economic market (for families with an income ranging from 3 to 6 minimum wages, later on increased) was assisted by housing Co-operatives (non-profit associations for occupational categories acting as intermediaries between the borrowers and B.N.H.). The medium market was designed to serve families with an income above 6 minimum wages and it was mainly operated by S.B.P.E. (Brazilian Savings and Loans System) serving the middle and higher income groups.

Therefore, we can assume that the relationship established between the state and the private sector was rather complex. The S.F.H. promoted private initiative and B.N.H. controlled the market, through building standards, terms for payment, interest rates for the voluntary savings and as the guarantor of funds for housing production.

B.N.H.'s performance shows that its policy was successful as an instrument for ideological domination (home ownership model), as a job generator in civil construction, (especially up to 1981), and as a promoter of the housing industry. Between 1964 and 1986 the Brazilian housing stock increased by 18.25 million units, of which 4.4 million utilised S.F.H. resources, that is, 24 per cent of the new housing benefited from B.N.H. resources. However, its social performance was rather affected, although 4.4 million units in 22 years are a significant figure, only a little over 1.2 million were allocated to low income families (up to 5 minimum wages) which form 67.7 per cent of the Brazilian families.

Due to its free market model S.F.H. has handled housing from the viewpoint of investment though it has also utilised subsidies. The Salary Variation Compensation Fund ended up operating as a large subsidy, in an indiscriminate manners — when it amortisated the debt balance, both for medium and high-income families and for poor families. Few of the workers that contributed with the F.G.T.S. benefited with houses.

S.F.H. did not respect the housing demand profile in the country where around 90 per cent of urban housing needs are represented by families earning up to 5 minimum wages (Albuquerque, 1985). In addition, efforts were made to minimise the final cost of housing by reducing the size of housing using cheaper building material and by densifying the housing estates.

It should be noted that the basic problem is not the Housing Financing System, but of *poverty*. The fact that one-third of national income is concentration in the hands of 5 per cent households (1985) while 34.04 per cent of Brazilian families live at poverty level (with monthly income of up to 2 minimum wages) is shocking, in a country where the per capita income is of about US$ 2,000. This situation is a result of an unfair distribution of opportunities and wealth. Given this income distribution, the task of providing each citizen with decent housing is impossible without subsidies. Considering that families need to pay for food, transportation to work and school, they are left with no money to purchase a house. According to a survey of family expenditure, families earning from 2 to 3 minimum wages can spend in the range of 10 to 16 per cent of their incomes on housing.

In addition, construction costs are rising in higher proportion than inflation and salaries. According to SINDUSCON (Union of the Civil Construction Industry for Large Structures in the State of Sao Paulo), construction materials prices rose by 388.1 per cent in 1987, as compared to general price rise (365.95 per cent). Until a few years ago, it was possible to provide houses of 50 sq m affordable for individuals in the range from one to three minimum wages. After this, Brazil went to "core-houses", with 23 sq metres. Today, this has been reduced to units with 7 sq m, containing only a kitchen and sanitary facilities, and now even this has become unaffordable. (Zastrow, 1987).

In relation to product, except for the Itaquera housing estate in Sao Paulo, S.F.H. did little to improve the quality and to reduce the cost of construction by investing in technological innovation. It favoured the principle that intensive labour technology contributed to job generation. Bolaffi (1983), was one of the few to state that capital intensive technology could reduce construction cost and simultaneously not reduce the number of jobs. With lower cost, the same amount of money could be used to build more. Then it would be possible to guarantee an equivalent number of jobs in the sector, probably more qualified and better paid jobs. In Itaquera, technologically advanced models and scale economies, thanks to the construction of over 40,000 apartments, permitted COHAB in Sao Paulo to sell its units at 69 dollars per square metre when the average price per square metre in Sao Paulo was 170 dollars. Of course, self-help housing and sites-and-services options are more in line with the resources available for housing but it would be unrealistic to think that the housing problems of a city such as Sao Paulo, with over 10 million inhabitants, could be solved with the division of land into small lots and technical help for self-help construction. High-rise solutions are also necessary.

Challenges of Brazilian Housing Policy

Today, what are Brazil's most important housing challenges? A brief estimate of the investments required to solve the problem is discouraging:

(a) in order to meet a 2.4 per cent per year demographic growth (3.15 million new inhabitants annually) and considering an average of 4.34 persons per dwelling, 725,000 new units need to be built each year.

(b) the housing stock consists 30.3 million units. Assuming an average lifespan of 30 years, 606,000 new houses need to be built per year only to replace deteriorated units.

(c) approximately 34 per cent of the existing stock needs improvement and assuming that the remodelling of each house is, on average, equivalent to one-half of new house, this amounts to the construction of about 5,151,000 units. Doing this in 10 years means building 515,000 new houses each year.

The first challenge is how to get more resources allocated for the housing sector to meet the present and future housing needs. The annually required construction including demographic deficit, replacement and quality improvement is estimated to be 1,846,000 units per year for the next ten years.

Based on the average 40 sq m per unit for popular housing, i.e. housing for the low-income people, 73.84 million sq m per year will need to be built. At an estimated unit cost of 15 UPC/sq m (US$ 110/sq m) (not taking into consideration the total wages of the self-help builder), the required annual investment in housing sector would be 1110 million UPC, or 8.1 million U.S. dollars. This investment could be reduced by using non-paid labour, (however, this would result in more horizontalisation, with the additional infrastructure costs) and the use of more advanced construction models, which presupposes an investment in technological research that has not been done to this date.

Considering that the total GNP amount to US$ 260 billion, the required housing investment represents 3.1 per cent of the GNP, (Including investments related to public services such as water, sewers, lighting and streets layout and paving but excluding land cost), thus forming 6.2 per cent of the GNP.

Brazilian savings capacity is between 16 and 18 per cent of the GNP. To invest one-third to solve housing problems is beyond the country's investment capacity, especially when it urgently needs improvements in the agricultural sector in order to maintain the growth in the food supply for a rapidly urbanising population, expansion of health care, social security and education services, and savings to update and expand its manufacturing industry. On the other hand, one should bear in mind that the Brazilian GNP rate, which was usually above 7 per cent per year, has decreased in the last 2 years.

The second challenge is related to another question: what segment of the population can afford a 40 sq m units, COHAB standard, even without paid labour? Such a house will cost 600 UPC or US$ 4,800. We can assume a monthly loan repayment over 20 years, free from interest, which would demand from the families a mortgage of 2.5 UPC or US$ 18.3 per month. Keeping in mind that in 1988 the minimum wage was equivalent to US$ 60 and that 34 per cent of the families earn less than 2 minimum wages (PNAD, 1984), there is an evident gap between the paying capacity and the cost of the house.

What modifications should be made in the urban and housing policies and practices to respond to the housing needs?

Firstly for decreasing the cost of land, it is necessary to review the land by-laws to control speculation. Secondly, assuming that the use of non-paid labour will continue, it is necessary to streamline and make cheaper the construction process. Why not invest in light pre-fabricated tax-free manufactured elements? Doing this would combine technological innovations and higher productivity with intensive labour. Also needed is research on highly productive work processes, new techniques for work site management, on assembling construction elements and on less expensive materials — wood, concrete or masonry panels and carboard. Finally, it is necessary to develop partnership between the national government, the society and the private market, where the role of the central government would be to foster and support local initiatives.

However, without touching the structural causes of the housing problem, the proposed policies will certainly be only palliative measures for an increasing rooflessness, in a country with an economic model that continuously increases both regional and social disparities.

REFERENCES

Albuquerque, M.C. (1985), *Popular Housing: Evaluation and Proposals for the Reorganisation of S.F.H.* Sao, Paulo, Escola de Administracao de Empresas da Fundacao Getulio Vargas, (mimeo).

Azevedo, S. and Game de Andrade, L.A. (1982), *Housing and Power*, Da Fundaco da Casa Popular ao banco Nacional da Habitacao, Rio de Janeiro, Zahar.

Bank, G.A. (1986), 'Poverty, Politics and the Shaping of Urban Space: A Brazilian example' *International Journal of Urban and Regional Research*, 10(4):522-540.

Blanck, G. (1980), 'Bras de Pina Experiencia de Urbanizacao de Favela' in Valladares, L. (ed.) *Habitaco em Questao*, Rio de Janeiro, Zahar : 93-124.

Bolaffi, G. (1977), 'A Casa das Ilusoes Perdidas, Socio-economic aspects of the National Housing Plan' *Cadernos Abap*, 27, Sao Paulo. Braziliense.

—— (1983), 'The Urban Issues: Housing Production, Civil Construction and Work Market', *Novos estudos CEBRAP*, Sao Paulo, 2(1):61-68.

Farah, M.F.S. (1985), 'The State and Housing in Brazil — the Case of Social Security Institutes', *Espaco e Debates*, 16:73-82.

Geiger, P.P. (1985), 'Expansion of Middle Class and of the Public sector and Urbanisation in Brazil', Paper presented in the Symposium '*Metropolis and crisis*', Institute of Geography, USP : 15.

Havel, J.E. (1968), *Habitat et Logement*, Paris, Presses Universitaires de France.

Jaguaribe, J. *et al*. (1986), *Brazil 2000 — Towards a New Social Pact*, Rio de Janeiro, Paz a Terra : 18.

Jastrow, J.L. von (1987), 'O Sistema Financeiro de Habitacao Agride a Classe Media' *Gazeta Mercantil*, July 13:4.

Marcuse, P. (1976), *Housing Policy and Social Indicators: Strangers or Siblings*? Department of City and Regional Planning, University of California, Berkeley, Working Paper No. 130.

Maricato, E. (1987), *Politica Habitacional oa Regime Militar*, Petropolis, Vozes.

Pasternak Taschner, S. (1978), 'Favelas do Municipio de Sao Paulo : Resultados de Pesquisa' in E.A. Blya, *Luta Pelo Espaco* Petopolis, Vozes : 125-148.

—— (1983), *The Dwelling of Poverty: Housing Without Health*, Doctorate thesis, University of, Sao Paulo.

—— (1986), '*No land people*' city-Symposium 9, Sao Paulo, FAU, USP : 268-304.

Rush B.S. (1974), *From Favela to Conjunto the Experience of Squatters Removed to Low-Cost Housing in Rio de Janeiro, Brasil*: Cambridge, Mass,(mimeo).

United Nations (1964), *Handbook of Household Surveys*, New York, Series F n 010.

—— (1967), *Methods of Estimating Housing Needs*, New York, Series F n 212.

Valladares, L. P. (1978), *Passa-se uma casa Analise do Proanama de Remocao de Favelas do Rio de Janeiro* Rio de Janeiro, Zahar.

—— (1983), *Repedsando a habitacao no Brasil* Rio de Janeiro, Zahar.

——, (1985), 'Politicas alternativas de habitacao popular : um voo sobre a literatura internacional'. *Espaco E Debates* 16(33):52.

Veras, M.P.B. and Bonduki, N. (1986), 'Politica Habitacional e a luta pelo dineito and habitacao' In M.L.M. Couvre, (org.) *A Cidadania que nan tenos*, Sao Paulo, Brasiliense, 39:62.

Vetter, D. and Simoes (1980), 'Acesso a infrastructura de saneamento basico e mortalidade', *Boletim Demografico*, 10.

PART II

CONTEXTS

5

LOW-INCOME HOUSING POLICIES IN THE DEVELOPMENT OF BRASILIA : A Critical Review

CLAUDIO ACIOLY JR.

HISTORICAL BACKGROUND

During the second half of the nineteenth century, certain concepts of city models started to flourish as rapid industrialisation takes place in Western Europe. Included in these concepts, there was a claim for the provision of adequate housing for the emerging urban labour and a great concern on salubrity and efficiency in the organisation of the living environment. Later on, during the first half of the twentieth century, through the CIAMs-International Congresses of Modern Architecture, these ideas gained strength among architects and urban planners, and were brilliantly summarised in the famous Charter of Athens (1933); then the four basic functions of the city were defined: living, working, recreation and communication.

The Charter became a reference book for all prominent modern architects involved with city planning in this period. However, it was Le Corbusier who systematised the guidelines and recommendations in the forms of a theoretical structure and concepts for city planning, and was the person who was responsible to widespread the new trend at international level. Although the problems of deterioration in city life, which he was so concerned with, had strong socio-political components, he put a lot of emphasis on architectural and urbanistic solutions. His call was for a bold expression, through urbanism, of society's confidence in the future. For him, city planning, besides of being a science, was the noblest of the arts; the expression of the activity of an epoch (Sarin, 1982).

It is quite explicit in his works a centralised top-to-bottom planning scheme and a decision-making process in which the elite of technicians could hold the control of the planning process. Then, cities and all changes in the physical environment could be under the guidance of competent expertises.

This conceptual framework generated several experiences not only in the continent that it was born, but also sponsored and still sponsors great amount of projects in urban planning and design in Third World countries. Most well-known examples are Chandigarh and Brasilia, as fully pre-planned cities implemented in the fifties in India and Brazil, respectively.

As well as in Chandigarh, the construction of the Brazilian capital evoked all sorts of bombast and pride nationalistic sentiments through which the construction of the city could be transformed into a symbolic step of the Brazilian society towards a new era of development and self-determination and the rise of a modern nation.

It was during this period that the concept of modernisation and economic development of Brazil through the increase of industrialisation and substitution of import policies, colonisation fronts in the new western frontier and regional development gained acceptance among politicians, intellectuals, militaries and lay citizens.

Juscelino Kubitschek, an experienced politician, intelligently perceived the situation and was able to put forward these aspirations in his political programme, and with that, he was able to aggregate a relevant political support for his campaign for president in 1955. As Brasilia was a main component in his political strategy, his election formalised the decision to change the capital from Rio de Janeiro to the hinterland of the central west region. It was during his administration that planning activities, with a strong ideological character, gained real support and became, at the same time, an efficient instrument for state control and a tool to conduct the modernisation project promoted and sponsored by the Brazilian state.

From the fifties onwards and particularly during the Kubitschek government, the ideology of planning took shape inside the Brazilian state under a process of modernisation; an ideology in which the act of planning is represented as a strictly technical-scientific action, neutral, through which one can foresee and control, that is to say, to administer in a rational way (Bicca, 1985).

However, as practised in market economies, urban planning has consisted of the imposition of a framework of rules, presented as being neutral, and legitimised on the grounds of being in the 'public' interest.

However, within the urban Third World, characterised by extreme social and economic inequalities, it is not difficult to show that the neutrality is a myth (Sarin, 1982).

In reality, the planning strategy gave priority to the increase of production and maximisation of the process of development and capital accumulation, and disregarded sharp economic differences among social groups and serious problems of distribution of wealth. In this apolitical technocrat scenario, the CIAM standpoints, as explicitly explained by Le Corbusier, found firm ground to flourish among the selective club of prominent Brazilian architects and urban planners, whom have played great influence on governmental officials, politicians, intellectuals, artists, and in many cases on the public opinion. The consequences of that can still be observed today in several plans and planning processes in different Brazilian cities, particularly, and more evident in the case of Brasilia.

The national competition of projects for the construction of the city, showed already clear evidences of this fact. All the 26 projects presented had very strong similarities among them as they were based on CIAMs concepts. They established a comprehensive set of objectives, land use control schemes, by-law building regulations, a strong concern with visual expressions and aesthetic concepts on city form, and a remarkable state control in the following development and consolidation of the new capital.

It was the work, known as Plano Piloto de Brasilia (see Fig. 5.1), submitted by Lucio Costa, a Brazilian urbanist who had worked with Le Corbusier more than a decade before, which was awarded with the contract and implementation began immediately.

In order to house thousands of building workers, governmental employees, technical staff and so forth, a network of labour camps, as a type of housing accommodation, was established on the site by governmental agencies and building contractors responsible for different projects. Fully sponsored by the Brazilian Government, the new capital was officially inaugurated on April 21, 1960, after three years of intensive construction, and has had an outstanding performance both in terms of development and population growth (with 1,700,000 inhabitants), and in terms of the problems which emerged with it.

The experience of building the new capital and the peculiarity of the urban plan and design applied in the city, represents a significant urban innovation and a turning point in the history of town planning in

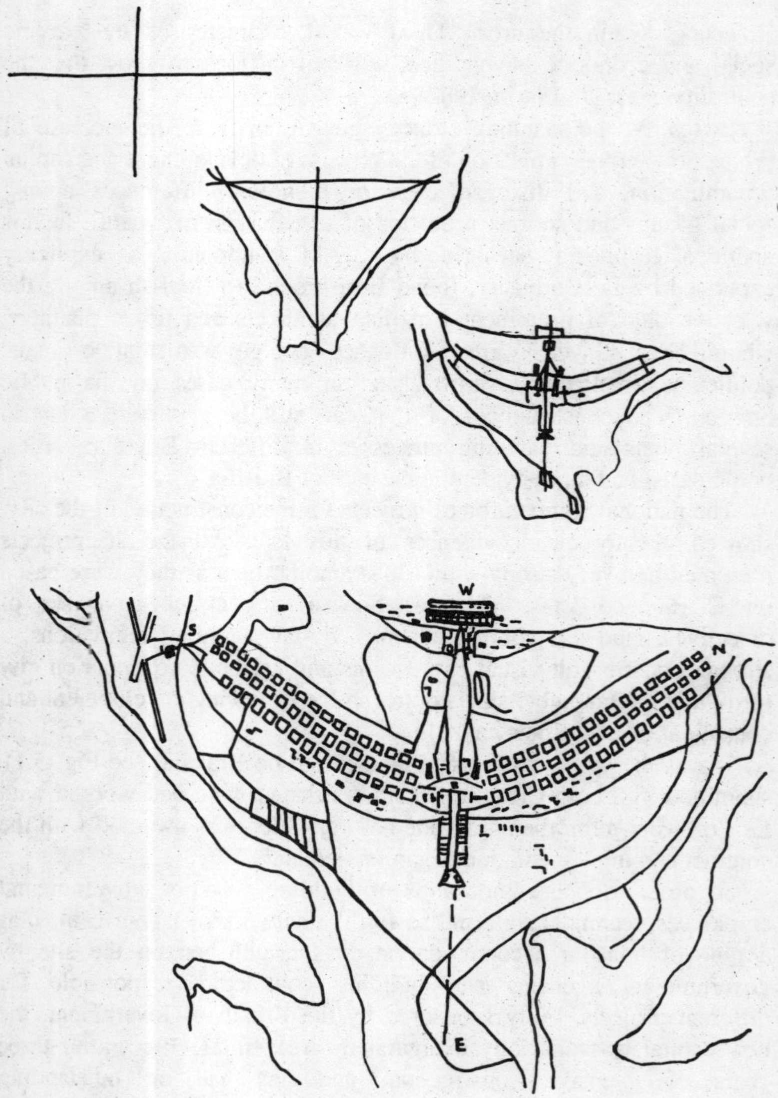

FIG. 5.1: Plano Piloto

Sketches of Plano Piloto by Lucio Costa (Revista Modulo, no. 8, Jul. 1957)

Brazil. There are also other aspects that make Brasilia a very peculiar case: the Government owns more than 60 per cent of the land stock; it maintains strict control over land use in order to avoid any type of illegal occupation and subdivision; it has had a significant participation in the development and consolidation of the city, with a relevant production of housing addressed to the popular sector; the city has been basically a tertiary city, relying its development on a great amount of Federal Government's subsidy, and has the State played a major role in the job market; the city governor is nominated by the president, there is no forum for political decisions (city council or similar system) and political participation of the inhabitants has been always very limited.

At the international level, Brasilia is undoubtedly the most expressive example of urban design in which the principles and concepts established by the CIAMs were applied in its extreme.

BRASILIA AS A FIRST STEP FOR REGIONAL DEVELOPMENT : A MYTH

Among several arguments that sustain the decision to transfer the capital to the hinterland of Brazil, one seems to stand out with relevancy: the idea that the appearance of the city in the territory would favour development at a regional scale and would create possibilities for the development of the municipalities that surround the Federal District of Brasilia.

Apparently, due to the network of communication through air, rail and roads which connects the city to the north, west, east and south regions and facilitates both the access of goods and passengers' transportation, and due to the increase of productive agricultural land in the Central West Region, one might have the impression that the city has indeed fulfilled its designations. However, the effect was exactly the opposite. The great majority of the cities located within the limits of the so-called geo-economic regions, an area of influence of the city, are facing serious difficulties. In this part of the territory, almost the totality of small size cities are presenting a decrease in their rate of urban development, except Goiania and Anapolis (which are the largest cities), some small urban centres located in areas of frontier expansion and those which are located just outside the limits of the Federal District (Barbosa Ferreira, 1985).

On one hand, because of a series of constraints in the housing sector in Brasilia, the cities located next to the limits of the Federal District became an outlet solution for low income residents who can hardly have access to housing accommodation in the capital. It became the only one alternative, and in such a scale that only in the municipalities of Luziania – a city located just few km away from the border of the Federal District, the population reached 80,000 inhabitants with an increase of more than 600 per cent in the last decade (Barbosa Ferreira, 1985). According to Paviani (1985), private sponsored projects implemented in these localities could provide opportunities for housing a population equivalent to 1,500,000 inhabitants, precisely the population of Brasilia in 1985.

On the other hand, small size cities have not been able to provide adequate infrastructure and job opportunities that could stop the flux of population that moves towards Brasilia every year. They have been unable to achieve reasonable degree of development and cannot compete with the high possibilities that the capital offers in terms of services and facilities, income generation and employment, that continues to attract waves of migrants.

BRASILIA AS A CAPITAL CITY OF 500,000 INHABITANTS : A DREAM

According to Costa's Plano Piloto, the city was expected to reach 500,000 inhabitants in a period of 25 years, maintaining its main characteristics as a tertiary city, seat of the national government. However, the dynamic process of consolidation showed a completely different situation 25 years later. The population reached 1,579,000 inhabitants in 1985, three times more than what was estimated by the initial plan. The population did not want to return to their homeland, despite all the measures planned in order that, at least, one-third of it would return, another third would be occupied in local activities in the city and, finally, the other third part would be employed in agricultural activities because it was a population with rural background (Costa, 1984). Not only the existing residents remained in the city but also Brasilia followed the outstanding process of urbanisation taking place in the country as a whole (By the end of the seventies, roughly 70 per cent of the Brazilian population was living in urban areas). The population growth rate in the capital was among the highest rates registered in other parts of the country, jumping from 140,165 inhabitants in 1960 to 537,592 in 1970, and 1,198,142 inhabitants in

1980. It is today one of the 10 largest cities of Brazil.

This remarkable growth can be explained through several lines of arguments with socio-political and economic components and are related to the overall context of Brazil in this period e.g. lack of an effective and continuous rural policy towards land property and production systems that could possibly slow down the pace of migration, deterioration of job market in the rural and urban areas; the world oil crisis and the increase of foreign debt which caused extreme government centralisation, and emphasis on export policies; military intervention, economic stagnation, lack of job creation programmes in the regional scale, etc. . . . and an overall process of capital accumulation and monopolisation, typical of the capitalistic development model applied in Brazil.

In this paper, attention has been concentrated to the local situation of Brasilia. What attempts have been made by the government of Brasilia to cope with the emerge of a serious housing problem in a city that, from the planning point of view, had at its disposal one of the most ideal set ups: an immense land stock, a considerable amount of financial resources, a very fresh institutional framework with recently created public agencies? Intension of the paper is to highlight the development of Brasilia from the point of view of housing policies, and look at the different strategies carried out by local authorities in order to respond to housing demands.

In this respect, Brasilia is a typical example of the Third World. Despite all the efforts made by the government and despite a significant state participation in housing production, these actions have not been able to cope with the increase of housing demands. A demand which is not only present in the low income sector, mainly located in satellite cities, squatter settlements and remaining labour camps (from construction period), but also in the middle income sector. This sector already faces serious difficulties to find housing accommodations in the highly developed Plano Piloto.

The existing critical housing problem in Brasilia, and a constrained housing sector is, in a great deal, related to the incapacity of the public sector to design more appropriate policies and programmes which could give opportunities for decentralisation of planning and more independence for the actors involved. This argument is discussed in the following pages.

THE EMERGENCE OF SQUATTER SETTLEMENTS: EARLY CONFLICTS WITH PLANNING

The existence of low-income settlements (labour camps-acampamentos) and squatter settlements – within the urban framework of the new capital was not accepted by the authorities and the planning team. Several of these settlements were bulldozed off and residents evicted to recently created satellite cities before the inauguration of the city. Even though these towns were planned to exist only after the moment that the Plano Piloto would be fully occupied, political decisions taken by the government, sustained efficiently by technical expertises, seemed to have layed the basis for a continuous slum clearance programme that would accompany the development of the city from that moment onwards.

According to Lucio Costa 'the NOVACAP – the city urbanisation company, Israel Pinheiro – the project manager, and the others decided to proceed like that because there were favelas (Brazilian denomination for squatter settlements) surrounding every construction site in the city which involved the families of the workers. From this fact derives the creation of peripherical settlements where individual plots were provided, and to where the population could be housed in one way or another. As a consequence, these sites became cities, the so-called satellite cities that took place of the satellite cities that were planned to exist' (Costa, 1984).

Before the official inauguration of the city, three satellite cities had already been planned and implemented: Taguatinga, Gama, and Sobradinho. Two old historical villages already existed and gained status of satellite city in the following years: Brazlandia and Planaltina.

The first one, Taguatinga, had its implementation immediately decided in 1958, after a site visit of President Kubitschek where he was faced with a demonstration of residents of squatter settlements. This fact marks the beginning of a long struggle of the urban poor in order to achieve their rights to stay in the city which they helped to build and consolidate. Other squatter areas received more vehement treatment and wherever occurred resistance, a group of social workers and sometimes special police forces were put in action to convince residents to move to new sites. At the labour camps, other conflicts for better lodging, food and respect of labour rights started to take place as well. At that moment, it highlighted clear contradictions between the interests of the State and the mass of workers which formed the basis of the human force employed in the construction of the city. Sometimes, violence outbroke with losses of human lives.

In this period, there was already an incipient popular organisation that made possible a long resistance against eviction in Cidade Livre (Free City). Despite the fact that this wooden town had been built in a provisory character, it already had all the features of a small size city: water, electricity, houses, commerce, shops, banks, hotels, a population of approximately 60,000 inhabitants, and was already surrounded by squatter settlements which kept on receiving newcomers attracted by the construction of the capital.

When the government attempted to demolish the city, a long resistance was organised and legalisation was finally obtained in the forms of federal law in 1961, with the name of Nucleo Bandeirante. It is a remarkable event because it represents the first real physical intervention of social forces in the land occupation process foreseen by the original plan. A residential area with popular characteristics in the limits of influence of Plano Piloto was imposed to planners and authorities by mechanisms that they could not have the control yet.

However, planning strategies became sophisticated and slum clearance policies became stronger and stronger in order to safeguard the "purism" of the the Plano Piloto, and protect, at the same time, the Federal Government from any kind of delicate political situation that a confrontation with popular forces would bring.

MASSIVE EVICTIONS: POLICE OR POLICIES?

In the beginning of the seventies, a slum clearance commission was formed and called CEI "Comissao de Erradicacao de Invasoes". It controlled labour camps and squatter settlements through systematic inspections and set up a series of measures for massive evictions. CEI was responsible for one of the most spectacular actions regarding low-income housing occurred in the history of the city. Residents of a gigantic squatter settlement located in the fringe of Nucleo Bandeirante (called IAPI) and from some other places, were evicted to a new satellite city created with the main purpose of housing all squatter residents of Brasilia. Located next to Taguatinga, 35 km from Plano Piloto, it was a large land division development project called after the name of the commission: Cei landia. By 1972, 80,000 people had already been resettled.

Coincidentally, this is a period that the military regime assumed extremely radical procedures, and established stronger centralisation of planning and decision-making without any possibilities for democratic participation. In Brasilia, this was more visible than in any other city. The following years demonstrated that slum clearance polices were not sufficient to solve the dilemma of housing the poor, nor the strict surveillance and control mechanisms over "invasoes" and "acampamentos" were sufficient to stop these settlements from growing.

By mid-seventies, some aspects became more evident. First, the urban design applied in the Plano Piloto, rigidly regulated by building and land use bylaw enforcement mechanisms caused an absurd rise in the costs of housing, and turned the area excessively class selective and prohibitive for low-income residents. The architectural and urbanistic assumptions applied in the city, preserved and reinforced by planning authorities who ruled the city in the following years, swept away any chances for informal land subdivision and densification. This is quite a common mechanism used by low-income groups to have to housing in the majority of Brazilian cities, and in the Third World.

Brandao (1976) was a pioneer in Brasilia in this line of arguments. "On one hand, the high levels of qualification of space, specialisation of functions, dimensions and urbanistic requirements for land occupation as well as the costs resulted from that, have become mechanisms to inhibit the poor population to live in the Plano Piloto, and on the other hand, it has not created facilities for middle-income population to have access to housing standards established in the plan" (Acioly *et al.*, 1986).

Indeed, during the seventies, some satellite cities e.g. Guara and Nucleo Bandeirante, started to experience the phenomenon of new-comers. Residents who could not cope with the high costs of housing in the Plano Piloto, moved towards the nearest satellite cities and established a displacement process of economic weaker groups by wealthier ones. "It is worth to note the extreme situation in Guara where practically 100 per cent of the existing housing stock had been gone through one commercial transaction and more than 50 per cent of the apartments were rented in 1976" (Gonzalez, 1985).

Second, the significant amount of government sponsored housing projects addressed to the popular sector never reached the poor despite the numbers of housing units produced by the governmental Social Housing Agency – SHIS. By 1979, with the conclusion of P-Norte extension of Ceilandia, the number of housing units reached 65,952

(Gonzalez, 1985). The poorest groups were never able to meet income requirements established by the programmes and therefore remained outside from all projects implemented. This was not a peculiarity of Brasilia but one of the evidences of the failure of the National Popular Housing Plan – PLANHAP designed and sponsored by the National Bank – BNH. According to Bolaffi (1986), from the total amount of resources collected by one of the (once) largest housing financial institutions in the world, only 18 per cent was invested in the construction of houses addressed to families earning less than 5 minimum wages (5 × US$ 55.30 in December 1986).

The massive production of housing, which was the basis of a policy for employment generation and for capital accumulation by the building sector, was not able to sustain itself as a policy nor was it able to solve the problem of housing the poor (Acioly, 1987a).

Third, the economic difficulties due to high rates of inflation, and the decrease of project/building activities in the city caused a serious decline in the building sector, consequently restraining employment opportunities and increasing the economic difficulties of low-income families. There were indications that the densification in some "invasoes" was linked with this process.

Fourth, the lack of employment policies and appropriate housing programmes, that could meet the needs of a growing low-income sector, caused the appearance of a relevant informal market regarding housing and employment. From the point of view of the job market, the informal sector was estimated to have 150,000 workers (Paviani, 1985). From the point of view of housing, not only squatter settlements and labour camps were under processes of densification but it was also visible that an over-occupation of residential plots in satellite cities was occurring. The practice of subletting rooms/houses made possible the emergence of a new category of low-income resident – *o inquilino de fundo de lote* – tenants who occupy rooms/houses located in the backyard of plots. Some empirical estimations revealed that by the mid-seventies, 50 per cent of the population was already living in rented accommodations (Gonzalez, 1985). By 1987, the Government of Brasilia assumed publicly that the population living in rented accommodations could reach the amount of 150,000 families, which means an estimated population of 750,000 inhabitants, or almost half of the capital's total population in this year.

At last, the effort made by the government to maintain the city as capital metropolis, became indeed an indirect stimulus for the development of informal mechanisms that could facilitate the access to housing and income generation by low-income residents. The fear to have urban densification in the surroundings of the capital city, and the excessive care showed by the government when it had to deal with the issue of industrial activities suitable for Brasilia, gave signs that it was not really willing to tolerate shifts that could put in danger the character and the designations of the city. "In this scheme, the Plano Pilcto could be preserved for some functions of the Federal Government, released from universities (students) and industries (workers) that could be replaced in other urban sites, and this would give it the characteristics of an administrative suburb of a larger conurbation, calm and pleasant, and distant from daily problems faced by the rest of the country . . . just like many politicians have idealised the country's national capital, centre of national decisions" (Cordeiro and Kohlsdorf, 1985).

On the other hand, the development process taking place more sharply in the satellite cities was giving evidences that, sooner or later, the functional characteristics of Brasilia would have to be revised, and the central role played by the Plano Piloto in the job market and in the supply of urban services and facilities would necessarily have to suffer a relevant shift.

A PLAN AND THE RISE OF LOW-INCOME RESIDENTS' ORGANISATIONS

Three relevant aspects occurred by the end of the seventies which influenced the housing sector drastically: a master plan, a political decision to decrease and stop housing production and the rise of residents' associations.

A comprehensive master plan was designed and approved in the very beginning of 1978 and, for the first time, the problems of Brasilia were treated in a more global view. Instead of referring only to the problems of Plano Piloto, the plan was concerned with the satellite cities and with existing vacant land without destinations in the Federal District. There were also some considerations over the geo-economic region and the municipalities located next to its limits.

PEOT – Expansion and Territorial Organisation Plan of the Federal District was characterised as a broad land use regulation plan which would guide urban development towards the southwest, in the direction of Gama, locating new residential areas far from Plano Piloto, and connecting them through a network of mass transportation system. By the time of plan implementation, the urban network of Brasilia was already composed of 8 satellite cities. The plan proposed another one – Samambaia.

PEOT had a strong sanitary basis with a series of technical arguments against urban settlements within the Paranoa lake basin, because the lake was already giving signs of high degree of pollution, and the existing network could not support an increase of population in this location. Although it was never very explicit, these arguments seemed to be used as political instruments to preserve Brasilia on the national political administrative capital. In this respect, with PEOT, this "preservationism" became much stronger inside the planning framework of the government and seemed to have guided a series of administrative and political decisions in the following years.

On one hand, the land use control regulations established by PEOT ignored completely the existence of "illegal" low-income settlements. On the other hand, the plan stimulated control mechanisms over these settlements. By doing that, it severely repressed the low-income housing sector because these settlements represented indeed a large informal sector and the only one alternative for housing out of governmental schemes. And since the housing production was decreasing, alternatives for accommodation in this sector became scarce: to invade public vacant land or to share accommodations in residential plots in satellite cities. The growth of an informal rental sector in the satellite cities seems also to be linked with enforcement mechanisms of PEOT.

A political decision taken by the government reinforced this process. There was a belief that the increase of migration towards Brasilia, and consequently the growth of squatter settlements was related with the amount of government sponsored housing projects. It was generally accepted within the Local Government that the existence of easier mechanisms to apply for a house motivated people to migrate to Brasilia. And so, between 1978 and 1982, there was not a single housing programme addressed to the popular sector with serious consequences to be evaluated in the coming years.

From the point of view of the population, there was a reorganisational process taking place inside several residential areas and consequently, residents' associations were formed in squatter settlements and labour camps. They claimed for legalisation of tenure or for implementation of basic infrastructure. Demonstrations for housing began and extremist actions such as mass invasions of vacant land took place in the beginning of the eighties. In the context of satellite cities, residents' associations were formed as well, but occurred a very peculiar fact: one tenants' association was formed per satellite city and by mid-eighties they were organised in an Union of Residents' Associations of Brasilia.

These movements gave indications that the policies formulated until then by the Government had been unable to meet the needs of the low-income population. Never were they asked to inform their needs to planners, nor were they able to give any input in the design of such policies.

The high costs for housing, the growth of illegal settlements, the densification of residential plots in satellite cities, the use of commercial areas for housing purposes in the Plano Piloto, squattering taking place in vacant land of Plano Piloto, the high costs of land, political struggles for housing, the growth of informal job and housing markets, etc. . . . demonstrated that there was an urgent need for shifts in governmental polities. Just out of the limits of the Federal District, particularly in the cities of Luziania and Santo Antonio Descoberto, a reflect of restrictive policies of the Government of Brasilia was also visible as well. The appearance of private housing development projects was filling the gap in terms of housing but was forcing residents to make daily trips of more than one hour, at high costs of transportation, and consequently bringing the costs of housing to levels almost unbearable (Acioly, 1987b).

HOUSING THE POOR : A NEW APPROACH

In 1983, a housing programme named PAPE –Programa de Assentamento Populacional de Emergencia – was set up, and was addressed to families living in labour camps and squatter areas. An independent planning and implementation unit was formed to run the programme and develop strategies related to low-income housing. It was called GEPAFI (Grupo Executivo de Assentamento de Favelas e Invasoes). The appearance of an independent unit in the institutional framework of the Government gave evidences of three facts: the need for an institutional reform, the stagnation of the Social Housing Agency–SHIS and the need for a radical change in public policies, especially those affecting the Housing sector.

The unit carried out a socio-economic survey and registered close to 18,000 families, an estimated population of 90,000 inhabitants living in 89 mapped settlements (GEPAFI, 1984).

A quick look at the census showed that former governmental decisions had instead increased the problems in these settlements. Despite all the measures to control and avoid the growth of illegal settlements during the past four years, not only existing structures had grown in terms of area and population, but also new settlements appeared in the urban scenario. A great number of them were subject of the seven projects of PAPE implemented in seven different satellite cities. They reached 47.96 per cent of the target population in less than three years time.

The programme set up the idea of upgrading existing settlements for the first time in the history of the city. Even though several squatter settlements were also relocated, GEPAFI took always into consideration and satellite cities where they were located, thus maintaining the existing links with services and facilities and with the places of employment of residents.

Although this approach had been used long before in other cities of Brazil, and had been discussed in specialised international literature since the sixties, the progressive development approach applied by GEPAFI can be considered, for Brasilia, a very innovative way of dealing with low-income housing. The centralised planning process that have ruled over the city in the past years have allowed very little space for participation of private and individual initiatives. The legacy left by CIAM inside government machinery have facilitated the rise of a planning process dominated by mighty planners, who have ruled over the city as competent expertises, just like Le Corbusier imagined. The practice of planning the city has neglected completely the existence of the population and its organisations. In this respect, it is not surprising to realise that the technical determinism that grew among planning authorities became a pathway for authoritarian practices carried out by the government. Constantly, lay residents have played the role of passive participants in urban development and, indeed, have had very little opportunity to influence the decisions, and the projects which are directly concerned with them.

GEPAFI (1984) put emphasis on self-initiatives of residents in the solution and improvement of their housing conditions, and established a clear concept of housing as a process. Every individual household had a role to play in the process of housing improvements. However, PAPE and its planning process can be characterised as typical top-to-bottom scheme, but it stimulated residents' organisations to play a more active and participative role. Even though there were several types of consultations, talks and meetings, residents' participation took place more strongly during implementation phase. Anyhow, residents' associations took advantage of this fact and were able to influence some decisions at this level.

There are some relevant aspects brought by PAPE. The emphasis on localised solutions was a clear contradiction with the urban development proposed by PEOT. This duality of the government generated internal conflicts of interests among public agencies involved with urban development and provided an excellent opportunity for residents' organisations to request individual solutions for their localities.

From the point of view of the building sector, PAPE became a great stimulus by providing work for several building contractors and consequently increasing job opportunities. It also stimulated the low-income housing market through the provision of 8,329 plots at subsidised values. A household survey, which was carried out in two of PAPE projects, revealed that the market was indeed stimulated. Conducted in the first and in the last project implemented by GEPAFI, Itamaraca and Candangolandia respectively, the survey revealed commercial transactions involving plots in both settlements. In the case of Itamaraca, after 3 years of project implementation, for every ten families, two were newcomers, and according to the leader of the group, this number was even higher than what the survey could reveal.

Although these transactions were illegal, news publicised by the press affirmed that the displacement process was happening in every project of PAPE, and was caused by the entrance of middle-income groups in the scenario of these settlements. In the case of Itamaraca, this was not correct because the majority of newcomers were former tenants living in the satellite city of Gama, under the pressure of very high rents. The survey revealed clearly that exists significant income differences and particularities among subgroups within the low-income sector, which the Government seemed to disregard when designed the programme e.g. differences in income and employment situation between squatter and labour camp residents, peculiarity of tenants, etc. . . . This shows the strong tendency to look at social groups as compact entities, common attitude in governmental programmes in Brasilia. In respect of tenants, although there were sufficient indications of the renting and subletting practices and the critical housing situation of tenants e.g. demonstrations, petitions, talks, meetings, public news, etc. . . ., PAPE reached a very insignificant number of them.

It was not difficult to realise that these transactions would have to occur at a large-scale because there was already a great demand for housing; the pressure on the existing housing stock was high enough to facilitate profitable deals; and the price of land was extremely high as a consequence of government control over the land stock (plots were actually sold at prices which were between 400 and 600 per cent above the values stipulated by the government in its land public auctions). Due to this land policy, low-income residents were automatically excluded because they could simply not fulfil legal requirements e.g. down payment, official/legal source of income, employment status etc.

In regarding to the process of housing consolidation, some preliminary conclusions came out from this survey. In the case of Candangolandia, the progressive development approach made possible the emerge of self-generated activities related to housing improvements and building construction materials. It stimulated the appearance of small size building materials firms and informal credit systems. The process of housing improvements involved a great amount of private savings of residents used to purchase building materials and to hire building contractors. However, when looking at a broad sequence of steps of improvement on the uncompleted red brick core house, only 10 per cent of the families surveyed were able to reach the end of the sequence, and declared a lot of difficulties to have access to financial resources. This sequence was identified according to the order given by residents' preferences in implementing relevant improvements. Due to the importance given by residents to certain improvements made in the core house, the sequence was divided in nine steps involving the following categories of improvements: (1) plot division walls, (2) connection to infrastructure networks, (3) excreta disposal systems, (4) roof extension for service area, (5) internal divisions, (6) core house extension, (7) demolition of core house, (8) replacement of core house and (9) construction of a new house. For these activities, no financial arrangement as well as no building materials loans were offered by PAPE which could reinforce and facilitate the consolidation of the settlement, fully in the hands of residents. Another aspect made the situation more critical: the costs of housing expenditures (land taxation, water, electricity, transportation) in both projects already reached the borderline of 20 per cent, without taking into account the costs of housing improvements and the monthly mortgage payment. There was an agreement that the latter would stay below 10 per cent of minimum wage, but by the time the survey was conducted, it had not started to be charged.

In case a cost recovery scheme is applied on the basis of 5 per cent annual interest in an agreed period of 25 years, then in Itamaraca, the total expenditures on housing would reach above the limits commonly established by housing institutions i.e 25 per cent of family income. Also if the costs of projects are to be calculated on the basis of market land price, it would push the prices to unaffordable levels for low-income residents. In both the cases it would lead to the displacement of the target group at a higher rate.

CONCLUSIONS

As the survey revealed, residents claimed for non-conventional housing approaches and demanded facilities to have access to finance and material resources. Despite of being poor, residents managed to create informal mechanisms to achieve housing improvements which could have been supported by the State through an efficient framework of loaning. From the point of view of project design, the standards introduced in terms of urban layout and infrastructure networks, increased considerably the total costs of projects and consequently the amount to be charged from the beneficiaries whenever cost recovery is implemented. In this respect, there is a need to revise the building codes and land use regulations which affect seriously the life of a low-income resident. Concerning the expenses of families on housing, both projects gave clear evidences of disregardness with the costs of improvements of the core house, fully sponsored by residents, and this was a contradiction to early policy statements of GEPAFI. If a participatory framework could have existed, perhaps the gap between programme objectives and final realisation would not have existed so sharply. The progressive development approach applied in Candangolandia provided opportunities for income generation and highlighted the close link between housing and income, housing and employment, which is a relevant relationship that all government sponsored programmes, including PAPE, have disregarded completely. The informal rental market in the satellite cities had already stressed these relations and, together with the development of small-scale industries and commercial enterprises taking place in low-income residential areas, gives evidences for the present administration of

Brasilia that the city can no longer be maintained as a strictly administrative paradise. Examples in the Plano Piloto and satellite cities demonstrate that there is a need for opportunities to individuals achieve some levels of self-determination in the solution of their housing problems, and fulfil their aspirations with the support of the government that will act as a facilitator in urban development.

In a context of democratisation taking place in the country from 1985 onwards, expectations for changes in local governmental policies grew significantly among sectors of the population. The political changes have made possible the appearance of political negotiations and more opportunities for participation of NGOs (Non-Governmental Organisations) already involved with urban problems. However, despite institutional reforms and small shifts in public policies, the return to Brasilia of Oscar Niemeyer (the architect who designed the famous buildings of the city) and Lucio Costa (the designer of the city), as special advisers of the governor, brought back the predominance of technical decisions and the hegemony of the elite of technical expertises over the problems concerning the city. Never before was the legacy of the CIAMs' recommendations so evident, and with that, the preservationism of the Plano Piloto became very strong. All attempts were made to preserve the original concept of the city at the costs of squatter evictions from the area, stricter building control regulations, and finally the approval of UNESCO to declare the city plan as a world patrimony. The fear that socio-political forces would penetrate and make interferences in the "master piece", horrified the planning structure of the city (governmental officials, authorities, planners, designers, etc. . .).

When politics entered the city in 1986 with the election of city representatives for the National Constitution Assembly, and the first elections for city council in 1988, there is a possibility that urban socio-political movements may influence the decision-making process. Consequently it will make Brasilia look like any other city in Brazil, with its conflicts and political negotiations that affect the physical and socio-spatial characteristics of the living environment. And so, the character of the Brazilian capital has a possibility to be revised, and hopefully, with some benefits for low-income residents.

REFERENCES

Acioly Jr., C. *et al.* (1986), *Politica de Aao de Governo e Propostas Para o Setor Habitacional*, Brasilia: SEH-Secretaria Estraordinaria da Habitacao. GDF :6.

Acioly Jr., C. (1987a), 'Possibilidades e Limitacoes da Autoconstrucao Para Solucao do Problema Habitacional da Populacao Desabrigada'. Concurso Nacional de Monografias do Ano Internacional de Habitacao Para Desabrigados, Brasilia: (mimeo).

—— (1987b), 'A Comparative Analysis of the Consolidation of Two Low-income Projects in Brasilia: An evaluation', Rotterdam, Institute for Housing Studies.

Barbosa Ferreira, I.C. (1985), 'O Processo de Urbanizacao e a Producao do Espaco Metropolitano de Brasilia', in: A. Paviani (ed.), *Brasilia, Ideologia e Realidade/Espaco Urbano em Questao*, Sao Paulo, Projeto Editores : 43-56.

Bicca, P.R.S. (1985), 'Brasilia: Mitos e Realidades', in: A. Paviani (ed), *Brasilia, Ideologia e Realidade/Espaco Urbano em Questao*, Sao Paulo, Projeto Editores: 101-134.

Bolaffi, G. (1986), 'Os Mitos Sobre o Problema da Habitacao', *Espaco e Debates*, VI, (17):24-31.

Brandao, A.B. (1976), 'Aspectos da Habitacao Popular em Brasilia', *Revista de Planejamento*, 8:19, 52-58.

Cordeiro, L.A.; Kohlsdorf, G.R. (1985), 'Brasilia: Algumas Especulacoes Prospectivas', in: A. Paviani (ed.), *Brasilia, Ideologia e Realidade/Espaco Urbano em Questao*, Sao Paulo, Projeto Editores :215-248.

Costa, L. (1984), 'Consideracoes em Torno do Plano Piloto de Brasilia', in: Comissao do Distrito Federal, *I Seminario de Estudos dos Problems Urbanos de Brasilia*, Brasilia: Senado Federal :21-28.

GEPAFI (1983), 'Referencia Para Acao do Governo no Setor Habitacao', Brasilia, GDF, mimeo :65.

—— (1984), 'Demonstrativo Geral do Cadastramento Socio Economico da Populacao Residente nas Invasoes do Distrito Federal', Brasilia, GDF (mimeo).

Gonzalez, S.F. (1985), 'As Formas Concretas da Segregacao Residencial em Brasilia', in: A. Paviani (ed.), *Brasilia, Ideologia e Realidade*, Sao Paulo, Projeto Editors: 81-100.

Paviani, A. (1985), 'A Metropole Terciaria', in: A. Paviani (ed.) *Brasilia, Ideologia e Realidade*, Sao Paulo : 57-80.

Sarin, M. (1982), *Urban Planning in the Third World. The Chandigarh Experience*, London, Mansell : 1, 33.

6

URBAN POLICY, HOUSING MARKET AND URBAN REGENERATION

LUCIA MARIA M. BOGUS

INTRODUCTION

Studies analysing the structuring of Brazilian cities, the processes of urban space occupation by different social groups during different historical periods, and the role played by the State in the conjugation of factors which are involved in the urbanisation process, have assumed over greater importance in the explanation of the social processes underway in Brazilian society (Villaca, 1978; Low-Beer, 1987).

This paper aims at contributing to the analysis of urban space-population relationships based on a case study of State intervention, whose mechanisms, once known, permit a broader reconstruction of those relationships, using the city of Sao Paulo as a backdrop and larger reference point.

This reconstruction is, in turn, impossible unless the parcel of space under consideration is inserted into the context of the city, thought about as a totality expressing the body of social relationships. Such relationships are historically and socially constituted and their spatial location expresses the characteristics of the society, at the level of the social division of work, the distribution of economic activities and the location of social classes, reflecting the structure of the society in the configuration of its urban space (Lipietz, 1982).

In the analysis of the process, the discussion of questions linked to land-use and occupation in the capitalist city, as well as the mechanisms for generation and appropriation of income from urban land, is important in order to understand how the forms of social-spatial population segregation are produced, which are responsible in large part for the configuration of the city of Sao Paulo, setting for the study in question.

The city of Sao Paulo, in its process of territorial structuring, reflected from early on, at the spatial level, the social relationships engendered by the factory production process. Thus, while the areas most valuable for residential purposes, because of their location, were occupied by the population with higher incomes, the lowlands and areas near the rivers were occupied by the working classes, living in proximity to the factories.

The productive process, historically and spatially situated, generates a body of social relationships which in their concrete expression translate the form in which the society is organised (Souza and Santos, 1986). In this manner, with each technological innovation, with each alteration of the social division of labour, which in the urban environment touches different branches of activity, changes are produced at the level of social dynamics and in the physical-spatial configuration of the city, having a direct reflection on the processes of urban land valuation, according to the uses for which it is destined and its differential location. Such factors condition demand for land as well as its prices, affecting, with regard to housing, the location possibilities of the great majority of the urban population.

The State, through its multiple forms of action, also interferes in the mechanisms of space occupation, whether through the expansion of the network of public services, supporting private enterprise, or through specific legislation concerning land-use and occupation, promoting the increased value of certain areas and/or the devaluation of other, with consequences for the resident population, whose access to a certain portion of urban space will depend on their income.

SCOPE OF THE WORK AND THE OBJECT OF THE STUDY

Starting from the central theme of the reproduction conditions of the labour force and the spatial location of the working population in the urban environment, it was taken as the initial premise that the external pressures acting upon individuals greatly affect the strategies adopted for their reproduction.

In the urban-industrial complex, these pressures, – which are of different types, – have mainly fallen on one of the items considered central for the reproduction of the labour force, also being the most expensive one in the family budget – housing. In these conditions, the working family must constantly create and recreate strategies of its own to resolve the housing problem, always being limited by the occupation process of urban land, a process in which it generally does not participate as an agent. The increased value of land which is dependent on the characteristics of the occupation process itself tends to segregate the working population into areas which are more and more removed from the urban centres, or in deteriorating central areas, creating a burden which again falls on the worker himself and his family.

The option of subdivisions in the outlying areas, – where the price of land is lower due to clandestine developments or very poor conditions of infrastructure, – means an increase in physical wear on the resident, who must travel a long distance to his job, higher transportation costs, in addition to the usufruct of precarious basic installations of sanitation and services.

With this in mind, we propose to analyse through a case study, the implications of the urban land occupation process on the fixation alternatives for the working population, – above all those of low income, – generating continuous moves within the space which, we believe, directly reflects on the reproduction strategies of the family, as a group (Patara and Bogus, 1981). In order to do this, it is important to consider the role played by the State in the process of distribution and redistribution of specific social groups in the urban fabric, insofar as, through its intervention, certain portions of land can undergo great alterations in their forms of occupation.

If it is true that the State, through its public policies, can bear part of the reproduction costs of the labour force, (for example: health, education), in the case of housing the action of the State has expressed itself almost always in terms of legislation or management of resources drawn from the population itself through the process of work, with the cost of housing falling exclusively on the resident. On the other hand, while it intervenes in the space, through public policies, the State ends up interfering in a negative manner in the housing problems of the working population. In actual fact, when establishing programmes for urban regeneration and improvement in areas which are deteriorated or lack public services, the State acts as an agent of real estate speculation, provoking a true exodus of lower income families to areas where the price of housing is still accessible to them. Such policies become inefficient in terms of the objectives proposed, insofar as the State ends up not being able to combine the actions of the different political-administrative jurisdictions necessary in order to accomplish its objectives, nor even to control the effects unleashed by such policies (Bogus, 1981).

The study of an area which underwent direct State intervention through a urban regeneration project: the CURA Project (Urban Communities for Accelerated Recuperation), – makes it possible to evaluate the effects of State action on the resident population and to analyse the causes of the expulsion of part of this population.

This area, – Vila do Encontro, – located in the southern zone of the municipality of Sao Paulo, became the setting for enormous transformations beginning with the construction, within its boundaries, of the metro terminal for the north-south line. The transformations were accentuated when the area was inserted into the priorities of the CURA Project, as part of the land whose occupation needed to be denser in order to justify the investments made by the metro. With the beginning of construction for urban renewal, or even the simple public announcement of it, land speculation began and prices rose rapidly. Rents, accompanying these increases, also underwent big increases and the presence of vacant land in an area in the process of increasing in value, attracted various private firms which began to build houses and apartment buildings to house the new residents.

In the case of the original resident population, a large part was made up of migrants, mainly from the North-East part of Brazil, who came to the metropolitan region of Sao Paulo[1] in search of better working and living conditions. With the transformation of the area, their possibilities of remaining became quite reduced, above all for those who had come into the area most recently who didn't have access to real estate ownership. These migrants, together with other intra-metropolitan migrants, many of them natives of Sao Paulo, have one condition in common: that of being low-paid workers, residents of a metropolis where the expansion of urban services and the subsequent increased value of urban land arise as a consequence of the domination of space by capital, producing and reproducing processes of segregation of social classes in space.

In fact, the historical configuration itself of Sao Paulo and of the metropolitan region show movements of different social groups which, in their spatial location, obey at one moment a pattern of "peripheralisation", extending the urban boundaries to areas ever more distant from the centre and lacking in infrastructure, and at another, a pattern of incorporation of areas which were previously in the periphery into central areas, with the extension of the services network and the establishment of specific public policies.

On the other hand, the expansion of urban-metropolitan space according to conflicting class interests and following a specific model of capitalist expansion, introduces, of necessity, the theoretic association between space (of capital), reproduction of the labour force and survival strategies, the latter constituting the expression of the subordination of family and individual life to objective conditions of existence in the urban-metropolitan environment.

In this respect, to remain living in an area which undergoes urban renewal can mean reformulating the strategies adopted up to then by the family with regard to the composition of the domestic group, the insertion of members into the work place and even the patterns of biological reproduction, making clear the relationships existing between space and population, mediated by elements of a conjunctural nature, such as certain aspects of State intervention and resulting waves of increased values and real estate speculation.

The case of Vila do Encontro is the fruit of more general mechanisms which act upon capitalist cities, above all in the Third World. Because of this, the determinations present there should be understood as part of the broader processes of space occupation, of generation and appropriation of income from urban land by different social groups, of action by the State; in summary, of the space-population relationships with all the ramifications contained therein.

SPACE-POPULATION RELATIONSHIPS IN THE URBAN POLICY PROCESS

The transformation process for which Vila do Encontro was the setting brought with it serious consequences for the resident population, above all in the case of families living in rented dwellings, whose prices sky-rocketed.

It is worth pointing out that the case study, with its specifics, reveals the more general mechanisms in the process of increased real estate values which affected other points in the city of Sao Paulo, a result of the actuation of different production agents in the urban space. In Vila do Encontro the establishment of the CURA Project accentuated a process of increased values already set in motion by the construction of the metro, accelerating the change of the profile of the area and of its population (Bogus, 1988).

In this paper only some of the dimensions of this process are addressed, seeking to evaluate the intensity of the upward real estate valuation in the area and its importance for the substitution of residents, observed there.

As to the solutions adopted by the resident population with the intent of remaining in the area, it is known that answers of the same type can be found in other areas, as regards the questions linked to survival and reproduction of the low-income social groups. In the case of Vila do Encontro, such questions are being strictly tied to housing and the possibility of continuing to reside "in a neighbourhood which has improved", as voiced by the residents themselves.

Fixation and Expulsion of the Resident Population

With the objective of accompanying the transformation process in the area studies, three surveys were taken in Vila do Encontro, – in 1978, 1980, and 1985, respectively, together with a populational sample itself.[2] The objectives which guided the stages were of two types: first, to find out if the same family continued living in the same house and, secondly, if this were the case, to detect any internal changes in the family organisation, such as: insertion of new members into the work force, change in the economic activity of the members previously inserted and alterations to the dwelling, through remodelling, rental of rooms, or other expediencies which could contribute to the domestic budget. Using these elements, an attempt was made to reconstruct the impact of the changes which took place in the area on its residents.

The verification, – through the first stage of work (done in 1978), – that this was a population with low purchasing power (70 per cent of the working individuals received 3 minimum salaries monthly or less) and with a history of extended migration, led to the supposition that in light of conditions in the area, the spatial relocation of this population would tend to continue, aggravating the situation of the poorest of them.

The survey taken in 1980 showed that at the end of two years, starting from the beginning of the urban renewal project, a fourth of the resident families had left the area, which constituted a considerable spatial mobility.[3] In the later period, between 1980 and 1985 the number of moves was relatively small, assuming different characteristics as well, as will be seen.

Considering, initially, the families who continued to reside in the area, throughout the entire period studies (1978-85), it can be observed that there were important changes with regard to the composition of the domestic group, above all in the case of renters, many of which were adopted as strategies in order to remain in the area:

(a) The reorganisation of the domestic group[4] by joining two families, – not related to each other, – in order to be able a pay a higher rent.

(b) The increase of the domestic budget, – when possible, by new members entering the work place, whether the wife, who had not worked outside the home, or the younger children unemployed up to that time.

(c) Adoption of the "extended family" model with the entrance into the family of nephews, in-laws, married children and grandchildren who attach themselves to the initially resident group with the goal of dividing the expenses related to housing, although in many instances this aggravates the already precarious living conditions.

For those tenants who left the area, alternatives were few, being divided between those who rented cheaper places in the outlying metropolitan region of Sao Paulo, those who went to the central pockets of poverty, to reside in "favelas" (shanty-towns) and slums, and those who went to live temporarily with relatives or friends until they could resolve their housing situation.

The situation of eviction of tenants has been in evidence since the beginning of the CURA work, continuing through the 1978-85 period, and analysis of the data show that the principal factor in population retention throughout the period studied was the ownership of property.

It is important to point out that 75.4 per cent of the families who left the area between 1978 and 1980 (1st phase of the study) resided in rented dwellings. Furthermore, a considerable portion of those who remained, resided in houses which were loaned or on invaded land.

Looking at Table 6.1, which shows a general picture of the permanence or moves of the resident population, according to ownership of property – it is seen that it is ownership of the dwelling which allows the possibility of staying there, which is very clear especially in the first period studied. In fact, only 23.1 per cent of the families who moved before 1980 resided in their own homes against 75.4 per cent who resided in rented dwellings. In addition to this, of those who stayed during this period, 15.9 per cent resided in houses which were loaned or in shacks built on invaded lands. The latter make up the poorest families, with a family income of between one and two minimum salaries per month.

It should be pointed out that in the first period studied, the association between length of residency and the possibility of staying in the area was clear. This is because the longer residency period also meant access to the purchase of a house or to a low rent which had been little readjusted. In fact, the greater percentage of families who left Vila do Encontro between 1978 and 1980 were those who had arrived after 1975 (47.6 per cent) followed by those who had arrived in the first half of the 1970's (17.2 per cent).

In the case of the families who stayed in the first period studied, the largest percentage (48.5 per cent) of them arrived during the 1960's, the period of the greatest influx of residents into an area where the price of housing was still accessible to low-income workers (Patara and Bogus, 1981).

TABLE 6.1: Heads of Family According to Ownership Status, Following Their Permanence or not in the Area, Vila do Encontro, Sao Paulo.

Ownership Status	1978-80						1978-80						1978-80					
	Left %		Stayed %		Total %		Left %		Stayed %		Total %		Left %		Stayed %		Total %	
Owned	15	23.1	113	56.2	128	48.1	37	51.4	76	58.9	113	56.2	52	37.9	76	58.9	128	48.1
Rented	49	75.4	56	27.9	105	39.5	27	37.5	29	22.5	56	27.9	76	55.5	29	22.5	105	39.5
Loaned or invaded	1	1.5	32	15.9	33	12.4	8	11.1	24	18.6	32	15.9	9	6.6	24	18.6	33	12.4
Total	65	100.0	201	100.0	266	100.0	72	100.0	129	100.0	201	100.0	137	100.0	129	100.0	266	100.0

Source: Field research in Vila do Encontro. Surveys in 1978, 1980 and 1985.

Some important differences are noticed during the period between 1980 and 1985.

It is necessary, above all, to stress that the population sample selected in 1978, based on the whole of families resident in the area, was no longer representative of the population which lives in Vila do Encontro during the period. The areas changed and its population changed. The process of verticalisation seen in the past years, with the construction of innumerable apartment buildings, attracted to the area a different social group from the one which had originally lived there and which, in turn, has started to leave the area. It may be because it is unable to handle the expenses, above all the rent, in a neighbourhood increasing in value, or because of the transfer to their own property of a parcel of value generated in the area, causing the sale of the house and appropriation of the benefits generated by the whole of the improvements.

The number of owners who sold their properties increased during the recent period (Table 6.1). The group of tenants continued leaving the area in a very accentuated fashion, characterising itself by being the group that throughout the entire period studied showed the lowest index of permanence in the area (27.6 per cent) against 59.4 per cent for the owners and 72.7 per cent for residents in loaned houses or invaded lots, as shown in Table 6.2. This occurred because, in most cases, the houses were demanded back by owners who could get much higher rents after doing some minor remodelling.

TABLE 6.2: Index of Permanence for Families Residing in Vila do Encontro by Ownership Status.

(Percentage)

Ownership status	Periods 1978-1980	1980-1985	1978-1985
Owned	88.3	67.3	59.4
Rented	53.3	51.8	27.6
Loaned or invaded	97.0	75.0	72.7
Total index of Permanence	75.6	64.2	48.5

Source: Field research data, Vila do Encontro. Surveys from 1978, 1980 and 1985.

Analysing the data regarding the second period of the study (1980-85), a weak link is also seen between the length of residence and permanence in the area. The owners who sold their houses were precisely the oldest residents, having arrived for the most part during the decade of the 1960s, the same thing happening with some long-term residents of loaned houses and invaded lands which began to be demanded back by the owners for sale or new construction.

The Process of Increased Real Estate Values: Vila do Encontro in the Context of the City

The whole process of substitution of residents and increased population density which took place in Vila do Encontro can be better understood starting with the analysis of the evolution of land prices in the area, in comparison to prices in Sao Paulo. The data for Vila do Encontro show that the process of increased real estate values was quite accentuated there, above all during the periods from 1974 to 1976 and from 1982 to 1984 (Bogus, 1988).

As shown in Table 6.3 and the Fig. 6.1, starting in 1973 a rapid process of increased prices per sq m of land in the area (Endo and Carmo, 1985) was unleashed due to the work on the metro, – already in its final stages, and the announcement of the establishment of the Jabaquara-CURA pilot-project (1972), with the major portion of the work occurring precisely in Vila do Encontro.

TABLE 6.3: Evolution of Prices Per sq m for Land Located in Vila do Encontro and in the Municipality of Sao Paulo, 1972-85

Year	Price per sq m in Vila do Encontro 1972 = 100	Price per sq m in the municipality of Sao Paulo* 1972 = 100
1972	100.00	411.27
1973	301.39	–
1974	369.34	459.22
1975	653.11	–
1976	476.05	508.23
1977	349.91	–
1978	286.54	420.59
1979	276.53	424.79
1980	167.61	388.92
1981	203.71	452.28
1982	493.88	–
1983	634.16	246.97
1984	543.29	207.55
1985	406.25	193.27

Source: For Vila do Encontro, data from EMBRAESP, Sao Paulo. For the Municipality of Sao Paulo, data from EMBRAESP apud Marcondes, M.J.A., – Formacao do Preco do Solo Urbano no Municipio de Sao Paulo, Masters Dissertation, PROPUR, UFRJ, Rio de Janeiro, 1986.

* Prices per square metre for land in the municipality of Sao Paulo had as a base the year 1975. For comparison purposes these data were transferred to 1972 using the Consumer Price Index from FIPE, Sao Paulo, 1985.

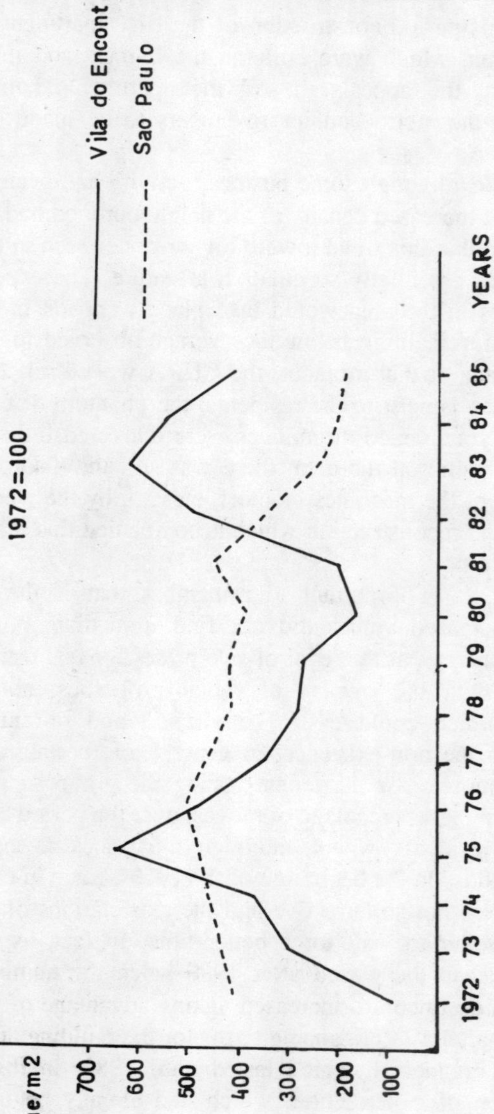

FIG. 6.1: Graph comparing the Evolution of land prices in the municipality of Sao Paulo and in Vila do Encontro, Sao Paulo, from 1972-85.

Source: Data from EMBRAESP, Sao Paulo and Marcondes, M.J.A. – Formacao do Preco do Solo Urbano no municipio de Sao Paulo. Masters Dissertation, UFRJ, Rio de Janeiro, 1986.

During this period construction of the first apartment buildings in the area began, which were built on the highest and therefore most valuable part, the appeals to sell the apartments being based on proximity to the metro and improvements to be made by the State, through CURA.

Meanwhile, although some business activity had been affected and the process of increased density of the neighbourhood had begun, it can be considered that this trend toward higher prices seen in the middle of the 1970s was essentially speculative in nature. The expectations that rapid changes in the area would take place were not met, and prices tended to fall, remaining below the average observed for the city (see Graph). In fact, at that moment, the CURA work itself brought more disruption than benefit to the residents: the phantom of expropriations worried everyone, since the notices were delivered little by little and hit different points in the area; there was still the disorder caused by the presence of the machines, tractors, etc. . . . by the whole picture of demolition and reconstruction which accompanied this process of local urban regeneration.

However, it is important to remember that if the expectations regarding increased values did not find immediate possibilities for becoming concrete, at the level of sale prices for real estate, it quickly germinated with the owners of rental properties, above all slum properties, which could easily be vacated and re-rented at higher prices, given the non-existence, in general, of formal contracts. This reveals the motive for the tenants being the group of residents who showed the highest percentage of moves, over the period analysed.

For the resident owners, although the prices at that time were higher than those in the beginning of the 1970s. Even in earlier periods, the offers were not so attractive and the expectations of new increase caused the seller to wait for a better time. In fact, as research data shows, it was in the period after 1980 when the number of owners leaving Vila do Encontro increased, taking advantage of the new price rise. In fact, after 1980 financing terms for the building and sale of real estate were broadened, which lasted until 1982. In this period, the verticalisation of construction, which had already begun in Vila do Encontro in the middle of the 1970s, underwent a tremendous increase. The number of new houses built for sale also increased along with the apartment buildings.

In 1982 there was a new drop in financing of real estate through the Sistema Financeiro da Habitacao (Housing Finance System) and consequently, in real estate production, which lasted until 1985. From all indications, the prices of land in Vila do Encontro continued to rise until 1983 simply due to the fact that the property owners insisted on keeping them artificially high. Meanwhile, the fall in prices began in 1983, given the impossibility of concluding deals which had kept prices at their formers levels.

Another point considered important for formation of prices in the real estate market is the location of land according to the Zoning Law (Marcondes, 1986). In the case of Vila do Encontro, the greater part of the land finds itself in Zone 2, which makes possible a good coefficient of utilisation for construction, principally of apartment buildings. Furthermore, because of the characteristics themselves of most of the lots which exist in the area, with very little frontage (approximately 8.0 metres), but with great depth (50.0 or 60.0 metres), the joining of two lots already allows construction of buildings with a large number of living units. Due to these aspects directly linked to land-use, in addition to those already mentioned in regard to established urban services, the average prices of land in Vila do Encontro, approach those found in other neighbourhoods with older settlements and an already consolidated occupation.

The fact that the curve for average prices for the city of Sao Paulo shows a more "stable" behaviour, when compared to the tremendous oscillations found in Vila do Encontro, does not mean that the same thing did not take place in the other areas of the city. It so happens that in the calculation of this average (with aggregated data) lands located in different zones, with different uses were also included which kept the prices at low level.

Nevertheless, the comparison shows the process of increased valuation in Vila do Encontro starting with the changes in the space and population.

CONCLUSIONS

The production of urban space takes place in a coherent fashion with the method of production being predominant and according to the interests of the different income groups and social classes. It falls to the State to reconcile these interests, adding infrastructure and public services and installations to the space, and passing laws for land-use and occupation, measures which as a whole will influence "the value of urban land".

When the State intervenes with urban regeneration programmes, such as in the case of Vila do Encontro, this intervention generally results in an increase in land value, with direct effects on the housing question, expelling part of the resident population who is then substituted by other social groups with higher incomes.

Thus, the public policies play a dual role: on the one hand, they start the process of urbanisation, which theoretically should benefit all the citizens; on the other hand, they expel the population from urbanised areas, since the urban improvement programmes are not as a general rule, accompanied by work of a social nature, particularly where housing is concerned.

NOTES

1. The Sao Paulo Metropolitan Area, also known as Greater Sao Paulo, is made up of 38 municipalities, with a population of 12,588,439 inhabitants (according to Census-1980) of which 67.5 per cent are residents of the City of Sao Paulo. With a surface area of 7,951 square kilometres, it is one of the most important Latin American urban complexes. From 1970 to 1980 its geometric growth reached 4.46 per cent per year.
2. Probabilistic and dual-phase methods were used to form sample groups in 1978. Phases were composed from a random balloting of blocks, and then of houses on each block. In the first phase, a systematic method was followed, and in the second a random sample was taken. The completed sample group consisted 266 households, or 35 per cent of the 745 households and 9 of the 45 blocks i.e. 29 per cent of the area. The resulting sample fraction represents 7.3 per cent of the total household/block universe.
3. While other studies of the same type do not exist, which would permit comparative analyses to be carried out, the percentage of resident families who left the area during the first two years of the study was considered high (about 25 per cent), a percentage which increases to 51 per cent when the total for the period studied is taken into consideration.
4. A domestic group is understood to be the body of people linked by family ties, affinity or economic ties, who live under the same roof, being considered a family based on unity of consumption or a sub-group of people in the domestic group who enjoy the same family budget.

REFERENCES

Bogus, Lucia M.M. (1981), 'Vila do Encontro: A Cidade Chega a Periferia. Notes on the relationships between Urban Policies, Family, and Reproduction of the Work Force'. *Cadernos PRODEUR*, (4), FAU-USP.

—— (1988), '(Re) urbanizacao: Por que e Para Quem'? Doctoral Thesis presented to the Graduate Programme at FAU-USP, Sao Paulo.

Endo, Seiti K. and Carmo, Heron C.E. (1985), *Breve Historico do Indice de Precos ao Consumidor no Municipio de Sao Paulo*. Sao Paulo, FIPE-USP.

Lipietz, Alain (1982), 'Alguns Problemas da Producao Monopolista do Espaco Urbano', *Revista Espaco e debate*, (7), Sao paulo : 5-27.

Low-Beer, Jacqueline D. (1987), 'Dinamica do Mercado Fundiario x Investimento Publico: Uma Analise da Valorizacao em Areas Proximas ao Metro'. Masters Dissertation, EAESP, FGV, Sao Paulo.

Marcondes, M. Jose A. (1986), 'Formacao do Preco do Solo Urbano no Municipio de Sao Paulo'. Masters Dissertation, PROPUR-UFRJ, Rio de Janeiro.

Patara, N.L. and Bogus, Lucia M.M. (1981), 'Percursos Migratorios e Ocupacao do Espaco Urbano: um Estudo de Caso'. *Anais do segundo encontro nacional*, ABEP, Sao Paulo : 823-849.

Souza, M. Adelia A. and Santos, Milton (org) (1986), *A Construcao do Espaco, Sao Paulo*, Nobel.

Villaca, Flavio (1978), 'A Estrutura Territorial do Metropole Sul Brasileira', Doctoral Thesis, FFLCH-USP, Sao Paulo.

7

INCORPORATING APPROPRIATE TECHNOLOGY IN SELF-HELP HOUSING: The Dominican Republic Experience

PATRICIA KLOBUS EDWARDS*

The incorporation of appropriate technology in housing programmes is emerging as a central policy in many Third World nations. This strategy represents a departure from approaches which tend to mirror low-income residential construction in more developed countries. Because of the experimental nature of these programmes, successful application and transfer of appropriate technology in the housing sector is problematic.

Most of the literature on appropriate technology deals with its utility in economic development activities. However, the implementation of technologies which are specifically relevant to Third World self-help housing requirements has received scant attention, despite the facts that numerous Third World housing programmes are adopting the approach and proponents of appropriate technology maintain there is a need to understand social, economic and technical obstacles to its application (Cooper, 1979). Moreover, the preponderance of extant literature does not deal with empirical studies of programme delivery (Lodwick and Stommel, 1984; Evans and Adler, 1979). This is a critical oversight, particularly when some writers assert that the delivery system is, perhaps, more important than the technology itself (e.g., Eckaus, 1977). Drawing on material

* The author wishes to acknowledge M. Nanita-Kennett for her substantial contribution to the second evaluation of CETAVIP and Susan Jones for her comments on a draft of the manuscript.

obtained from two evaluations of the Centre for Appropriate Technology for Popular Housing (CETAVIP), a division of the Dominican Republic Inter-Institutional Council for the Coordination of Housing Programmes, Inc. (CII-VIVIENDAS), this article discusses the role of appropriate technology in Third World development and assesses an USAID programme designed to foster dissemination of appropriate technologies in Dominican self-help housing. It concludes with an examination of issues relevant to the generation and transfer of appropriate technology in Third World housing.

THE ROLE OF APPROPRIATE TECHNOLOGY IN DEVELOPMENT

Appropriate technology is an umbrella term which incorporates an array of development approaches, including low-cost, traditional, intermediate, self-help, environmentally sound, labour-intensive, and progressive technology (Usui, 1976; Baron, 1978; Jequier and Blanc, 1983). Consequently, the relative nature of the term has fostered a wealth of literature examining definitional nuances of the concept, as well as its proper role in Third World development (e.g. Robinson, 1979; Jequier, 1976; Ghosh, 1984). For the purpose of this study, which focuses on a programme designed to use indigenous construction materials and local human resources in self-help housing, Morawetz's broad perspective of appropriate technology as "a set of techniques which make optimum use of available resources in a given environment" is an applicable definition (Robinson, 1979).

In practice, appropriate technology encompasses a coalition of concerns expressed by an array of professionals involved in innovative development activities worldwide (Baron, 1978). The concept includes a diversity of activities such as products research, delivery systems, educational and management techniques, and even credit strategies (Thormann, 1979). Each of these activities are integral components of housing programmes. According to Robinson (1979), there is no single system of technologies appropriate for all Third World countries because they are not homogeneous in terms of resources, needs and skills. Family patterns, social structure, and cultural practices, which differ widely among developing nations, also affect the choice and applicability of technologies (Thormann, 1979). Furthermore, what appears to be innovative practice in some countries may be traditional in others (Jequier, 1976). Thus, the choice of technologies that may be considered "appropriate" for a given region or nation requires consideration of a range of physical, social, and economic variables.

Objectives

Despite the multiplicity of appropriate technology approaches, there appears to be some consensus regarding the purpose of appropriate technology in development. Reddy (1979) has aptly summarised these objectives as: "(1) the satisfaction of basic human needs (starting with the needs of the neediest) in order to reduce inequalities between and within countries; (2) indigenous self-reliance through social participation and control; and (3) harmony with the environment." Cooper (1979) adds that the implementation of appropriate technology should foster the "fullest employment of resources and labour" and "a more equitable distribution of income". Finally, Veldhuis (1979) urges that technology must be consistent with national policies and plans as well as community aspirations. Each of these objectives are relevant to the Dominican Republic housing programme assessed in this study.

Scope

While it is impossible to calculate the amount of money and number of organisations involved in the appropriate technology movement, it is evident that efforts to stimulate the approach have been extensive in recent years. Jequier (1976) estimated that, in US dollars, approximately 10 million was spent world-wide by a fairly small number of agencies in 1975. However, he maintained that many organisations, although not formally concerned with appropriate technology *per se*, were, in fact, involved in the development of these technologies. A 1977 survey indicated that the main fields of activity of 1,550 appropriate technology centres, located in both industrialised and Third World nations, concentrated on the development and promotion of small industries, building materials, agricultural tools, cultivation techniques, and training (Ghosh, 1984). It was estimated that over $ 300 million was being spent by respondent organisations; about one-half of this amount funded projects in Third World nations. Seven years later, the Centre for Business Information (1984) compiled a world-wide directory, listing 1,977 organisations and agencies from 113 nations directly involved in appropriate technology activities. The vast majority of these organisations were in Third World countries.

In the late 1970s, U.S. policy began to shift toward the enhancement of appropriate technology approaches in donor programmes (Evans, 1979). For example, Section 306 of the International Development and Food Assistance Act of 1975 appropriated funds to the Agency for International Development (USAID) to expand its activities with respect to appropriate technology. Currently, USAID's strategy is to integrate appropriate technology activities into the mainstream of the agency's programmes, making it difficult to estimate the precise extent of the effort. Funds are also channelled to AT International (ATI), a private, non-profit corporation established by an act of the U.S. Congress in 1977 to assist Third World countries in improving their own capacity to develop and apply technologies deemed appropriate to their needs. Although the fiscal resources of ATI are minimal, these resources are leveraged by developing cooperative projects with USAID and other organisations. Additionally, U.S. agencies such as the Department of Agriculture, National Bureau of Standards, National Technical Information Service, and National Science Foundation fund appropriate technology activities (Ghosh, 1984).

THE DOMINICAN PROGRAMME IN CONTEXT

According to the census of 1981, the year CII-VIVIENDAS was created, the population of the Dominican Republic was slightly over 5.6 million (EIU, 1985). The country ranked 9th out of 25 Latin American and Caribbean countries in terms of its population growth rate of 2.9 per cent annually (Ghosh, 1984). Approximately 55 per cent of the population lived in rural areas, but urban areas were growing at a rapid pace. In 1982, the unemployment rate was estimated at 25 per cent; estimates of underemployment accounted for another 30 per cent of the labour force. The government and service sectors were the largest employers (EIU, 1985).

Construction, particularly that sponsored by public funds, was a major factor in the Dominican's economic growth throughout the 1970s. Although activity in the industry slowed between 1975 and 1978, the need for reconstruction after hurricanes David and Fredrick in 1979 fostered an increase in construction over the next two years. Despite the importance of construction in the nation's economy, only 3.5 per cent of the labour force was employed in the industry in 1980, and by 1982 unemployment in this sector was at record levels (EIU, 1985).

At the beginning of the 1980s, the National Housing Institute (INVI) shifted its priorities from building middle-class apartments to providing low-cost housing for urban migrants and, nominally, for the rural poor. The new government elected in this period made an effort to increase jobs, by calling for the construction of 5,500 housing units in 1983 and 18,000 additional units by the end of 1985. However, large capital expenditures by INVI had substantially contributed to the overall operating deficits of the central government. As a consequence, plans for increased housing construction went unrealised due to the freeze on government spending required to obtain a new loan agreement with the IMF (EIU, 1985). In 1985, the IMF agreement was approved, requiring devaluation of the Dominican Peso. The result was high inflation, new taxes, cuts in public investment, and political dissent. With respect to the housing sector, the country's economic crisis caused a marked increase in the price of construction materials and skilled labour, a situation which severely reduced the ability of the informal sector to obtain materials and technical assistance for housing construction.

The extensive damage by hurricanes David and Fredrick was a clear indication that much of the Dominican housing stock was vulnerable to natural disasters due to its poor quality and inappropriate design. In addition to the need for reconstruction, substantial population growth added to the demand for housing. Official estimates in 1981 set the housing deficit at 13,000 units annually; 80 per cent of the deficit was estimated to be in rural areas. The National Planning Office projected that the country would need to replace 190,000 housing units and build an additional 78,000 new units. These figures exclude the substantial level of upgrading that would be needed in the housing sector to improve the quality of living conditions. The existing housing situation made it virtually imperative to develop innovative strategies to foster more efficient housing construction projects which could produce dwellings resistant to the ravages of hurricanes and floods. In this context CETAVIP was conceived.

THE CENTRE FOR APPROPRIATE TECHNOLOGY FOR POPULAR HOUSING (CETAVIP)

CETAVIP was created in 1981 as a division of CII-VIVIENDAS, a non-profit coordinating agency for 20 national and international organisations devoted to the improvement of housing construction, building materials, and community development for the low-income population in the Dominican Republic. Eleven of the organisations affiliated with CII-VIVIENDAS are from the private sector, seven from the public sector, and two are international in scope. The CETAVIP division was designed to execute CII-VIVIENDAS' projects as a response to the existing need, both internationally and nationally, for information and experience sharing in the field of appropriate technology. In pursuing its responsibility, CETAVIP developed five programmes each based on a specific strategy designed to foster the use of appropriate technologies in Dominican self-help projects: basic research; promotion; diffusion of information; technical assistance; and demonstration through the construction of housing models.

In May 1983, CETAVIP obtained a three-year Operational Programme Grant (OPG) for US $ 478,000 from USAID. The purpose of the grant was to strengthen CETAVIP by supporting its Diffusion Programme. Oversight for the grant was given to Cooperative for American Relief Everywhere (CARE) and the contract stipulated that INVI, the Dominican National Housing Institute, should provide fiscal support and technical assistance to the project. Two separate evaluations of the Diffusion Programme were undertaken: one by PADCO, a private consulting agency (PADCO, 1984), and the other by independent consultants (Nanita-Kennett and Edwards, 1986). Data obtained from these evaluations, which utilised personal interviews, programme materials, agency records, and observations of demonstration and construction sites, illustrate the potential and problems associated with the implementation of appropriate technology in Third World self-help housing.

Organisational Structure and Goals

During the period spanning the evaluations, CII-VIVIENDAS managed the activities of CETAVIP and a second division, Inter-Institutional Operations, which was responsible for developing agreements and securing resources for the creation of new projects. In addition, plans for two new divisions were being developed (see Fig. 7.1). The Centre for the Improvement of the Quality of Life (CEMCAVI) was proposed to collect and analyse socio-demographic

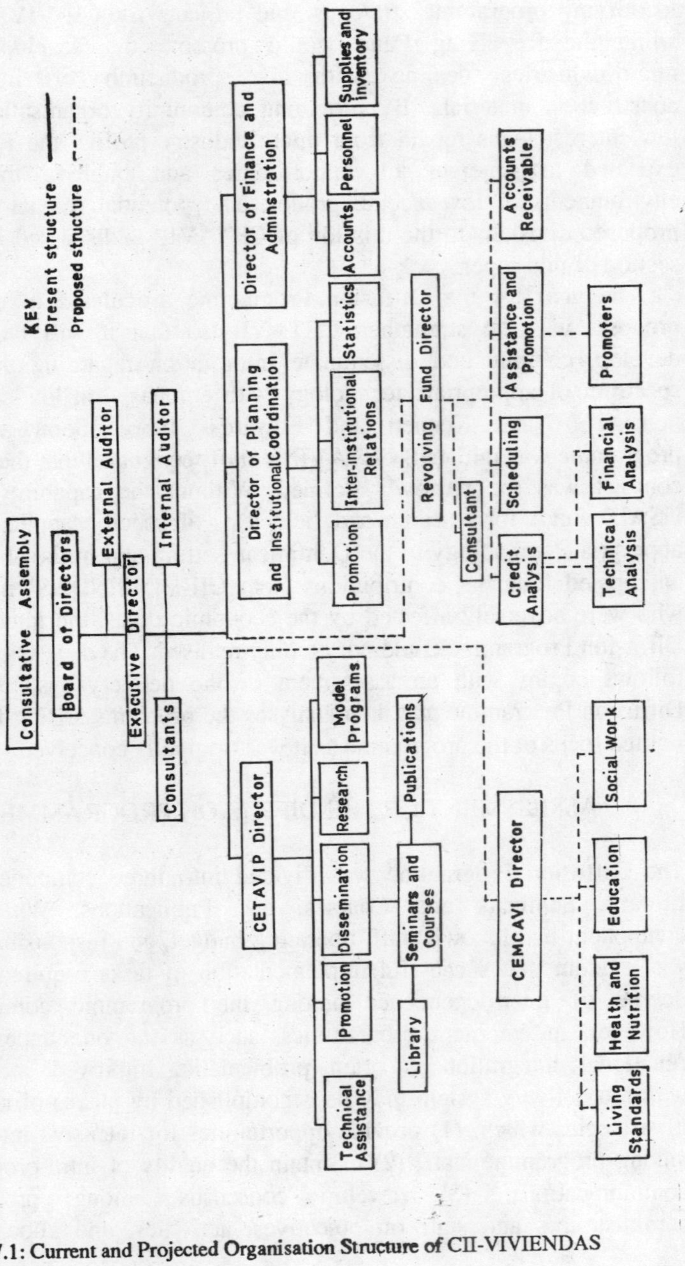

FIG. 7.1: Current and Projected Organisation Structure of CII-VIVIENDAS

data bearing on needs of low-income communities for the purpose of identifying programme strategies and projects for CII-VIVIENDAS, while the Revolving Fund would promote the development of micro-industries dealing with the production of indigenous construction materials. By providing community organisations with low interest loans repaid from micro-industry profits, the Fund was expected to generate job opportunities and improve the living environments of low-income groups. The potential impact of these proposed divisions to the mission of CETAVIP is discussed in a later section of this paper.

The goal for the Diffusion Programme articulated in the OPG proposal was "to strengthen CETAVIP so that it will be able to develop, compile and disseminate information regarding the entire spectrum of appropriate technology with emphasis on low-cost rural housing" (Nanita-Kennett and Edwards, 1986). Soon after the programme was initiated, CETAVIP's staff recognised that the USAID contract was too narrowly defined. Without the capability to use USAID funds for research and field tests of specific applications of appropriate technology in the Dominican setting and in the absence of anticipated financial contributions from CII-VIVIENDAS' members, who were adversely affected by the economic crisis, the intent of the Diffusion Programme could not be fully realised. The discussion which follows begins with an assessment of the delivery system of the Diffusion Programme and then analyses the problems arising from the limited focus of the programme as it was originally conceived.

ASSESSMENT OF THE DIFFUSION PROGRAMME

The Diffusion Programme was divided into three components: the Library, Seminars and Courses, and Publications. While each component had its own staff, operating budget, and responsibilities, it was evident that successful implementation of tasks required a high degree of inter-dependence among the programme components. However, in emergent programmes, such as the one under study, functional integration is often problematic. Improved integration within a delivery system may be accomplished by means of a variety of strategies which: (1) provide opportunities for intensive interaction among programme staff; (2) maintain the quality of intra-programme communications; (3) develop consensus among programme administrators and staff on objectives, activities, and allocation of resources; and (4) facilitate access to available resources. These strategies were not sufficiently in place after the first two years of CETAVIP's operation.

Library

The primary objective of CETAVIP's library was to acquire and catalogue documents on appropriate technology and housing construction innovations for the use of CII-VIVIENDAS and its member organisations. By the end of 1985, the library had collected approximately 2,400 documents. Most of the materials were identified through SATIS (Socially Appropriate Technology Information service) and some documents were exchanged with other interested national and international institutions. However, CII-VIVIENDAS staff did not assist the librarian in selecting literature suitable for the library collection. Acquisition of new documents also posed a problem. Procedures set out by the OPG required receipt of materials before payment, although many publishing houses require advanced payment for books and documents. This procedure restricted the source of library acquisitions.

Due to a space shortage in CII-VIVIENDAS' main facility, the library was located in a shopping centre, a distance of approximately 15 minutes by car. Because the library could not obtain a telephone, as a result of a freeze on new installations by CODETEL (the Dominican telephone company), this unit was virtually isolated from other CETAVIP functions. Records showed that, on the average, only three individuals used the library daily; the vast majority were students and professors from local universities. Interviews with CII-VIVIENDAS staff indicated that they had limited knowledge of the library's resources, despite the availability of a recently updated catalogue. A major problem was that the catalogue listed titles in the original language of a publication, although the primary language of CETAVIP staff was Spanish. As indicated previously, staff rarely used the library, but only in part because it was not conveniently located. They complained that many of the documents in the collection were written in English, posing a deterrent to their use.

It was evident that the library was underutilised due to the inadequacy or absence of mechanisms to facilitate communication and functional integration among programme units. Perception of the unit's inaccessibility was the consequence of a large problem – that of undervalued resources. In order to make the library a viable part of the organisation, it was necessary to improve the utility of the materials and increase staff awareness of benefits that could be derived from the library's resources.

Several strategies were devised to remedy the situation: (1) To strengthen communications between the library and other components of the organisation, an advisory committee was formed to select acquisitions and deal with policy issues pertaining to the unit. All CII-VIVIENDAS staff were asked to recommend suitable library acquisitions identified in seminars and/or courses they attended. In addition, summaries of library holdings related to specific topics and projects of interest to staff were published in Spanish in the organisation's bulletin, FOCO. (2) Plans were made to translate future editions of the library's catalogue into Spanish with a notation that the text was in another language. Revenues received from the sales of library materials were allocated for translation of documents identified by the staff as relevant to their work. (3) A project was initiated to convert the library catalogue to a computerised system, presenting bibliographic information in both the original language of the document and in Spanish. When completed, the system will be available in the main offices and staff will be instructed how to use it. (4) A strategy was recommended to promote the library through local presentations made to CII-VIVIENDAS' member organisations, as well as to other government and private agencies that had an interest in appropriate technology. Additionally, plans were made to use the mass media and staff referrals to publicise the library's resources. (5) A procedure was instituted to allow CII-VIVIENDAS to pay for materials by invoice, drawing on funds directly appropriated to the library. This increased the breadth of resources potentially accessible to the organisation.

Seminars and Courses

One component of the Diffusion Programme had responsibility for two separate activities: seminars and courses. While these activities were perceived as highly interrelated, and even covered similar topics, they were intended to reach very different audiences. According to the OPG proposal, seminars would be directed at the professional level (i.e., architects, engineers, and housing programme administrators) and would focus on integration of appropriate technology into agency plans and programmes. Courses, on the other hand, were intended to address a more "nuts and bolts" approach oriented to the needs of artisans. Four staff were responsible for this component of the programme.

The OPG required that two regional seminars be conducted annually. In the first year, the Diffusion Programme held two seminars for professionals and a workshop on construction methods for skilled construction supervisors. The second year, CII-VIVIENDAS, in collaboration with five agencies – Dominican Association of Engineers, Architects and Surveyors (CODIA), National Housing Institute (INVI), Rochester Institute of Technology, USAID, and German Society for Technical Cooperation (GTZ) – sponsored a more ambitious international seminar on "Low-cost Housing in the Informal Sector". The objectives of the seminar were to: (1) promote awareness of low-income housing construction needs in the informal sector; (2) capitalise on the experiences of other national and international institutions engaged in appropriate technology projects; (3) develop recommendations to improve programmes; and (4) establish a plan for the coordination of institutions engaged in work on housing problems. Thus, the seminar was conceived as an opportunity for professionals to exchange ideas and develop cooperative activities to enhance their work.

Seminars are effective in establishing valuable contacts with international and national agencies involved in appropriate technology projects and facilitate the initiation and clarification of CETAVIP's own policies and approaches. However, staff felt that the seminars were not useful in generating ideas for new technologies that could be used in the Dominican Republic. Perhaps, the emphasis on policy formulation versus technological innovation is appropriate during the initial stages of an organisation's development. But the viability of CETAVIP ultimately rests on the Division's ability to identify and adopt a broad array of housing technologies and designs relevant to the needs of their target population. Furthermore, organising two annual seminars consumed time and effort, on the part of the small staff, that might be more effectively spent on providing courses for local self-help organisations. Thus, after developing administrative and staff consensus on programme priorities, the OPG was amended to require only one annual seminar, focused on innovative construction methods and materials.

Courses offered by the Diffusion Programme involved empirical learning and demonstrations presented to local self-help organisations and artisans, such as carpenters and masons. They focused on design and construction techniques sensitive to regional needs and resources. The purpose was to train a group of people in a community who can then pass on their knowledge and skills to other residents. Each course was based on studies conducted by CETAVIP's research component. Support materials, consisting of booklets containing detailed drawings depicting construction techniques, procedural manuals, and slides were prepared by the programme's staff for use in the courses. The following are examples of the courses offered: Construction of energy efficient stoves; design of site plans and foundations; manufacture of suelo cement blocks using the Cinva Ram machine and steel molds; manufacture of roofing sheets and panels utilising sisal, a vegetable fiber; construction and maintenance of traditional and dry fertiliser latrines; and production and installation of cement flooring.

Courses were offered on request by CII-VIVIENDAS' members institutions and community self-help organisations. Promoters employed by the Dominican Office of Community Development (ODC) made the contacts and scheduled the training programmes. However, despite the fact that there were written agreements with ODC, cooperation between the two agencies was problematic.

The necessity of a viable promotion strategy was demonstrated in a rural housing project sponsored by CII-VIVIENDAS. Participants were trained and materials were provided to produce corrugated sisal cement sheeting for roofing used in the construction of housing in the community. Research by CETAVIP had demonstrated that sisal cement sheeting was stronger than traditional fiber roofing and more heat resistant than the popular, but costly, tin roofing. But residents of the demonstration project were strongly opposed to using this material for several reasons. First, they were concerned that the sheeting would deteriorate over a period of time or cave in during tropical storms. Second, tin roofing appeared to be a conspicuous symbol of a family's relative affluence, and thus, a priority in terms of housing investment. It was clear that the ODC promoters had failed to adequately demonstrate the strength and durability of sisal cement sheeting. However, the ODC promoters did not have sufficient opportunities to learn about the benefits of the technologies developed by CETAVIP. Additionally, their primary responsibility and commitment centered on ODC activities. Because promotion is essential to the diffusion of appropriate technology, CETAVIP staff proposed that funds be allocated to employ promoters hired by the agency to carry out the necessary community organisation functions of the division. While the evaluators agreed that the relationship with ODC was not meeting the needs of CETAVIP, they were concerned about the potential consequences of severing linkages with the organisation.

The Diffusion Programme was still in its infancy at the time of this study, so it was impossible to predict the impact of the training strategy on participating communities. However, transfer of technology was observed in Honduras, a community involved in CETAVIP's training and demonstration projects. After completing the self-help housing project in their community, local participants, on their own initiative, used the techniques they had learned to repair the school, build a recreation centre, and construct a pond for cultivating fish. Moreover, in the surrounding area, persons who had not been trained directly were making use of construction techniques disseminated via the courses. It was evident that information and skills were being disseminated to others by the course participants.

Publications

The objectives of the publications component of the Diffusion Programme were to: (1) publicise the activities of CII-VIVIENDAS and its member organisations; (2) publish information oriented toward research and application of appropriate technology systems; and (3) promote and influence the development of low-income communities in the Dominican Republic. To achieve this intent, a quarterly bulletin, FOCO, was distributed to approximately 750 individuals and institutions, including libraries, national and international organisations, and centres involved in the study of appropriate technology. FOCO contained technical articles, a section on new developments in the field, announcements of training programmes and conferences throughout the world, and descriptions of activities in the housing sector that are undertaken by institutions affiliated with CII-VIVIENDAS. The publication was professionally printed; articles were written in a journalistic style and quality photographic material was included.

Prior to this study, the publications component extended its scope to publish monographs on research and applications of appropriate technology directed to middle level technicians and professionals. In addition, the staff produced three video tapes. The first, "What is CII-VIVIENDAS?" was used to present the aims and activities of the organisation to possible funding sources. The other videos, dealing with sisal cement roof construction and regionally suitable housing models using appropriate technology, were used for promotion and training purposes.

Adequate communication and linkages with staff from the larger organisation was essential to the publications personnel. While other CETAVIP personnel did assist in preparation of some of the media presentations, the publications staff did not have a reliable source of articles for the bulletin. As a consequence of the lack of material and the number of auxiliary projects initiated, FOCO was not published on a regular basis. To remedy this situation and editorial council, advisory to the head of publications, was formed to assist in strengthening coordination with other departments of the organisation. All CII-VIVIENDAS staff, as well as those from member organisations, were encouraged to identify and contribute material relevant to FOCO's aims. It was also recommended that the public perspective of FOCO could be enhanced by adhering to a standardised format and consistent publication schedule. Publications staff were encouraged to limit their activities to a smaller number of projects in order to maintain quality.

A HOLISTIC PERSPECTIVE OF THE DIFFUSION PROGRAMME

It is clear that the USAID-sponsored Diffusion Programme was not a programme that can operate independently. Without strong support from other programmes within CETAVIP, as well as the housing sector institutions represented by CII-VIVIENDAS, the programme could not utilise donor aid efficiently or effectively. Figure 7.2 illustrates the interrelationships between the Diffusion Programme's functions and the system within which it operated.

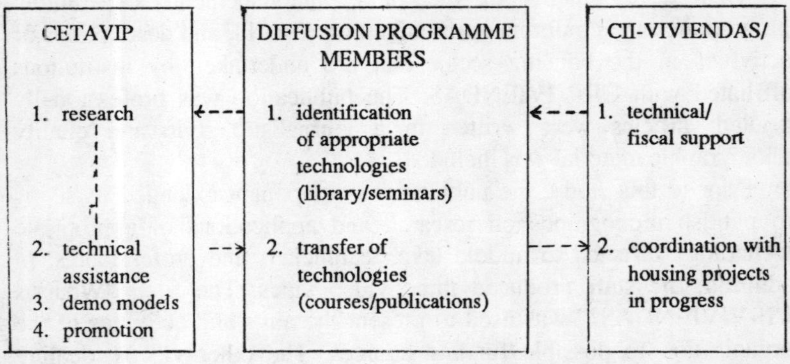

FIG. 7.2: Functional Interrelationships of Diffusion Programme to CETAVIP and CII-VIVIENDAS Activities

Success of the Diffusion Programme depended on an array of assumptions that were not fully realised, due to the economic crisis in the country. To illustrate, it was anticipated that USAID funds would leverage technical and financial contributions from CII-VIVIENDAS' member organisations to support the remaining programmes in CETAVIP. The OPG stipulated that the National Housing institute (INT) contribute RD $20,000 annually, in support of CETAVIP's programmes. In addition, INVI's Project Department was expected to lend technical personnel to CETAVIP to carry out research on appropriate technology. CETAVIP did not foresee that it would have to fund and staff its own research programme. According to the OPG, INVI resources would be funneled through the Diffusion Programme to CETAVIP, which would then coordinate the research activities with its other programmes. However, due to the freeze of government funds immediately after the contract approval, the bulk of payments were not made and the transfer of personnel did not occur. Consequently, the research programme intended to support the Diffusion Programme suffered from limited resources. CETAVIP was obliged to develop its own research capacity by securing donations from other sources.

The fact that USAID appropriated funds for the dissemination of information as opposed to the research and development (R&D) efforts of CII-VIVIENDAS was consistent with the findings of Jequier and Blanc (1983) which indicated that the U.S. allocates approximately 26 per cent of its fiscal expenditures for appropriate technology to information-oriented activities and only 15 per cent to R&D. The apparent intention of the OPG was to insert funds at an intermediate stage in the appropriate technology delivery system in order to leverage private sector and government resources for the initial and final stages. However, since it was obvious that R&D is the initial task in the process, the USAID strategy carried a high risk factor. In the case of CETAVIP, the research component was one of its weakest links. Only a few research projects had been completed, and resources to undertake new projects were insufficient to meet the information needs of the Diffusion Programme. In light of this finding, USAID needed to reconsider its priorities for allocating appropriate technology funds. Moreover, successful appropriate technology research could prove to be more efficacious than information transfer programmes in stimulating public and private investment in housing projects.

A second issue relates to the lack of both horizontal and vertical integration of the Diffusion Programme within the larger system. As discussed previously, interdependencies among CETAVIP's programmes had not coalesced sufficiently. While the personnel assigned to the courses and seminars component worked closely with the research, technical assistance, and promotions programmes in CETAVIP, the library and publications components of the Diffusion Programme were not utilised effectively. This aspect of the problem was relatively easy to solve by including staff from each programme on the advisory committees to the library and publications components and improving communications networks among CII-VIVIENDAS staff.

In contrast, CETAVIP's ability to improve the inter-institutional arrangements necessary for the Diffusion Programme's effective operation was more questionable. For example, the OPG agreement had stipulated that the government's Office of Community Development (ODC) would assume responsibility for mobilising and organising community groups to work on appropriate technology projects. This promotional assistance was not carried out to the satisfaction of CETAVIP staff, because the division virtually had no control over the ODC staff who worked with them. While CETAVIP staff felt it was imperative to hire their own employees for promotion as a short-term solution, this strategy could hinder future cooperative arrangements between ODC and CETAVIP.

The problem of implementing the Diffusion Programme was further compounded because the Dominican's economic situation severely limited the housing construction initiatives of INVI and other public and private agencies in the country. Thus, it was not possible to coordinate the transfer of appropriate technology with ongoing projects, as was contemplated in the OPG. On one hand, the limitation of the OPG to diffusion of appropriate technology was a severe constraint. As Fig. 7.2 illustrates, research generation, demonstration and promotion are prerequisites to technological diffusion. On the other hand, the Diffusion Programme, as it was conceived in the OPG, was overly ambitious. The expectation that a staff of 10 could carry out the broad agenda outlined in the contract (i.e., two seminars, training, development of a library, publication of a monthly newsletter, cooperative activities with other institutions) simply was unrealistic.

For these reasons, CII-VIVIENDAS was seeking funding for the two new divisions. The Revolving Fund would provide capital for development of CII-VIVIENDAS' own housing programmes, while the Centre for the Improvement of the Quality of Life could identify the needs of communities and work with promoters hired by CETAVIP to organise residents who could carry out the projects. Successful implementation of these two programmes most certainly would enhance the self-sufficiency of CII-VIVIENDAS. But just as there are dangers in too much interaction with and reliance on other agencies, there is the risk of isolation when agencies "look inward" (Jequier and Blanc, 1983). The scale of CII-VIVIENDAS' operations will be limited by the amount of resources it can generate, unless the policy of inter-institutional cooperation is maintained. Moreover, the organisation must avoid undue competition with other housing agencies for scarce resources and community alliances. Thus, a balance between the extremes of self-sufficiency and dependency is essential.

LARGER ISSUES CONFRONTING APPROPRIATE TECHNOLOGY APPROACHES

Among the multitude of controversies surrounding the adoption of appropriate technology in Third World development, several issues are of particular import to this case study. The first relates to the substitution of appropriate technology for the capital-intensive technologies of more developed countries. Evans and Adler (1979) note that there is a preference for foreign technology in developing countries. Imported technology is perceived by many Third World officials as the most efficient and reliable strategy to compete in a world market and improve the standard of living, while appropriate technology may represent an inferior approach (Jequier, 1976). Others perceive appropriate technology as "technological imperialism", an approach that will keep "poor nations in their place" (Thormann, 1979). Proponents of appropriate technology have countered these views with strong arguments based on economic, environmental, and social equity issues (Evans and Adler, 1979; Thormann, 1979). They contend that capital-intensive approaches are not as efficient as labour-intensive strategies, adversely affect the natural environment, and fail to improve employment opportunities of non-elites. The lack of support in the case of CII-VIVIENDAS, may be attributed, in part, to the opposition of some officials to the bottom-up approach that appropriate technology strategies represent. At best, INVI and ODC staff viewed CETAVIP's programmes as experimental. CETAVIP needed to enhance its image in this regard by developing a clear economic and political rationale for its projects.

A second issue concerns who determines or controls decisions regarding the development and implementation of appropriate technology. The debate centres on the relative power and influence of an array of participants, from donor agencies, government officials and R&D institutions to private corporations. Some (i.e., Reddy, 1979), argue that the elites of Third World countries (including businessmen, bureaucrats, and professionals who often have been educated in more developed countries) exert a strong influence on decisions regarding technological choices, and that these choices do not reflect either the desires or the resources of the poor. Technological choices were, in effect, controlled by bureaucrats and researchers in the case of CII-VIVIENDAS. Our site visits indicated that, while some of the technologies were acceptable to community residents, others were firmly opposed. We saw some evidence of this resistance with respect to sisal cement sheet roofing. A more striking example was the failure of CETAVIP to promote building of dry fertiliser latrines. Community residents unequivocally refused to use human excrement to fertilise their crops. While the development of appropriate technology is clearly the role of CETAVIP technician and advisors, decisions regarding what is deemed "appropriate" should be the purview of their potential beneficiaries.

Successful implementation of appropriate technology must not only be consistent with community aspirations, but also should have a strong relationship to national policies and plans. CETAVIP's emphasis on rural housing may not have been in concert with the concerns of INVI regarding the burgeoning urban housing deficit caused by increasing migration to the cities. Moreover, CETAVIP's plans to initiate and control its own housing projects could have been perceived as creating competition for the already scarce housing resources in the country. Certainly, cooperation and programme linkages between INVI and CII-VIVIENDAS required strengthening.

Finally, the redistributive properties of the appropriate technology approach need examination. Obviously, the breadth and scale of CETAVIP's projects were limited due to financial constraints. Recipient communities were targeted in terms of three basic criteria: poverty, housing needs, and the presence of a cooperative organisation in the community which could manage and implement a project. Since the first two criteria were present in most communities, the latter proved to be the most significant in terms of selecting targets, and it was evident that leaders in the communities were the beneficiaries. CETAVIP's project in Honduras illustrates this point. The limited resources of the project provided materials for construction of homes for less than half the residents of this community. These homes were occupied by the community's elites. It should be noted that the project did generate some benefits for the remaining residents because those who were trained later used their skills for community projects. Still, the most substantial benefits – new hurricane resistant homes – were obtained by the leaders of the community. Thus, existing social disparities within the community were reinforced by the project. In order to mitigate this kind of situation, the application of appropriate technology in self-help housing projects must be linked to strategies which foster the redistribution of resources, continuity of employment, and an integrated mix of programmes and services.

REFERENCES

Baron, C. (1978), 'Appropriate Technology Comes of Age: A Review of Some Recent Literature and Aid Policy Statements'. *International Labour Review*, 117: 625-634.

Center for Business Information (1984), *Appropriate Technology Organisation: A Worldwide Directory*. London, McFarland & Company.

CII-VIVIENDAS (1985), *Document for the Creation of a Revolving Fund for the Construction of Housing in the Informal Sector*. Santa Domingo, Inter-Institutional Council for the Coordination of Housing Programmes.

Cooper, C. (1979), 'A Summing Up of the Conference'. In A. Robinson (ed.), *Appropriate Technologies for Third World Development*. London, Macmillan: 404-409.

Eckaus, R.S. (1977), *Appropriate Technologies for Developing Countries*.Washington, D.C, National Academy of Sciences.

Economist Intelligence Unit (EIU) (1985), *Quarterly Economic Review of Cuba, Dominican Republic, Haiti, Puerto Rico, Annual Supplement*. London, The Economist Publications.

Evans, D.D. and Adler, L.N. (1979), *Appropriate Technology for Development: A Discussion and Case Histories*. Boulder, Westview Press.

Ghosh, P.K. (1984), *Appropriate Technology in Third World Development*. London, Greenwood Press.

Jequier, N. (1976), *Appropriate Technology: Problems and Promises*. Paris, Development Centre of the Organisation for Economic Co-operation and Development.

Jequier, N., and Blanc, G. (1983), *The World of Appropriate Technology*. Paris, Development Centre of the Organisation of Economic Co-operation and Development.

Lodwick, D. and Stommel, M. (1984), 'Appropriate Technology, Selected References and Abstracts from Empirically Relevant Studies' in P. Ghosh (ed.), *Appropriate Technology in Third World Development*. London, Greenwood Press : 425-455.

Nanita-Kennett, M. and Edwards, P.K. (1986), *Diffusion Programme, Centre for Appropriate Technology for Popular Housing: Second Year Evaluation.* Blacksburg, Virginia, Virginia Polytechnic Institute and State University.

PADCO (1984), *AID Project: Appropriate Technology for Rural Housing*. Washington, D.C: Padco.

Reddy, A.K. (1979), 'Problems in the Generation of Appropriate Technologies' in A. Robinson (ed.), *Appropriate Technologies for Third World Development*. London, Macmillan : 173-189.

Robinson, A. (1979), *Appropriate Technologies for Third World Development*. London, Macmillan.

Thormann, P. (1979), 'Proposal for a Programme on Appropriate Technology Prepared by the United States Agency for International Development' in A. Robinson (ed.), *Appropriate Ttechnologies for Third World Development*. London, Macmillan : 278-299.

Usui, M. (1976), 'Introduction' in N. Jequier (ed.), *Appropriate Technology: Problems and Promises*. Paris, Development Centre of the Organisation for Economic Co-operation and Development : 9-13.

Veldhuis, K.H. (1979), 'Transfer and Adaptation of Technology: Inilever as a Case Study' in A. Robinson (ed.), *Appropriate Technologies for Third World Development*. London, Macmillan : 219-238

8

WHO OWNS, WHO RENTS:
Tenure Choice in a West African City

A. GRAHAM TIPPLE and KENNETH G. WILLIS

The private rental market has been a major provider of housing across the world for many generations. In the United Kingdom, while the incidence of home ownership has been high in recent years, private rental housing nurtured the great majority of households from cradle to grave prior to 1918.

Over the past two decades, owner occupation has dominated the attention of housing specialists, encouraged by the pioneering work of Abrams (1964), Turner (1968, 1976), and others. Little attention has been paid to the private rental market despite its large contribution towards the accommodation of low-income households. Over the past decade, however, increasing though still fairly sparse attention has been paid to rental markets in Third World cities. Notable contributions have flowed from the University of London (Gilbert and Ward, 1982; Gilbert, 1983, 1987; Edwards 1982) and research staff at the World Bank (e.g. Malpezzi *et al.*, 1985; Mayo *et al.*, 1986). Together, they have begun to establish some frameworks within which rental housing can be examined.

Writers who have concentrated on the advantages accruing from owner-occupation have seen renting as a short-term measure for newly arrived urban migrants until they achieve an economic position where they can buy or build, especially in the informal sector. Turner (1968) argued that most households spend their first few years in the urban area in inner city rented accommodation (his "bridgeheaders") but are on a trajectory towards ownership which can be satisfied by moving to peripheral squatter settlements (his "consolidators"). This pattern, Turner argues, is not only favoured by households but also should be favoured by governments as owner occupation has advantages as a means of consolidating wealth, maximising capital investment in housing and securing greater occupant care of property. Those who do not succeed on the path to home ownership in the periphery are seen as failures excluded by income or misfortune. Thus, the rental market is seen as residual and accommodates those households less able to own (Gilbert, 1983).

Later work, however, has shown that the distinctions between owners and renters are not as clear as this, neither locationally nor economically. In Bogota and Mexico City owners and renters do not have significantly different incomes (Gilbert, 1987). Many squatter areas have considerable renter populations (Schlyter, 1987; Gilbert and Ward, 1982). Indeed, Gilbert (1987) reports squatter settlements in Bogota where housing is being built on the lines of inner city tenements specifically for rental.

It is clear that not all households who value owner-occupation succeed in owning a house during their lifetime. It is also clear that there is more to the achievement of ownership than income. Local conditions may allow low-income households to obtain land; e.g. by invasion or through assisted land allocation schemes. In addition, policies enabling land acquisition may be short-lived or only open to particular groups; e.g. forces personnel, war veterans, or government officials; leaving a fortunate few with great advantages over their peers.

As owners consolidate their housing, they may be able to build extra rooms to rent to households not dissimilar from themselves. While it is clear that there are rich landlords who exploit poor tenants, there are also many ordinary households who let a few rooms to people with whom they are on cordial relations.

The World Bank staff have contributed to the rental debate by pointing out the need for encouraging the positive effects of landlordism in order to generate investment in housing. They point out that private landlords provide a large proportion of housing in developing countries at little or no cost to governments. The current World Bank research on rent control shows that, where rents are kept artificially low, investment has been foregone in new starts and maintenance and the benefits which accrue to renters are probably much smaller than costs incurred by landlords (Malpezzi and Rydell, 1986; Tipple and Willis, 1988; Willis and Tipple, 1988).

A second strand of World Bank research concentrates on people's willingness to pay rent. Data from many cities has been collected to show that poorer households pay a higher proportion of their income on rent than higher income groups. Furthermore, the average rent to income ratio rises as city average income increases; i.e., Engels curves of rent to income ratio against income shift upwards as cities develop (Malpezzi *et al.*, 1985), (see Fig. 8.1).

In Africa, very little data on rental markets are available although renting is the most common form of tenure in many countries. Notable among these is Ghana in which the great majority of urban housing is provided by private individuals for rental. The purpose of this paper is to, explore the differences that exist between households who own and those who rent, to examine the quality and quantity of housing services consumed by each group, and to model tenure choice to try and determine why some households own while others rent.

The data used in this analysis were collected in a survey of 1469 households carried out in Kumasi in 1986 under the auspices of the World Bank's International Comparison of Rent Control. In addition, a broadly similar survey conducted in 1980 (presented in detail in Tipple 1987) will be referred to where appropriate.

The paper is in four parts. Part one introduces housing in Kumasi and defines six tenure groups; part two describes the households in the six groups and the housing services they consume; part three examines the variables found to be influential in tenure choice in Latin America to test how far they have been influential in Kumasi; and part four applies discriminant analysis in order to identify the household characteristics which most influence tenure choice and tests the likely influence in changes in two significant characteristics on tenure choice.

INTRODUCTION TO HOUSING IN KUMASI

Housing in Kumasi is characterised by privately owned compound houses, usually single storey and about thirty square metres, consisting of three rows of rooms ranged around a rectangular courtyard with kitchen, bathroom and toilet facilities on the fourth side. Access to all rooms is via the central courtyard which is reached through a single door at the side or rear of the building. Two and three storey compounds have balcony access to upper floors reached from a staircase in the courtyard. Less than ten per cent of the rooms in the city have been provided by the government sector despite a programme of estate building beginning in the 1940s. Detailed descriptions and illustrations of the compound house form can be found in Rutter

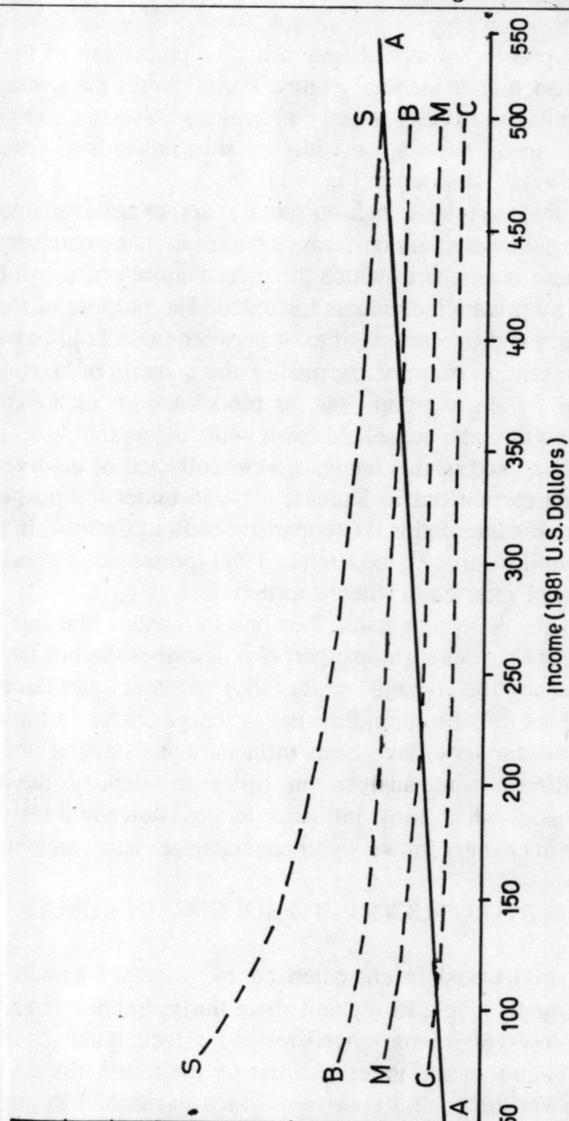

FIG. 8.1: Rent-Income Ratios by Income for Renters

Key: A-average for each city at its average income; B-Bogota; C-Cairo; M-Manila; S-Seoul

Source: Malpezzi *et al.* (1988).

(1971), Schreckenbach (1982), and Tipple (1987). Examples of social life in compound houses in urban Ghana can be found in Sanjek (1982) for Adabraka, Accra, and Schildkrout (1978) for the northerner dominated Zongo in Kumasi.

Rental levels have been controlled since World War II to levels set by central government edict. The rent control legislation sets specific rents for single room accommodation which shared services as it dominates rental housing in urban areas. The most recent, PNDC Law 138 (and L.I. 1318), sets the rents for this type of accommodation at C300 per month (C2.5 per square foot) for those built of sandcrete and C200 (C1.7 per square foot) for those built with mud. Two such rooms *en suite* rent for C400 (C1.7 per square foot) or C300 (C1.3 per square foot) respectively.

Although rental housing appears to have given a reasonable return on investment up to the early 1970s (Schildkrout, 1978), the last 15 years have seen rents fall far behind other prices (Tipple, 1988). Current controlled rental levels give a landlord only 1.25 per cent return on capital used to construct a single room in local materials (Tipple and Willis, 1988).

Definition of Tenure Groups

For this paper, tenure in Kumasi has been disaggregated first into three: two types of ownership and renting. Each of these has been further divided into two according to whether the household has exclusive use of services or not. Use of kitchen has been used as a proxy for use of services because exclusive use of a kitchen is most likely to show which accommodation is self-contained as a dwelling or apartment, and which is part of a communally occupied larger building such as a compound. Only sixteen per cent of households have exclusive use of a kitchen in Kumasi of whom just over half are not renters.

Owners (Exclusive) and Owners (Non-Exclusive)

About ten per cent of households in Kumasi own the house in which they live. Three quarters of these have exclusive use of a kitchen, one quarter do not. These households are described as owners in this paper but house ownership is not necessarily limited to them. No data were collected on whether a household owned any house other than that which they occupied, whether it is in their home village, another town, or elsewhere in Kumasi. As ownership of a house in the home village is regarded as a priority by many Ghanaians, and as landlessness is extremely rare, it is likely that many urban dwellers have a house in the village which they own either outright or in common with other family members, or have the right to occupy land on which they could build a house. Furthermore, no record has been kept of whether an adult other than the 'head'; e.g., a wife; owns a house – a not impossible occurrence where spouses do not have common budgets (Fapohunda, 1987).

Family Housers (Exclusive) and Family Housers (Non-Exclusive)

In Ghanaian culture, ownership of houses, like that of most property, often involves members of a lineage rather than individuals especially in financing such a large structure as a compound. Thus, outright ownership by one individual or household is likely to be clouded by lineage claims. In this way, there are many people who have the right to demand accommodation in a house. Although new laws encourage inheritance through nuclear families and more individual control over self-acquired property (Tipple, 1986), many houses in Kumasi have already been inherited in common by a lineage, under the care of the senior male (abusua panyin). Lineage members have a strong claim to live in these houses rent free. Family claims to accommodation are so deeply ingrained in Ghanaian culture that the Rent Act, 1963, allows eviction of tenants if a room is required for a family member. In this paper, households who live in a family house rent free are referred to as 'family housers'. In 1986 they constituted about twenty-five per cent of all households in Kumasi. This is a marked growth since 1980 when only 12.8 per cent of households lived as family housers. About ten per cent of family housers have exclusive use of a kitchen and ninety per cent do not.

Renters

Renters are those households who pay rent for a dwelling with exclusive use of services. The type of accommodation renters occupy in Kumasi can be divided between single dwellings built as bungalows and apartments in buildings of two or more storeys (but no higher than four storeys). They can be further divided between government-built dwellings, which are rented out by the State Housing Corporation at subsidised rates, and privately owned dwellings let to employees, private individuals, or major employers for a rent determined by the Rent Control Committee or by agreement between the owner and the renter according to the quality of the accommodation (rent control has only intermittently been applied to the most expensive houses). In turn, the renter may pay either the rent determined by the Committee or, when paid to an employer, one based on a fixed percentage (usually ten or 12.5 per cent) of his salary. If the house is a large, well-equipped one, the difference between what a worker pays to his employer and what the employer pays to be landlord may be very great indeed, the latter being the larger amount. However, we have no data on the rents actually paid by employers for the accommodation which they rent on to their employees.

As both rents and wages are low, many renters pay surprisingly little for some of the best accommodation available in Kumasi (Median C300, Mean C324 per month). About seven per cent of households are renters.

Roomers

Roomers are classified as those households who occupy rooms singly, or occasionally in pairs (known as a hall and chamber), usually in a compound house, sharing facilities with other households.

Kumasi roomers have a similar position in the housing market to Edwards' (1982) roomers in the *inquilinatos* of Bucaramanga. They are not, however, confined to city centre tenements. Indeed, the Kumasi equivalent of *barrio* rental housing in South America, though not strictly squatting (Peil, 1976; Tipple, 1984), provides accommodation of a quality similar to tenements with ten or so households sharing services with each other and a landlord. About fifty-five per cent of all households in Kumasi could be classified as roomers in 1986.

A further group was identified in the survey: renters who pay rent to someone other than the house-owner. This is a very small group (only three per cent of households) and has not been included in this analysis.

HOUSEHOLD CHARACTERISTICS AND HOUSING SERVICES CONSUMED

It will be seen in the data that the tenure groups with similar access to services are more like each other than those with different levels of service. Therefore, the tables in this and subsequent sections are arranged first by use of kitchen and second by tenure. Data for medians are shown with interquartile ranges in parenthesis below. For example owners (exclusive) have a household size of six at the median, five at the twenty-fifth percentile and eight at the seventy-fifth percentile.

Household Size

An occupier of property is likely to receive requests for accommodation from members of his lineage. Unless his rooms are already crowded, such requests cannot easily be resisted. However, many rooms there are 'en suite', the occupier will, in this way, acquire a household large enough to fill the rooms. Jibir (1985) found the same behaviour filled the three-, four-, and five-roomed apartments in Abuja to occupancy rates of three persons per room. As the law in Ghana allows tenants to be evicted to make room for family members (Ghana, 1963), an owner will be unable to resist pressure to accommodate more family members. If, his house is designed as a single dwelling, his household size will increase. If, however, all the rooms have independent access, as from the courtyard of a compound house, it is possible for the relatives to be housed but to form separate households. Table 8.1 demonstrates that households in rooms with shared services (kitchen) or none are smaller than those in rooms with exclusive use of services.

As there is a strong relationship between number of rooms occupied and household size, the least independent households [family housers (non-exclusive) and roomers] are the smallest households.

Where a householder has accommodated members of the extended family, these relatives will often be at least partly dependent upon him or her. Some measure of this can be seen in the number of adults in the household (the data on number of workers per household shows a median of two across all tenure groups but non-sampling errors are probably high on this variable). The owning groups (owners and family housers) have smaller ratios of adults to total household members than the tenants; roomers are the least liable to be supporting many children or non-workers. The three tenure groups who enjoy the most rooms per household (see Table 8.1) – owners (exclusive), owners (non-exclusive) and renters – all have large households.

TABLE 8.1: Measures of Household Size, Composition, and Occupancy by Tenure; Medians (and IQRs) and percentages

Median (IQR)	Exclusive use of kitchen			Non-exclusive use of kitchen		
	Owners	Family housers	Renters	Owners	Family housers	Roomers
Household size (persons)	6 (5, 8)	5 (4, 8)	5 (2, 7)	5 (3, 9)	4 (2, 5)	4 (2, 5)
Number of adults (persons)	4 (3, 5)	2 (2, 4)	3 (2, 4)	2 (1, 3)	3 (2, 3)	2 (1, 3)
Rooms occupied	4 (3, 6)	3 (1, 4)	3 (2, 4)	2 (1, 3)	1 (1, 2)	1 (1, 1)
Percentage in one room	7	40	24	42	74	87
Occupancy rates (persons per room)	1.5 (1, 2)	2 (1.3, 4)	1.7 (1, 2.5)	2.1 (1.5, 4.5)	3 (2, 5)	3 (2, 5)
Percentage with 3 persons per room or more	13	41	25	44	54	64

Rooms Occupied and Occupancy Rates

Owners (exclusive) are able to obtain more rooms per household, and achieve lower occupancy rates per room than any other tenure group, but only marginally more so than renters. Both they and renters have enough rooms to offset their larger households in achieving occupancy rates which are generally under the mean for Kumasi of 3.3 persons per room. Roomers and family housers, however, rarely obtain more than one room for their households and, consequently, are severely crowded. Twenty-nine per cent of roomer households (sixteen per cent of all households in Kumasi) live at more than five persons per room.

Access to Services

In this analysis, a household defined as being without access to a service means one which cannot use a service (whether inside or outside the house) which is for the specific use of households living in the house. Their lack of access to the service is usually because it is absent, but it may also be because members of one household or a group of households reserve use for themselves. Households without access to kitchens will store their cooking utensils elsewhere, perhaps on their verandah, those without bathrooms may wash in their rooms. Households without toilets or water supply will 'go for bush' or use public latrines and standpipes.

TABLE 8.2: Households *without* Access to Services (Percentage frequencies)

Services	Exclusive use of kitchen			Non-exclusive use of kitchen		
	Owners	Family housers	Renters	Owners	Family housers	Roomers
Kitchen	0	0	0	21	27	26
Bathroom	2	0	0	4	3	2
Toilet	10	20	3	20	46	27
Water supply	14	19	1	24	41	31

We will take the left and right sides of Table 8.2 separately. On the left side, it is obvious that not all households with exclusive use of a kitchen have any access to toilet or water supply in the house. As the kitchen need not have any fittings or water supply, it is very cheap and simple to provide even in areas without any public utilities. Family housers (exclusive) fare worst while renters are generally well provided for because their accommodation is dominated by self-contained apartments with western-style kitchens and bathrooms which include a toilet and water supply.

On the right side of Table 8.2, we can see that, of households who do not have exclusive use of a kitchen, considerable percentages are without any use of services within the house. Apart from bathrooms which are fairly universal (and may be only a tiny room with no tap or fittings), over twenty per cent of households in each tenure group lack each service. Family housers again fare worst, especially for toilet and water supply where over forty per cent of households have no access. It is interesting, however, how little difference there is between owners (non-exclusive) and roomers.

VARIABLES INFLUENTIAL IN TENURE CHOICE

Gilbert (1983 and 1987) suggests that the variables which influence tenure choice are:

(a) Household income, sources of income, and number of workers in the household which allow us to test whether ownership is related to economic factors;

(b) Ability to obtain land through economic, political or ethnic qualification or privilege or opportunity and willingness to be involved in a land invasion;

(c) Age of household head, and age at which the head arrived in the city (and, therefore, length of stay in the city) to test whether tenure choices change as a household absorbs urban values.

These characteristics are dealt with in the Kumasi context in turn.

(a) **Household Monthly Incomes**

For this work, expenditure is taken as a proxy for income. Previous work in Kumasi (Tipple, 1984) had demonstrated the problems of collecting income data, thus it came as no surprise that stated incomes in the 1986 data were only 42 per cent of stated expenditure. We have no reliable data on sources of income. We realise the problems attendant on using expenditure as a straightforward proxy for income which include a tendency towards underestimation for the higher income groups because marginal propensity to consume declines with income. However, experience from the 1980 survey and living in Ghana indicated that expenditure was reliably reported and we feel that the advantage of using it outweigh any known disadvantages.

It would be expected from Edwards (1982) and Gilbert (1983) that owner households would have higher incomes (and, therefore, expenditure) than tenants, and that tenants of apartments (renters) would be better off than occupants of rooming accommodation (roomers).

Table 8.3 shows that in Kumasi, owners (exclusive) and owners (non-exclusive) have higher household expenditure than tenants (both renters and roomers), and that family housers have the lowest. However, the differences between exclusive and non-exclusive in each tenure group are, perhaps, more significant than those between tenures. The difference between renters and roomers is very marked: only twenty per cent of renters consume less than the roomers median of C11,850 per month. Within the non-exclusive category, family housers and roomers display a marked similarity at the foot of the consumption pyramid.

TABLE 8.3: Household and Per Capita Expenditures by Tenure Group, Cedis Per Month (Median and IQR Rounded)

Median (IQR)	Exclusive use of kitchen			Non-exclusive use of kitchen		
	Owners	Family housers	Renters	Owners	Family housers	Roomers
Household	21900 (12600, 30300)	14650 (11990, 21150)	19100 (13670, 24500)	14600 (10990, 19200)	11350 (7800, 15570)	11850 (8870, 15750)
Per Capita	3280 (2360, 4380)	2930 (2200, 3640)	3830 (2690, 5820)	2740 (1830, 3900)	2940 (1990, 4330)	3350 (2140, 4880)

However, as Datta and Meerman (1980) indicate, the picture changes markedly when per capita monthly expenditure is examined. The reasons for major differences between the distributions of household and per capita incomes are likely to be found in part in the effect of household size on the two measures and in part to the extended family system and house design in urban Ghana.

Because of their greater propensity to have their households increased in size by migrant family members (Table 8.1), owners have lower per capita expenditure than renters and roomers. Furthermore, households in self-contained apartments and houses also have their higher household incomes (expenditures) reduced by large mean household sizes.

(b) **Ability to Obtain Land**

Ability to obtain land free or cheaply was found to be a very important determinant of whether relatively low-income households could be owners in Latin American cities (Gilbert, 1983). This has been achieved either through subdividing the land into small plots or through invasions of state land.

In Kumasi, land is obtainable on lease in two ways. Members of the village communities which are subsumed by Kumasi (e.g. Tafo, Amakom, Ayigya, Oforikrom, Bantama, etc.) can obtain the use of land in perpetuity as a right, through their chief, on payment of an annual ground rent to the chief. 'Strangers', who are not from Kumasi villages, can obtain the right of use of land for 90 years through the payment of a tribute, known as 'drink money', which, although strictly only the price of a sacrifice to the local 'stool' and a tribute to the Golden Stool (the apical symbol of the Asante nation), has come to represent a notional market price. There is evidence, however, that this 'price' varies according to whether or not the applicant belongs to the local major tribal group, the Akan (Asabere, 1981).

There are, therefore, major land price advantages in being a native of a Kumasi village and smaller advantages in being an Akan. In the light of this, it would be expected that ownership (both outright and through shares in family houses) would be more common amongst locals and would reach further down the consumption range. Table 8.4, which separates Akans from non-Akans, shows little evidence of the former being particularly dominant in ownership, but also show fewer roomers than would be expected *ceteris paribus*. When respondents who claimed to come from Kumasi are separated from the remainder (Table 8.6), it is obvious that owners (non-exclusive) and family housers (exclusive and non-exclusive) are far more common amongst natives of Kumasi than in the population as a whole. The data do not show conclusively whether or not Akans are more likely to be owners at lower incomes than non-Akans.

TABLE 8.4: Ethnic Group by Tenure group (Percentage Frequencies)

Median (IQR)	Exclusive use of kitchen			Non-exclusive use of kitchen		
	Owners	Family housers	Renters	Owners	Family housers	Roomers
Akan	87	92	91	81	83	72
Other	13	8	9	19	17	28

(c) Age and Establishment in the City

Evidence from other cities (Gilbert, 1983) would suggest that owners are likely to be older, to have migrated to the city at an earlier age, and to have lived in the city longer than tenants. These features support the notion that migrants to the city embark on a trajectory which, through time, leads at least some of them into ownership. The Kumasi data support this in so far as both sets of owner household heads are older than, and they tend to have lived in Kumasi at least as long as, other groups. Family housers are also long-established in Kumasi many having always lived in the city. There is certainly support for the notion that renters and roomers are younger and more newly arrived than owners (Table 8.5).

However, these data show no conclusive evidence to support the idea that renters and roomers are in those tenures temporarily and will strive to attain ownership by the time the head is fifty to sixty years old. The discriminant analysis below shows that, while ownership is indeed likely to increase and renting decrease if households have had longer stays in Kumasi, the major change would be into family house occupation.

It is remarkable how few migrants to Kumasi intend their stay to be short. Migration to the city is most commonly from areas less than one day's journey away. Indeed seventy-eight per cent of household heads are Akans, originating from the area of Asante domination in the

TABLE 8.5: Measures of Age and Establishment in the City, by Tenure (Medians and IQRs)

Median (IQR)	Exclusive use of kitchen			Non-exclusive use of kitchen		
	Owners	Family housers	Renters	Owners	Family housers	Roomers
Age of head (Years)	52 (45, 62)	41 (35, 60)	40 (36, 52)	51 (42, 58)	38 (30, 50)	38 (30, 46)
Length of residence in Kumasi (Years)	26 (17, 40)	30 (18, 46)	16 (10, 30)	30 (20, 40)	25 (15, 35)	17 (10, 28)
Migration age (Years)	23 (10, 34)	14 (0, 21)	25 (15, 33)	16 (3, 30)	12 (0, 24)	20 (12, 28)

eighteenth and nineteenth centuries based on, and immediately surrounding, Kumasi (Wilks, 1975). Visits 'home' are frequent, particularly for funerals, and great emphasis is placed on a migrant keeping in close contact with his or her village and building a house there if at all possible. Brokensha (1966) stresses the social consequences of neglecting village obligations. Many households who do not own a house in the city will either already own, or be intending to build, in the village as a matter of priority. This has been unintentionally encouraged in recent years by the very low rents for which households can gain shelter in the city where they work while leaving their savings intact for building in the home village.

TABLE 8.6: Household Heads' Intention to Stay in Kumasi (Rounded Percentage Frequencies)

	Exclusive use of kitchen			Non-exclusive use of kitchen		
	Owners	Family housers	Renters	Owners	Family housers	Roomers
Temporary or target migrant	1	0	10	0	1	6
Long-term migrant or retire to village	39	50	72	59	39	67
Permanent resident	51	14	16	15	22	15
Kumasi born	9	36	2	26	38	12

It is obvious from Table 8.6 that most owners with exclusive use of a kitchen are committed to long-term or permanent residence in the city but it is inescapable that a large proportion of both renters and roomers are also intending to stay at least until retirement. They have not the same commitment to permanence as exclusive owners but nor have owners with non-exclusive use of a kitchen.

It can be seen from the above that many of the differences between owners and tenants found by Gilbert (1983, 1987) in Latin America are more pronounced in Kumasi between households with different access to services than between owners and tenants. In the following analysis, an attempt is made to assess to what extent the variables discussed above actually determine access to services and tenure or whether others are more influential.

MULTIVARIATE ANALYSIS AND TENURE CHOICE

The preceding univariate statistics have described the characteristics of households in different tenure in Kumasi. Multivariate statistics can extend the analysis and permit tenure choice to be modelled. But it needs to be modelled in a particular way, since the dependent variable, tenure, assumed discrete values. It is an unordered categorical variable.

Discriminant analysis begins with a situation in which individuals (households in this case) are categorised into discrete groups. Discriminant analysis tries to find a linear function, of *n* explanatory variables, that provides the best discrimination between the groups (Willis, 1987). It makes intuitive sense that the discriminant function should be chosen so that the variance between groups is maximised, relative to the variance within groups, and this is precisely what a discriminant function seeks to achieve.

Discriminant analysis has not been widely applied in the analysis of housing market issues; although a substantial number of applications of the technique exist in financial markets from assessing good and bad loans, to using discriminant analysis to predict firm failure (Storey *et al.*, 1987). An early study by Doling (1973) of the sale of UK council housing showed the ability of discriminant analysis to model or analyse the distinction between the following:

(1) households who purchased their house from the local authority,
(2) households who wished to buy but could not raise a mortgage or loan,

(3) households who did not buy, but who could have obtained a mortgage, and
(4) households who did not wish to buy and who in any case would not have been able to acquire a mortgage or loan.

But despite this promising start with discriminant analysis to model housing issues, and the large number of categorical situations in housing markets where individuals are already classified in some way, it is a relatively underused technique.

Discriminant analysis begins here with the existence of the six tenure groups identified earlier. The object is to find a model or number of variables which will discriminate between these six groups; i.e. correctly assign each household to its existing tenure group. This is accomplished by constructing linear function.

$$Z = a_0 + a_1x_1 + a_2x_2 + \dots a_nx_n$$

where $a_1, \dots a_n$ are positive or negative coefficients of variables $x_1, \dots . x_n$.

Two methods can be used in the selection of variables to include in the model. First, simply include all possible variables and select those which are significant on the basis of a specified statistical test, say an F value. Second, select those variables which, on *a priori* grounds or as indicated by work elsewhere, are thought to determine tenure choice. The actual selection procedure involved a combination of both methods: *a priori* variables were initially selected according to theoretical expectations of their influence on tenure choice, and then only those variables which were significant at a five per cent level were included in the discriminant function.

The variables which significantly influenced tenure choice correspond quite well with those from Gilbert (1983, 1987) discussed above:

(a) income (i.e. consumption as a proxy for income) and income per capita, which relate to economic factors;
(b) age of head of household, length of residence in Kumasi, and length of residence in the house, which relate to adoption of urban values by being in the city for a long period;
(c) year of construction of house, and dummy variables for whether a household had lived in a government built house in excess of 10 years (as a proxy for those likely to have been able to buy a

government built house), and for the home region of the head of household, which relate to access to land ownership; and

(d) number of rooms in the house, and a dummy variable for condition of house structure, which are unrelated to Gilbert's list.

These variables discriminated between households in the six tenure groups, and produced the results outlined in Table 8.7. It can be seen that the discriminant model based on the foregoing variables, classified 65.7 per cent of households correctly in their respective tenure groups. (This is calculated by summing the diagonal and dividing by the total number of observations in the matrix). The two tenure groups displaying the largest percentage of households classified correctly were owners (exclusive) (78 per cent) and roomers (82 per cent).

TABLE 8.7: Classification Summary of Kumasi Household Tenures (Number and Percentage)

No. Per cent	Exclusive use of kitchen			Non-exclusive use of kitchen			
	Owners	Family housers	Renters	Owners	Family housers	Roomers	Total
Exclusive access to kitchen Owners	39 78.0	1 2.0	0 0.0	0 0.0	1 2.0	9 18.0	50 100.0
Family Housers	2 9.1	5 22.7	1 4.6	1 4.6	5 22.7	8 36.4	22 100.0
Renters	6 15.4	1 2.6	5 12.8	1 2.6	3 7.7	23 59.0	39 100.0
Non-exclusive access to kitchen Owners	8 13.8	0 0.0	2 3.5	12 20.7	1 1.7	35 60.3	58 100.0
Family Housers	5 4.1	3 2.4	2 1.6	3 2.4	60 48.8	50 40.7	123 100.0
Roomers	11 2.9	4 1.0	8 2.1	8 2.1	37 9.6	317 82.3	385 100.0
Total	71 10.5	14 2.1	18 2.7	25 3.7	107 15.8	442 65.3	677 100.0
Priors	0.074	0.033	0.058	0.086	0.182	0.569	

There are some other notable features in Table 8.7. First, the discriminant model tries to allocate some households from their respective tenure groups and classify them into other groups, particularly the roomer group. For example, eighteen per cent of owners (exclusive) are deemed to be more like roomers. Second, a significant percentage of households from owners (non-exclusive) and renters are assessed as being more like owners (exclusive). Third, family housers (exclusive) and renters are particularly misclassified with this model. A high proportion of family housers (exclusive) were deemed to be more like the family housers (non-exclusive) category. Fourth, overall, the model classified a slightly higher percentage of the housing market as owners (exclusive) (10.5 per cent) than actually occurs in the Kumasi housing market (7.4 per cent); and a similar situation occurs with roomer households. In all other cases the model under estimates households in tenure categories compared with their respective percentages in the housing market. However, we believe that a 66.5 per cent correct overall classification rate achieved in this discriminant model, represents a good policy capturing equation; out performing prior probability assignment and intuitive judgement.

It should not be expected that the model ought to provide a 100 per cent fit: models are abstractions from reality, drawing out the principal features and determinants of particular phenomena. The housing market is dynamic. Some individuals in the renter category may be on the point of becoming owners: hence their characteristics will be more like those of owners, only they have not yet moved between tenures. For some owners, circumstances may have changed so that their socio-economic characteristics are now more like renters, although they still continue to own especially for cultural reasons.

Moreover, the decision as to what to optimise also determines goodness of fit of the model. Because there are more roomers, the discriminant analysis programme tries to assign as many of these correctly as it possibly can, to achieve a better goodness of fit overall. It does mean that a higher proportion of other tenures are misclassified, than could otherwise be achieved.

This links with the choice of what *a priori* probabilities to specify to undertake the analysis and to assign probabilities of group membership. There are basically two choices: specify *a priori* probabilities to reflect the percentage distribution of households among tenure groups in the Kumasi housing market (the approach adopted for the above analysis), or assume there is an equally probability that a household could be in any tenure group. Specifying equal probabilities with the same variables as in the original model, reduces the overall fit of the model to 48.4 per cent (i.e. the model correctly assigns forty-eight per cent of households) but the classification rate within all tenure groups except roomers is now improved. The model now classifies seventy-eight per cent of owners (exclusive) correctly (same as previously); thirty-eight per cent of owners (non-exclusive); fifty-nine per cent of family housers (exclusive); forty-nine per cent of family housers (non-exclusive) (same as previously); and forty per cent of renters. A comparison of these figures with the diagonals in Table 8.7, reveals the improvement in the classification of smaller groups as less emphasis is placed on correctly assigning households in the largest tenure category: renters with non-exclusive use.

Discriminant analysis can also be used predictively, to assess the influence that a change in one variable will have on the proportion of households in each tenure category. One of the principal variables influencing tenure choice is income.

TABLE 8.8: Classification of Households as Household Expenditure increases

No. Per cent	Exclusive use of kitchen			Non-exclusive use of kitchen		
	Owners	Family housers	Renters	Owners	Family housers	Roomers
Existing household expenditure	10.31	1.87	2.68	3.61	14.73	66.80
+ 20	11.78	2.14	3.88	3.48	14.19	64.52
+ 40	13.52	2.68	5.62	3.48	13.52	61.18
+ 50	15.80	2.81	7.10	3.35	12.85	58.10
+ 80	18.88	3.48	9.10	4.15	11.38	53.00
+ 100	21.15	4.15	11.51	5.09	10.04	48.06

Table 8.8 indicates how the distribution of households between tenure categories can be expected to change if income was to increase (in real terms). If income doubled, the percentage of owners (exclusive) would double from 10.3 to 21.2 per cent. The proportion of roomers would decline from 66.8 to 48.1 per cent; while there would be a large increase in renters category, from 2.7 to 11.5 per cent of households. Overall, increasing income results in more households in the owner categories; less in the renter categories; and leaves the family house categories unchanged, except that more households here would have exclusive use of facilities. Increasing income results in a greater proportion of households with exclusive use of services in all

tenure categories.

Gilbert (1987) suggests that it is important to determine whether there are large numbers of renters who would be owners if they had opportunity to obtain land cheaply. In Kumasi, members of local lineages have access to cheap land. A discriminant analysis which assumed all households were natives of the city showed little change in tenure pattern.

A second method of obtaining land cheaply is through being in the city at a period when land was cheap, either through lower levels of development in the past or through having the chance to benefit from some sort of scheme aimed at the low income group. The time for both of these may now be past and many households will have missed out during a period when others had benefited from favourable conditions for low income land ownership. Gilbert (1987) argues that, as informal settlements are legalised, land prices rise creating an ever higher barrier to ownership. There is certainly anecdotal evidence to suggest that land values have been rising in Kumasi.

TABLE 8.9: Classification of Households as Length of Stay Increases

No. Per cent	Exclusive use of kitchen			Non-exclusive use of kitchen		
	Owners	Family housers	Renters	Owners	Family housers	Roomers
Existing length of stay	10.31	1.87	2.68	3.61	14.73	66.80
+ 20	9.91	3.75	2.41	4.02	15.53	64.39
+ 40	9.37	6.43	2.14	4.28	15.39	62.38
+ 60	9.10	8.43	1.34	5.09	15.53	60.51
+ 80	8.84	10.31	1.34	6.83	14.73	57.97
+ 100	8.57	12.72	1.34	8.03	14.73	54.62

Through discriminant analysis it is possible to examine whether or not it is only a matter of time before appreciable numbers of households will own their housing. This can be done by interfering with the length of stay in the house, which is assumed to represent a minimum length of time which a household has been in its current tenure. Table 8.9 indicates how the distribution of households in each tenure category can be expected to change as length of stay increases. Increasing residence time (doubling length of stay) is associated with a lower proportion of both renters and roomers, indicating that these households transfer to tenure groups with at least some ownership rights, especially in family houses (from a sum of 16.6 to 27.5 per cent). The inevitability of individually owned houses passing to joint heirs through mortality probably explains the reduction in owner (exclusive) while any movement to ownership from tenancy is probably mainly into the non-exclusive category.

Both discriminant analysis and multinomial logit analysis can be used to predict the choices of a new individual (household) with given characteristics, land the probability that an individual will chose a different group (tenure), given a change in one of the characteristics. Because of the close relationship between discriminant analysis and the logit model, and also because the logit regression model has far fewer assumptions than the linear discriminant model (SAS, 1986), logit regression might be preferred over discriminant analysis. Even when all the assumptions of discriminant analysis hold, logistic regression is virtually as efficient as discriminant analysis. A logit regression model, using the same variables as in the discriminant model, was developed to predict tenure classification. Overall, the logit model correctly assigned 60.4 per cent of households, a figure slightly lower than the linear discriminant model; and moreover, the logit model failed to reclassify households completely to their existing tenure categories in some groups, concentrating on correctly assigning owners and renters. Hence, in this empirical case, discriminant analysis is to be preferred to logit analysis.

CONCLUSIONS

In the foregoing analysis of six tenure groups in Kumasi, we have shown that there are more differences between the households according to whether they have exclusive use of services than whether they own or rent. As in Latin America, owners do tend to be better off and more generously housed than most tenants, although the extended family system gives them large households and the consequent reduction in per capita income. The group we call renters are remarkably similar to owners and appear to find their tenure a valid alternative to owning even for the highest income groups. Renting as a residual tenure can be found among roomers – who are just a majority of households and include many of the poorest and least advantaged – but there is likelihood that many roomers have, or will one day have, a house of their own in their home village. As landlessness is virtually unknown in Ghana, the culture of poverty theory cannot be applied to roomers without major inaccuracies; indeed the owners of houses occupied by roomers are hardly better off than their tenants.

The variables related to wealth, ability to obtain land cheaply, and degree of urbanisation, do help to explain tenure choice. The application of discriminant analysis shows that the variables discussed by Gilbert (1983, 1987) are influential in tenure choice but there are also some characteristics of the houses themselves which are significant, especially those which separate the lower end of the 'market' from the upper. The evidence that access to services is increased as income increases illustrates that improvements in housing will probably only be achieved through economic development.

Policy-makers should note the polarisation of owners (exclusive) and roomers. Housing policies in Ghana and many other countries have attempted to turn ordinary low-income households into owners of self-contained apartments or bungalows. Evidence presented in this paper suggests that it would be easier to encourage roomers to become owners of compounds where services are shared and rental income is readily available than to try to intice them into the role of 'owner (exclusive)'.

REFERENCES

Abrams, C. (1964), *Man's Struggle for Shelter in an Urbanising World.* Cambridge, Massachusetts, MIT Press.

Asabere, P.K. (1981), 'The Price of Urban Land in a Chiefdom: Empirical Evidence on a Traditional African City, Kumasi'. *Journal of Regional Science*, November :329-39.

Brokensha, D. (1966), *Social Change at Larteh, Ghana.* Oxford, Clarendon Press.

Datta, G. and Meerman, J. (1980), *Household Income or Household Income per capita in Welfare Comparisons*, World Bank Staff Working Paper No. 378. Washington D.C., The World Bank.

Doling, J.F. (1973), 'A Two-Stage Model of Tenure Choice in the Housing Market', *Urban Studies*, 10(2): 199-201.

Edwards, M. (1982), 'Cities of Tenants: Renting among the Urban Poor in Latin America', in A. Gilbert *et al., Urbanisation in Contemporary Latin America.* Chichester, John Wiley.

Fapohunda, E. (1987), 'The Nuclear Household Model in Nigerian Public and Private Sector Policy: Colonial Legacy and Social-Political Implications', *Development and Change*, 18(2): 281-94.

Ghana, Republic of (1963), 'The Rent Act', Act 220.

—— (1975), 'The Public Servants' Housing Loans Scheme Decree', NRC Decree 319.

—— (1979), 'Public Servants' (Control of Provision of Bungalows) Decree', AFRC Decree 34.

Gilbert, A.G. (1983), 'The Tenants of Self-Help Housing: Choice and Constraint in the Housing Markets of Less Developed Countries'. *Development and Change*, 14(3): 449-77.

— (1987): 'Latin America's Urban Poor: Shanty Dwellers or Renters of Rooms?' *Cities*, (February): 43-51.

Gilbert, A.G. and Ward, P.M. (1982), 'Residential Movement among the Poor: The Constraints on Housing Choice in Latin American Cities', *Transactions of the Institute of British Geographers*, 7: 129-49.

— (1985), 'Housing, the State and the Poor: Policy and Practice in Latin American Cities' Cambridge, Cambridge University Press.

Jibir, S.D. (1985), 'Housing Provision and Housing Needs in Abuja, Nigeria', Unpublished M.Phil Dissertation, University of Newcastle upon Tyne.

Malpezzi, S., *et al.* (1985), *Housing Demand in Developing Countries*, World Bank Staff Working Papers No. 733, Washington, D.C., The World Bank.

Malpezzi, S. *et al.* (1988), 'Measuring the Costs and Benefits of Rent Control: A Case Study Design'. Draft Report, Urban Development Division, The World Bank, Washington D.C.

Malpezzi, S. and Rydell, C.P. (1986), *Rent Control in Developing Countries: A Framework for Analysis*, World Bank Discussion Paper, Report No. UDD-102. Washington, D.C, Water Supply and Urban Development Department, The World Bank.

Malpezzi, S. and Tewari, V.K. (1987), *Costs and Benefits of Rent Control in Bangalore, India*. Washington, D.C, Operations and Research Division, Water Supply and Urban Development Department, The World Bank.

Mayo, S.K. *et al.* (1982), *Informal Housing in Egypt*. Washington, D.C, Abt Associates.

Mayo, S.K. *et al.* (1986), 'Shelter Strategies for the Urban Poor in Developing Countries', *World Bank Research Observer*, (Summer): 183-203.

Peil, M. (1976), 'African Squatter Settlements — A Comparative Study'. *Urban Studies*, 13(1): 155-66.

Peil, M. and Sada, P.O. (1984), *African Urban Society*. London, John Wiley.

Rutter, A.F. (1971), 'Ashanti Vernacular Architecture', in P. Oliver (ed.) *Shelter in Africa*. London, Barrie and Jenkins.

SAS (1986), *SUGI Supplemental Library User's Guide*, Cary, NC, SAS Institute.

Sanjek, R. (1982), 'The Organisation of Households in Adabraka: Towards a Wider Comparative Perspective', *Comparative Studies in Society and History* (Jan): 57-103.

Schildkrout, E. (1978), *People of the Zongo, The Transformation of Ethnic Identities in Ghana*. Cambridge, Cambridge University Press.

Schlyter, A. (1987), 'Commercialisation of Housing in Upgraded Squatter Areas: The Case of George, Lusaka, Zambia', *African Urban Studies*, 2(3): 287-97.

Schreckenbach, H. (1982), *Construction Technology for a Tropical Developing Country*. Eachborn, Deutsche Gesellschaft fur Technische Zusammenarbeit (GTZ) GmbH.

Storey, D. *et al.* (1987), *The Performance of Small Firms*. London, Croom Helm.

Tipple, A.G. (1984), 'Towards a Culturally Acceptable Housing Strategy: The Case of Kumasi, Ghana'. Ph.D thesis, University of Newcastle upon Tyne.

— (1986), 'A Revolution in Property Rights (Ghana)'. *West Africa* 27th January, 179-80.

— (1987), *The Development of Housing Policy in Kumasi, Ghana, 1901 to 1981: With an Analysis of the Current Housing Stock*. Newcastle upon Tyne, Centre for

Architectural Research and Development Overseas, University of Newcastle upon Tyne.

—— (1988), *The History and Practice of Rent Control in Kumasi, Ghana.* Water Supply and Urban Development Department, Discussion Paper No. 102, The World Bank, Washington D.C.

Tipple, A.G. and Willis, K.G. (1988), 'Costs and Benefits of Rent Control in Kumasi, Ghana' World Bank Draft Working Paper, Washington, D.C.

Turner, J.F.C. (1968), 'Housing Priorities, Settlement Patterns and Urban Development in Modernising Countries'. *Journal of the American Institute of Planners* (November): 354-63.

—— (1976), *Housing by People: Towards Autonomy in Building Environments.* London, Marion Boyars.

United Nations (1979), *Review of Rent Control in Developing Countries.* New York, Department of International Economic and Social Affairs.

Wilks, I. (1966), 'Aspects of Bureaucratisation in Ashanti in the 19th Century'. *Journal of African History,* 7(2): 215-32.

—— (1967), 'Ashanti Government', in D. Forde & P. Kaberry (eds.), *West African Kingdoms in the Nineteenth Century.* London, Oxford University Press.

—— (1975), *Asante in the Nineteenth Century.* Cambridge, Cambridge University Press.

Willis, K.G. (1987), 'Discriminant Analysis', in C.S. Yadav (ed.) *Models in Urban Geography, Part II (Mathematical),* Perspectives in Urban Geography Vol. 4-B. New Delhi, Concept: 629-45.

Willis, K.G. and Tipple, A.G. (1988), *Effects of Rent Control: An Analysis of Impact on Low-Income Households in Kumasi (Ghana),* Working Paper Series No. 6, Department of Town and Country Planning, University of Newcastle upon Tyne.

9

HOUSEHOLDS AND THEIR HOUSING IN OAXACA MEXICO: The View from the Bottom

EARL W. MORRIS, MARY WINTER and ARTHUR D. MURPHY

THE THEORETICAL FRAMEWORK

The theoretical scheme used in this paper at the microsocial level of the household is based on an approach developed since the beginning of the 1940s in the study of household behaviour with respect to housing and residential mobility. The early use of the approach in sociology began with the publication of a number of papers on "maladjustment to the family home" by Riemer (1943, 1945, 1947). It was from those papers that the idea was derived that a disjunction (in Riemer's words, maladjustment) between a household and its housing is an appropriate topic for serious theoretical sociological work. This section of the paper is based heavily on Morris *et al.*, (1990).

Values as a useful concept in the explanation of the housing behaviour of households was shown by Cutler (1947) and Beyer *et al.*, (1955). Although it received little theoretical attention in the sociology of housing since those introductory efforts, the concept is an implicit part of the current approach.

Rossi (1955) conceptualised residential mobility as a process of adjustment between a household's current housing and changes in its housing needs. The changing needs were derived from life-cycle changes. An important concept from that work was the idea that it is not so much the objective housing that matters but rather whether the housing meets the household's needs. That idea, along with Riemer's "maladjustment" foreshadowed the concept of normative deficit discussed below.

Additional important concepts were introduced by Foote *et al.*,

(1960). The title of their work suggests its main conceptual contribution, the idea that there are constraints that limit a household's ability to freely make housing choices.

The role of satisfaction as an intervening concept between housing conditions and the propensity to engage in housing adjustment behaviour was introduced by Rossi but further developed by Speare (1974). Chi and Griffin-Wulff (1980) and Griffin-Wulff and Chi (1980) showed the usefulness of the concept of satisfaction in Latin American housing. Brown and Moore (1970) demonstrated the importance of viewing housing adjustment behaviour as a decision-making process that involves the decision (among others) whether to move or to make changes in the current dwelling.

The notion that housing needs can fruitfully be defined in terms of cultural norms and the inclusion of the concept of the normative housing deficit as the condition that motivated housing-adjustment behaviour were developed by Morris and Winter (1975, 1978, 1985).

A brief summary of the approach is the following:

> When a family's housing does not meet the norms a deficit exists. If the family is aware of the deficit and feels that it is important, they will be dissatisfied. Dissatisfaction, in turn, produces a propensity to remove the deficit. Given such a propensity, the family would choose between alternative adjustment behaviours: moving to a new residence, or altering or adding to the current dwelling; Constraints may inhibit perception of deficits, appearance of dissatisfaction, development of an adjustment propensity, or completion of adjustment behaviours (Morris and Winter, 1985).

A deficit can be removed either by changing the housing (adjustment) or changing the norms (adaptation). Likewise, a deficit can be created by a change in the housing or a change in the norms relevant to the current housing. There are conditions under which the constraints are so severe that adjustment behaviour is not possible. In that case the household is likely to engage in adaptation by (1) altering its version of the norms, (2) altering the role or demographic composition of the household, or (3) removing constraints through investment in material of human capital. If they are unwilling or unable to make those adaptations they are likely to be motivated to engage in social or political action to alter the general situation. This is particularly likely to occur when a significant proportion of others in similar circumstances become aware of the similarity of their circumstances and their unwillingness to adapt.

Housing Adjustment and the Response Types

Until now the housing adjustment literature contains no direct reference to conceptualisations related to housing and disasters such as those reported by of Bolin and Trainer (1977). It seems clear to us, however, that the notion of three response modes can be applied to routine housing behaviour as well as to post-disaster behaviour. When a household seeks to provide itself with housing it can do so with differing combinations of inputs from autonomous, kin, and institutional sources.

Households within a society can be seen to differ in their preferences for, ability to command, and ability to implement routine inputs from the three sources during the housing adjustment process. Societies can be seen to differ in their normative, organisational, and resource structures that prescribe and constrain the use of the three modes.

Households and Housing Adjustment

One of the main responsibilities of the household is the psychological nurture of its members. The household's ability to do so under trying circumstances is an important element in the response of the household to transitions in the life cycle. The dwelling serves as the centre for that nurturing as well as all the other aspects to household life. As a result, the dwelling takes on meaning far beyond what its sheltering function would suggest.

Over the life cycle of the household there is a progression of housing needs that results from the interplay of norms and standards with the composition of the household. Superimposed on that progression is a stream of resources and a historical progression of the social, political, and economic climate of the society. Policy making at the societal or city level needs to respond to the current and more importantly to the evolving balances among (1) the life-cycle composition of the population of the city or the nation, (2) the life-cycle composition of specific areas of the cities and the nation, (3) the social and economic levels of development of the cities and the nation, and (4) the processes of change occurring in each.

The main policy goal of households as they engage in the housing-adjustment process is to maintain housing conditions within acceptable limits as defined by the cultural norms of the society and the household's own norms. The household's norms and preferences as well as its ability to attain those standards are strongly affected by the current level of the household's resources. Realistically, many households are unable to do anything about their housing at particular times because of constraining factors.

There are five classes of constraints: (1) resource constraints including money, skills, and the like, (2) market constraints including prices and supplies of housing, materials, land, and financing, (3) household organisational constraints including the ability to marshal resources, make decisions, and implement them, (4) predispositions or psychological dimensions of the household similar to the personality of the individual (e.g. apathy, achievement motivation, and the like), and (5) discrimination (Morris and Winter, 1985).

When the constraints are severe, adaptive, rather than adjustive, techniques are necessary. Adjustive techniques involve changes in the housing situation; adaptive techniques involve changes in the household itself. The main adaptive techniques include (1) changing the household's norms and preferences to make them less demanding (Morris and Winter, 1985), (2) reorganising the household to produce a more effective assignment or roles, (3) reconstituting the household by sending some members elsewhere or bringing in new members (Morris, 1977), and (4) increasing or improving the material and non-material resources available to the household.

It is important to take cognisance of the priority of some other concerns (food, for example) over housing. Expenditure on housing often is postponed during times of scarce resources when most of the household's resources are used for food. Then, in better times, a portion will be diverted to housing improvement. Therefore, competing needs serve as an additional set of constraints on housing behaviour. This is one of the points at which the concept of values enters the analysis. Households differ in the importance they grant to housing relative to other life domains and therefore differ in the threshold at which resources are diverted to and from housing.

Resources available to the household include income, wealth, skills, and information. The ways in which such resources are developed for use in meeting the household's needs differ among households. They can be obtained by (1) using the time of household members to obtain wages, (2) using the monetary resources of the household for investments which presumably would yield gains, (3) by receiving them as transfers from kin, (4) by transfers from other households, and (5) transfers from governmental programmes.

THE EMPIRICAL ANALYSIS

Much more work has been done on the development of the theoretical analysis for this paper than on the empirical analysis. Therefore, the empirical analysis presented in this section explores only a small portion of the theory as it applies to Oaxaca. In addition to the survey data presented in the tables given below we make use a some of the ethnographic data we have gathered on household survival strategies and on their housing behaviour and attitudes. Other empirical analyses have and will explore other parts of the theory and will be published elsewhere.

The Data

The data for this analysis were gathered during 1987 in the city of Oaxaca in Mexico, as a part of the project, "A Decade of Change in Oaxaca, 1977-1987". The overall purpose of that project, funded by the National Science Foundation, is to assess the effects of the macroeconomic changes in Mexico and in Oaxaca in the past 10 years on a sample of Oaxacan households. Specific purposes of the project include the purposes of the present paper.

The sample for the 1987 study is a two stage cluster sample of the city of Oaxaca de Juarez. The first stage consisted of a random sample of the blocks within each of the 54 fiscal sectors of the city. The second stage was a systematic sample of the approximately 3600 households living on the blocks selected. Approximately 800 of the occupied dwellings of the 3600 households were selected for interviewing. Accounting for ineligible households (those with a male head without a spouse), refusals, sickness, and absence it was expected that interviews would be completed with about 500 households. Because the completion rate was higher than anticipated, interviews have been completed with about 600 households. In each of these households, an interview was completed with the females household head or co-head; interviews have been completed with 425 male heads, as well.

The interviews were conducted by a team of Mexican interviewers who received approximately 10 hours of training prior to commencement of the interviewing. Each interview lasted approximately one hour with a range from about 30 minutes to around two hours.

The Analysis

The analysis begins with noting the similarities and differences between housing norms and preferences for single-family home ownership in the U.S. and in Oaxaca. Then we examine the current housing and compare with the U.S. Finally, we present a series of tables showing the sources of assistance with building and sources of financing.

Norms and Preferences

The norms and preferences of Oaxacan couples (Table 9.1) are even more demanding of single-family dwellings and home ownership than are the norms and preferences of U.S. couples. About 99 per cent of wives and 97 per cent of husbands report that the appropriate tenure for the typical Oaxacan family is ownership not rental. About 97 per cent of wives and 96 per cent of husbands say that ownership is best for their family. Both norms and preferences for home ownership are nearly universal in favouring home ownership. The percentages in the U.S. are substantially lower perhaps averaging below 90 per cent for both.

TABLE 9.1: Percentage with Home Ownership and Single-Family Housing Conditions, Norms and Preferences

Norms	Wife	Husband
Home ownership	99	97
Single-family dwelling	100	99
Preferences		
Home ownership	97	96
Single-family dwelling	99	98
Current Conditions	Couple	
Home owners	70	
Single-family dwelling	87	

The norms and preferences for single-family dwellings are also nearly unanimous with 100 per cent of wives and 99 per cent of husbands favouring the single-family dwelling (detached or attached) for the average Oaxaca household. In terms of preferences, about 99 per cent of wives and 98 per cent of husbands say that the single-family dwelling is best for themselves. These percentages are likewise substantially lower in the U.S.

Current Housing

With respect to current housing about 70 per cent of the couples own their own residence (a small percentage of them do not own the land on which the dwelling sits because the dwelling may be located on *ejido* land (Ejidos are communally owned lands that are not legally permitted to be subdivided for housing) or is built on land owned by the parents). About 87 per cent live in single-family detached or attached dwellings. Higher percentages are owners and higher percentages live in single-family dwellings in Oaxaca than in the U.S. The figures in the U.S. in similar sized cities are about 60 per cent owners and 67 per cent single-family.

The average number of rooms in the Oaxacan dwelling is 3.7, well below the average for U.S. which is not quite double that of Oaxaca. The equality of the dwellings is much lower than in the U.S. by any reasonable measure.

The data require the analyst to separate questions of size and quality of housing from questions of ownership and type of dwelling. In reality, it is the number of rooms in a dwelling and the quality of the dwelling that are expensive. It is obvious from these data that home ownership and single-family dwellings are well within the reach of even the poorest Oaxaca families. This is not the customary way to think of housing among American housing experts.

Kin and Non-kin Sources of Assistance

The story begins with whether the respondents own or rent the dwelling they live in (Table 9.1) because renters would nor be involved in financing or construction of the current dwelling. About 70 per cent of the sample households own their dwellings. The remainder pay rent or use the dwelling free (the latter are very rare).

Then we asked the owners of dwellings if they own the land (Table 9.2). There were 30 households (7 per cent) who own the dwelling but do not own the land; none of them pay cash rent for the land. Of those 30 (Table 9.3), one household does not know who owns the land, relatives own the land for three of them, an official entity owns the land of six households, and twenty households say the land is owned by "others". Our interpretation is that the latter 26 most likely are lots located in either government housing projects or *ejidos*.

TABLE 9.2: Percentage Distribution of Tenure of Land Among Owners of Dwellings

Own land	92.9
Free rent	7.1
Total	100.0
N	(424)

TABLE 9.3: Owner of Land Among Those Who Use Land Free

(Percentage)

Not known	3
Relative	10
Official entity	20
Other	67
Total	100.0
N	(30)

We asked those who do not own their land how they came to own the dwelling (Table 9.4). Three received it as a gift (they are the ones who live on land owned by relatives). One of them bought the dwelling already built and sitting on the land. There were 25 who either built the dwelling or had it built.

TABLE 9.4: How Owners Came to Own Dwelling Among Those Use Land Free

(Percentage)

Gift from previous owner	10
Built it or had it built	83
Purchased it	7
Total	100.0
N	(30)

Next, we asked about borrowed money among those 25 households who built a dwelling on land they do not own (Table 9.5). Only 17 per cent borrowed any money. The source of borrowed money (Table 9.6)

for the four cases who borrowed was an official institution (generally a government agency) for two households and a private individual for the other two.

TABLE 9.5: Was Any Money Borrowed to Build Dwelling Among those Who Use Land Free and Built Dwelling (Percentage)

No	83
Yes	17
Total	100.0
N	(25)

TABLE 9.6: Who Borrowed From of Those Who Use Land Free and Built Dwelling (Number Who Used Each Source From Among the 4 Cases Who Borrowed Money)

Bank	0
Official institution	2
Private individual	2
Friend	0
Compadre	0
Relative	0
Other	0
N	4

The source of labour for building the dwelling for those who built on land they do not own (Table 9.7) is predominantly members of the immediate household. There were 9 households who hired labour to work on housing construction but only one each received help from relatives and friends.

TABLE 9.7: Sources of Help for Building of Those Who Use Land Free and Built Dwelling (Number of Households, Households may Use More Than One)

Household members	15
Relatives	1
Compadres	0
Friends	1
Hired labour	9
N	11

Perhaps more interesting are the majority of households own both the dwelling and the land (Table 9.8). About 24 per cent obtained the land with the dwelling already built. Most of them bought it but a small percentage inherited or received the dwelling and land as a gift.

TABLE 9.8: How was Dwelling Obtained Among Those Who Own Dwelling and Land (Per cent)

Bought land with dwelling on it	19.6	
Inherited land with dwelling on it	4.3	
Received as a gift with dwelling on it	0.3	
Subtotal		24.2
Bought land and built dwelling	66.3	
Inherited land and built dwelling	7.7	
Received as a gift and built dwelling	1.8	
Subtotal		75.8
Total		100.0
N		(392)

About three-fourths of the current home owners, however, built or had someone built their house on land they owned. Two-thirds of them purchased the land and then built. A sizeable proportion however either inherited or received the land as a gift.

With respect to borrowed money for construction (Table 9.9) a little less than 40 per cent borrowed money. The main source of financing (Table 9.10) is private individuals. These would be individuals who are in the business of lending money but are not connected with a formal lending institution. Perhaps they are the next thing to loan sharks in some cases. They are more likely to be individuals who receive interest on money outside of formal channels perhaps to avoid taxes. The second most common source is relatives with just under a quarter. The only other significant source is official institutions.

TABLE 9.9: Money Borrowed to Buy Land Among Those Who Built Dwelling (Per cent)

Paid cash	61.5
Borrowed money	38.5
Total	100.0
N	(296)

TABLE 9.10: Source of Borrowed Money to Buy Land of Those Who Built Dwelling on Owned Land and Borrowed Money to Buy Land (Per cent, Households May Use More Than One Lender)

Bank	0.9
Official institution	15.0
Private individual	55.8
Friend	1.8
Compadre	0.9
Relative	23.9
Other	2.7

The sources of labour (Table 9.11) mainly include members of the household (over 50 per cent) and hired labour (nearly 50 per cent). Very small proportions received help from relatives (7 per cent) and compadres (1 per cent) and none received help from friends.

TABLE 9.11: Source of Labour to Build Dwelling Among Those Who Own Land (Per cent, Households May Use More Than One Source)

Household members	53.2
Relatives	7.1
Compadres	1.3
Friends	0.0
Hired labour	48.8

Conclusions of the Analysis

There are two main conclusions from the empirical analysis. The first is that the preference of Oaxacan household for home ownership and single-family dwellings is even stronger than it is in similar sized cities in the U.S. The second is that Oaxacan households receive very little assistance from the government, and very little from kin (both real and fictive) and friends in the purchase and construction of their housing.

CONCLUSIONS

The differences between housing in Oaxaca and in U.S. cities is that often in Oaxaca the final form or tenure (ownership or rental) and the type of dwelling (single family or not) are determined soon after the household is formed and then the size and quality of the dwelling are added incrementally as the household is able tot afford increases in one or the other. In the U.S. it is more typical to rent smaller, lower quality housing early and then become a home owner later on. This difference is related to the difference in rates of residential mobility between Oaxaca and the U.S. which has a higher mobility rate. The move to an owned dwelling later on requires a residential move that is often avoided by Oaxacan households.

Oaxacan households are much more likely to postpone household formation for a time after marriage than are U.S. households. This pattern, to some extent, is a substitute for the U.S. pattern of rental early in the life of the household. It appears that first-time home ownership comes earlier in the life-cycle of Oaxacan households than it does in U.S. households. In other words, the time spent in rental is longer for U.S. households than the time spent in the parents' home for Oaxacan households.

It is notable however that the propensity to move among Oaxaca families is rather high with 21 per cent who have at least thought about moving and 8 per cent who have definite plans to move within a year (according to the husband). This is considerably less than the propensity to make alterations or additions to the dwelling. About 58 per cent have at least thought about it and 26 per cent have definite plans to alter or add to the dwelling within a year.

What can we say about housing policy based on the theoretical and empirical analyses? First, and most obviously, any policy based on rental or apartment housing will not be satisfying to the bulk of the families of Oaxaca. Of course, one can always find a small percentage of families who will accept nearly any kind of housing that has or will be invented. But the overwhelming majority of Oaxaca's families want single-family home ownership and most of them want detached single-family homes.

These ideas, when placed in comparative perspective, indicate that the latter come before considerations of size and quality of the dwelling. These can be added later in Oaxaca. It would not be reasonable to think that high quality rental projects could be used in Oaxaca to provide housing during early phases of the life cycle until money can be saved to buy high quality housing. The same goes for number of rooms.

The main technique likely to be used to improve quality of the dwelling by the individual household is alteration of the current dwelling. The current dwelling is very likely to have been built by or for the current occupants. Techniques for increases in the size of the dwelling to be used include both additions to the current dwelling and moving to a different dwelling. The low mobility rate and high rate of alterations and additions in Oaxaca may be due as much to differences in the vacancy rates in appropriate types and quality of housing between the U.S. and Oaxaca as to a cultural difference in preferences for mobility.

These conclusions provide a picture of the Oaxacan household as out in the open exposed to the ravages of the national economic crisis with little assistance from sources outside the household. That they manage to meet most of their needs including home ownership attests to the strength and creativity of the Mexican household as a major economic component of the nation.

The connection back to the theoretical analysis can be made by noting that the norms prescribing home ownership in Oaxaca are very strong. Therefore, households seeking a home will make great sacrifices to do so. Because quality and size of the dwelling is less important and can be added later to the basis dwelling households do not experience or perceive that they have deficits in terms of quality and quantity aspects of their housing until they have achieved their goal of home ownership. In the U.S. it is different in that households are more likely to rent than to compromise their quality and space standards.

There are market situations that explain a portion of the difference. In the United States there is an active, fluid, relatively inexpensive rental market. There is no such market in Oaxaca especially in that rental is relatively expensive there. The problem with that interpretation is that the market situation is at least partially determined by demand and it appears that Oaxacans are less likely to exert demand for rental housing than are Americans aside from supply considerations. In other words tastes (cultural norms) probably differ. We conclude that the housing adjustment approach is as appropriate for understanding housing in Oaxaca as it is for Omaha and can be fruitfully used in comparative analysis.

REFERENCES

Beyer, G.H. *et al.* (1955), *Houses are for People: A Study of Home Buyer Motivations.* Ithaca, NY, Housing Research Centre Publication 3, Cornell University.

Bolin, R. and Trainer, P. (1977), 'Modes of Family Recovery Following Disaster: A Cross-National Study. In E.L. Quarantelli (ed.), *Disasters: Theory and Research*, Beverly Hills, CA, Sage Publications : 234-247.

Brown, L.A. and Moore, E.G. (1970), The Intra-Urban Migration Process: A Perspective; *General Systems*, 15: 109-122.

Chi P.S.K. and Griffin, M.D. (1980), 'Social Indicators for Measuring Residential Satisfaction in Marginal Settlements in Costa Rica'. *Social Indicators Research*, 8: 453-465.

Cutler, V. (1947), *Personal and Family Values in the Choice of a Home*. Agricultural Experiment Station Bulletin 840 Ithaca, NY, Cornell University.

Foote, N.N. *et al.* (1960), *Housing Choices and Constraints*. New York, McGraw-Hill.

Griffin-Wulff, M.D. and Chi, P.S.K. (1980), 'Residential Satisfaction and the Propensity to Move: An Analysis of Potential Movers from Marginal Settlements in Costa Rica'. *Singapore Journal of Tropical Geography*, 1:16-22.

Morris, E.W. (1977, 'Mobility, Fertility, and Residential Crowding'. *Sociology and Social Research*, 61: 363-379.

Morris, E.W. and Winter, M. (1975), 'A Theory of Family Housing Adjustment'. *Journal of Marriage and the Family*, 37: 79-88.

— (1978), *Housing, Family and Society*. New York, John Wiley.

— (1985), 'Housing'. In D.D. Dillman and D.J. Hobbs (eds.), *Rural Society in the U.S.: Issues for the 1980s*. Boulder, CO, Westview: 196-204.

— (1985), The Microsociology of Housing. Paper Presented at the Annual Meeting of the Midwest Sociological Society.

Morris, E.W. *et al.* (1990), 'Adjustment, Adaptation, Regeneration and the Impact of Disasters on Housing and Households'. *Housing and Society*, 17: 1-26.

Riemer, S. (1943), 'Sociological Theory of Home Adjustment'. *American Sociological Review*, 8: 272-278.

— (1945), 'Maladjustment to the Family Home'. *American Sociological Review*, 10: 642-648.

— (1947), 'Sociological Perspectives on Home Planning'. *American Sociological Review*, 12: 155-159.

Rossi, P.H. (1955), *Why Families Move*. Glencoe, Free Press: 11.

Speare, A., Jr. (1947), 'Residential Satisfaction as an Intervening Variable in Residential Mobility'. *Demography*, 11: 173-188.

PART III

SOLUTIONS

10

THIRD WORLD SHELTER POLICY: Solutions and Problems for Housing the Poor

CHARLES L. CHOGUILL

Over the past 40 years, there has been an enormous increase in the level of urbanisation in the Third World. Whereas in 1950, 16 per cent of the population of these countries lived in urban areas, at present the level is over twice this rate (Lughod, 1977). In 1950, 38 per cent of the world's urbanised population resided in cities within the Third World. By 1980, the United Nations estimates that this figure had risen to 54 per cent and by 2000, it is projected that two-thirds of all urban population will be in the cities of the poorer nations of the world (UN, 1989).

The results of this massive growth have been profound. Whereas large cities in developed countries, such as New York and London, have stable to declining populations, in such cities as Lagos, Bandung, Nairobi, Bogota and Karachi, growth rates rise to over seven per cent per annum. Such growth results in high levels of urban unemployment and underemployment, extreme pressures upon urban services and infrastructure, congestion, pollution and significant shortfalls in the provision of housing for these new urban residents.

Not surprisingly, most governments have attempted to cope with these problems by a variety of means. It is the approaches and efforts that have been made towards squatters and slums, or the more all-embracing term of shanty towns, that is the focus of the present paper. There are perennial housing shortages in Third World cities and much of the housing stock that does exist is inadequate. In recent years, this problem, or more accurately, this set of problems, has received increasing attention from governmental authorities. Over time, their approaches to these problems have changed dramatically, and it is the reasons for these changes, as well as the key issues involved in various urban-based development projects that comprise the paper.

THE CULTURE OF POVERTY

Traditionally economists have given fairly low priority to housing issues in the national development planning process because this sector was considered to be unproductive. Instead, investment priorities were given to industrial investment, energy generation and transport, sectors which were viewed as growth-generating and hence able to "pay for themselves" over time.

In the 1960s, a change began to take place in a number of countries. In part, no doubt this was due to the high visibility of urban housing problems in Third World cities. When over half of a city was comprised slums and squatter settlements as was the case at that time in Abidjan, Bogota, Dakar, Ankara, Accra, Rabat, Donala, Lome, Ibadan, Addis Ababa and Mogadishu (World Bank, 1975), it was inevitable that politicians and government administrators could not avoid seeing the extent of the problem.

In addition, however there appears to have been another source of this recognition and this was the theoretical debate that was going on in the academic world over the causes and policy implications of such apparent poverty. Among social analysts, theories are frequently in conflict, based as they are on different perspectives, with varying assumptions and conflicting values. Normally, the outside world takes little notice of such debates perhaps feeling that if they are confined to the ivory towers of academia they can cause little lasting harm in the real world. Yet the 1960s were unusual in the sense that such arguments were not only noticed but actually had an impact upon government policy. In the United States, for example, efforts were being made not only to find solutions for domestic poverty through President Kennedy's New Frontier programmes and President Johnson's efforts with the New Society, but also internationally through the Alliance for Progress and the Peace Corps. Although these efforts were, unfortunately, prematurely terminated by the escalation of America's involvement in the Vietnam Conflict, for a few short years, academics and government decision-makers in both developed and developing nations were brought together to seek solutions to some of the underlying social problems that existed in both sets of nations at that time.

One theoretical contribution which attracted attention was Lewis's (1951, 1961, 1966a) concept of the "culture of poverty". Lewis was an anthropologist at the University of Illinois who had carried out micro-studies of households and individuals first in Mexico and then in Puerto Rico and New York. Lewis was interested in determining how individuals at the very bottom of the economic pecking order viewed their position and the future that they saw for themselves and their children. According to Lewis, this culture of poverty played a positive role in the lives of the poor in that:

> ". . . It has a structure, a rationale and defence mechanism without which the poor could hardly carry on. In short, it is a way of life, remarkably stable and persistent, passed down from generation-to-generation along family lines. The culture of poverty has its own modalities and distinctive social and psychological consequences for its members. It is a dynamic factor which affects participation in the larger national culture and become a sub-culture of its own."

Although Lewis (1966b) himself was very careful to limit the application of this concept of the culture of poverty to certain kinds of societies, any such theory which incorporated such strong feelings of fatalism, helplessness, dependence and inferiority was, not surprisingly adopted by those who advocated a much more active role by the state in helping the poor to cope with these problems than had been previously done. The reason for this can be derived from Lewis's writings. In the United States, where Lewis suggested only a small proportion of the population could be classified into such a sub-culture, the suggested solution was "slowly to raise their level of living and incorporate them into the middle class. Wherever possible psychiatric treatment is prescribed." In Third World, where the numbers involved were very much greater, Lewis felt that this solution was not feasible (the local psychiatrists, he suggested, had all they could do coping with the growing middle class). In these more serious situations, change might only be achieved by radically restructuring society, redistributing wealth, reorganising the poor — in short, by revolution.

Governments in power seldom take kindly to talk of revolution. Hence Lewis's talk of restructuring society by revolutionary means coupled with the distressing spectacle of expanding shanty towns throughout the capital city was extremely persuasive in casting doubt upon the earlier economic argument concerning the unproductiveness of housing as an investment. Unfortunately, recognition that an argument is valid does not necessarily mean that a unique policy solution exists. Poor people must always live in poor countries: nations where resources to cure poverty are simply not available. Yet one obvious, although partial, solution to the shanty town situation in developing countries is to build houses for the poor. And if a government could build houses that were better than those in which the poor resided, a complementary policy of bulldozing, or more popularly, of "eradicating" shanty towns, seems an obvious addition to the solution. It was indeed unfortunate that some governments seemed far more concerned with eradicating than in building for the understandable reasons that it was cheaper. This argument concerning cost-effectiveness could be linked to another powerful argument concerning survival. If shanty towns represented a revolutionary threat to the *status quo* and to vested interests, as Lewis seemed to suggest, the bulldozer seemed a most effective weapon to head off the coming battle.

The Lewis arguments also had appeal to those governments who had little intention of doing anything for the poor as it provided an apparent reason for their inaction and to wealthy elites seeking justification for their own positions. After all, carried to its extreme the argument suggested that the poor were poor because they were poor and it was their own fault. Only an irresponsible government, it was argued, would spend scarce resources on such a group when the money could be spent on nation-building investment such as industry and transportation systems.

Even those governments which took their involvement in improving urban conditions seriously through the use of well-organised and thought out projects found themselves on the horns of a dilemma through the poverty trap. To the 1960s, most of the experience governments of Third World nations had in building houses was confined to that gained by constructing accommodation for the military and the nation's civil servants, groups that were inevitably given high priority by the military and the senior civil servants. Yet if houses for the poor were to be built at these standards, bankruptcy of the nation was an almost inevitable result. By working within the constraints of available resources, on the other hand, only a small, probably insignificant proportion of the poor could be served. In either case, it was unlikely that the poor would be able to pay the rents that would necessarily be charged for the houses that were to be constructed. Some governments tried to bridge the gap between the two extremes, usually by vascillation between the two policies, with the result being that they neither satisfied the housing needs of their urban population nor did they succeed in improving the housing stock within their nations.

A World Bank study (Grimes, 1976) has illustrated the types of problems that are likely to arise in policies designed to deliver finished units to the poor. The study presents a comparative analysis of the urban housing market in six cities: Ahmedabad, Bogota, Hong Kong, Madras, Mexico City and Nairobi. An interesting point to emerge from the analysis was that although the six nations involved represented quite a wide cross-section of income levels and different cultures, between one-third and two-thirds of the populations of these cities could not afford even the cheapest new public housing unit which was built for them. The salient points of this study are worth reviewing.

The study noted that the economic cost of the cheapest new dwelling unit produced by the public sector in the six cities in the early 1970s varied from a low of U.S.$570 in Madras for a 17.5 sq m single-family detached house to U.S. $3,005 in Mexico City for a 47.3 sq m single-family detached house, all values being assessed at 1970 prices. Within the terms of the analysis, economic cost was defined as without subsidy or profit and before financing costs. Despite the relatively modest costs achieved it was found that a significant proportion of the lowest income groups in each of the six cities could not afford such a house. Even by assuming that households would be willing to spend up to 2½ times their annual household income on housing — an assumption far more realistic in the economically advanced West than in the Third World — it was found that the median income for this group was below that threshold where one could hope to afford such a cheap house in all six of the cities studied. Even among the lowest 40 per cent of the income distribution, the median income was insufficient for such a house in Ahmedabad, Mexico City and Nairobi and only just sufficient in Madras.

Once more realistic assumptions were added to the illustrative cases, the conclusions became more depressing. If a ten per cent interest rate was added to the cheapest house for a repayment period over 25 years, even without a down payment, it was found that 68 per cent of households in Nairobi, 64 per cent in Ahmedabad, 63 per cent in Madras, 55 per cent in Mexico City and 47 per cent in Bogota could not afford it. Even in relatively wealthy Hong Kong, 35 per cent could not afford this cheapest house.

It would appear that escape from the culture of poverty through the construction and delivery of housing to the poor is, in most parts of the world, unrealistic. Even governments which wish to act in good faith and possess a genuine desire to upgrade the living standards of the poor in their countries are generally unable to accomplish such objectives by building houses. The resource requirements for such a venture are just too high. Obviously increasing incomes of the poor might make some positive contribution to this situation yet income and employment generation have proved even more expensive than the alternative of providing houses. What would seem to be required is some sort of comprehensive programme aimed at across the broad improvement of the living circumstances of the poor. Yet since these countries became independent, that has been the overall objective of the entire national planning process. So far it has proved only partially successful. Is there a cheaper way?

A RATIONAL APPROACH TO POVERTY

At about the same time that Lewis was publishing his theories two other analysts were drawing rather different conclusions about their own observations from lengthy fieldwork in Peru, conclusions which were to have far reaching implications for future urban projects aimed at assisting the poor. One was an expatriate British architect, John Turner, while the second was an American anthropologist, William Mangin.

They argued that the poor were just as rational as the middle and upper income classes in terms of a response to their situation but that middle class observers misinterpreted their motivation because of a culture gap. Although the followers of Lewis suggested that the tumble down shanty in a slum area was threatening evidence of social malaise, Turner and Mangin viewed the shack in quite a different light as a rational step on the way to self-improvement. Turner (1967) noted that such families who earned erratic incomes in an unstable economy viewed property as a primary means of security in much the same way as the middle and upper classes viewed insurance, banking services and access to credit. In rejecting Lewis's structural rigidity, he argued that if the poor could achieve geographical stability then, as they became fully urbanised, they could be expected over time as their circumstances improved to add to and improve their existing houses — their primary asset — whether it be by adding another room, a better roof or merely wooden window frames. As Turner noted, ordinary families in urbanising countries prefer to live in large unfinished houses than in small finished ones of the type delivered by government agencies. Yet, Turner (1976) noted, certain prerequisites must be met if this self-improvement is to take place:

> "Secure possession of land where they can live now is far more important to them than the promise of a modern house that may never materialise. But given the land and the right circumstances — that is, adequately located, properly planned, and with a secure title — experience has shown that development to contemporary standards will surely take place, even if slowly."

INCORPORATING SELF-HELP IN HOUSING POLICY THROUGH SITES AND SERVICES

It is apparent that a number of these points could be readily adapted into housing policy, and hence projects, by Third World governments and indeed they have been. Turner's advice is make land available on a secure tenure basis and to pretty well leave everything else to the householder. There should be no need to impose standards as it is likely to take some time for the poor to improve their house to such an extent as to meet them. Standards can transform an opportunity into a burden. In the meantime, deficiencies in housing are much easier to bear if they are due to the plan of the owner/builder rather than something imposed by an outside body.

One proposed way of obtaining such advantages was through the design of so-called "site and services" projects. Schemes of this kind involved the provision of tracts of urban land which were divided into plots and provided with basic supporting services. Title to the plots could be either sold or rented to those who wished to build their own houses on them.

The advantages of such schemes were seen to be not only for the residents but for governments as well. Site and services schemes were viewed as a very economic way of formally shifting the housing burden from government, which had not coped with it very well anyway, to the households in need of shelter who traditionally had been the key movers in the field. Furthermore, it was felt that the quality of living in such projects would lead to improvement in living standards over the unplanned shanty towns they were designed to replace. In addition, site and services schemes could be used as a justification for imposing restraints upon the growth of unplanned squatter settlements.

The concept of site and services projects received a tremendous boost in 1972 when the World Bank decided to support the development and improvement of shelter for the urban poor. McNamara (1975) the then President of the World Bank noted that such projects "stimulate self-help, and make it possible for the poor to house themselves in a viable, cohesive community with a minimum of public expenditure". Between 1972 and 1975, the Bank granted U.S. $ 65.2 million in credits and U.S. $ 41.1 million in loans to projects in Senegal, Nicaragua, India, Botswana, Jamaica, Tanzania, Zambia, Indonesia, El Salvador and the Republic of Korea (World Bank, 1975). By 1983, the Bank had funded more than 70 such projects (Cohen, 1983). As a result of the World Bank's decision, the funding available for such projects increased and the documentation on certain schemes, especially World Bank projects, became more widely available. In addition, the entire concept of site and services underwent a subtle but significant change which felt it looking very much like a component part of the World Bank lending system, complete with costs, benefit and its own jargon.

The first of these shifts concerned the viability to which the then President of the World Bank referred. World Bank shelter projects, as with projects in other sectors, were required to meet the principle of affordability. In operational terms this meant that project designers were to view the cost of housing as a variable which was to be reduced until it came within the reach of the target population. As it was assumed that the poor could not afford to spend more than 15 per cent of their household budgets on accommodation, some idea of the severity of this particular constraint can be seen.

Two other terms which entered site and services jargon courtesy of the World Bank were accessibility and replicability. Accessibility means that households within the prescribed range of incomes for which a project is designed actually gain entrance to it. Replicability means that the recipients should pay for the project with little or no subsidy from external sources. The aim of the project design is to have all three of these objectives converge, with affordability playing the role of the central issue (Keare and Ziménez, 1983).

The inclusion of such principles represented a significant departure from past government practice. Under earlier housing policy schemes, units have been built by government of its agencies and allocated to recipients. If the new householder could not afford the rents charged, frequently he might very well be forced to return to the very circumstances from which the government housing policy had "saved" him. As incomes were normally low and full cost economic rents inevitably high, such a mismatch was almost certain unless subsidies were included in the rental price on an almost permanent basis. In fact, Charles Abrams (1964), who wrote the definitive book on housing in the Third World for the early 1960s correctly felt that subsidies were probably an inevitable part of the housing situation under such conditions. With the entrance of the World Bank onto the scene, the principle of full cost recovery became all important. Government officials and academics alike readily adopted this World Bank principle of cost recovery, representing a distinct break with earlier practice.

Of course, this spread of the principle of cost recovery was not universal. Some governments maintained their past policies. In Malaysia for example, it was decided that rather than design shelter programmes intended to meet income constraints, a decision was made instead to build housing that met what was termed the "minimum socially desirable standard" (Asian Development Bank, 1985). Whereas on one level this was totally understandable, some suggested that it was the cause of one undesirable consequence. Since their socially desirable standard raised costs to exclude as much as one-half of the urban poor and since the money available for subsidies was limited even in such a relatively wealthy nation as Malaysia, the only possible alternative outcome was squatting and in Kuala Lumpur, for example, over 35 per cent of the population was listed as squatters and slum dwellers.

HOLDING DOWN COSTS

If cost recovery has become a central principle in the design of shelter projects for the urban poor, then it is not surprising that ways of reducing the various costs concerned with such projects have become increasingly important as well. Although interest in cost reduction is not strictly due to World Bank involvement, adoption of the concept of replicability reinforced the search for finding cheaper ways of doing things.

A central issue in this area is the problem of standards and it is not unlike the dilemma faced in Malaysia as noted above. The problem of setting standards is a long-standing one in most developing countries and in fact, standards currently in use frequently date back to colonial times and all too often reflect the present day standards in use the former coloniser. Although most analysts agree that standards of some sort are required for fire prevention, public health, structural safety and possibly aesthetics, too few apparently seem to realise that as standards rise, so too do costs. Whereas developed countries may well be able to afford high standards in construction and layout to achieve perfectly understandable aims, it does not necessarily follow that a Third World nation should adopt these Western standards which might be totally inappropriate to their own climatic, cultural or economic circumstances.

In an important analysis of the problem of setting shelter standards in Third World nations, Mabogunje *et al.*, (1978) assert that the official standards in most developing countries can be criticised on at least eight grounds. First, very few such standards are based upon local experience but are either a remnant of colonial days or even a later import from the developed world. Second, current housing standards encourage the over-exploitation of what few local resources do exist, such as timber and minerals. Third, official standards are frequently irrelevant to the local culture. Fourth, Western-based standards inevitably involved Western technology, such as mass production, prefabrication and industrialised-system technology, rather than utilising the most abundant local resource: labour. Fifth, inappropriate standards are responsible for the high cost of open market housing which is beyond the reach of most poor residents. Sixth, such rigid and inflexible standards are largely unenforceable. Seventh, the adoption of such standards has widened the gap between the rich and the poor, hence increasing social stratification. Finally, eighth, although the vast majority of Asians and Africans still live in rural areas, the standards adopted for these areas contain a strong urban bias due to their Western origin.

Once standards are adopted which reflect indigenous conditions, one would expect costs to drop. Yet even if these were to be done, very serious problems might be expected to remain. Take land as an example. Most developing countries have experienced sky-rocketing land prices as urbanisation has taken place. This rapid rise in land prices within such areas inevitably greatly increases the cost of compulsory purchase of land by public authorities for shelter projects. This problem arises largely because land serves a source of wealth, resulting in more importance being given to the exchange value of land that its use value. With fixed supplies of land and unstable currencies, such an outcome is an almost certain result of such economic forces.

Yet public authorities come very close to encouraging such economic outcomes by their own high standards of land consumption in project design. In low-income housing project, plot sizes are frequently larger than necessary as planners wish to avoid the potential criticism of building slums. There also seems to be a tendency for the land provision to be designed not for the low-cost structures being built at the time but for some imaginary standard twenty years in the future. As a result, too much land is used and land prices are bid up. Although the cost of land as a percentage of total housing cost per unit varies widely, it can be substantial. As Grimes (1976) has noted, "Cost breakdowns for middle- and low-income housing in selected cities — Ahmedabad, Hong Kong, Madras, Mexico City, Nairobi and Seoul — of developing countries demonstrate that land makes up 12 to 46 per cent of total cost for-single family public housing unit and from 2 to 15 per cent for multifamily units".

Another problem sometimes occurs if land standards are set too high. In central city areas, pressure from the poor on existing land resources is usually greater due to their understandable desire to be near the employment opportunities that exist at those points. Projects in such areas which provide excessive plot sizes are likely to find that the residents subdivide the plots themselves and rent or sell them to others. This is a particular danger where full economic costs are charged for the plots. The result is the types of over-crowding and possibly even slum creation that the authorities were attempting to replace.

The important point with respect to land is not just the size of the plot. Good locations and a secure title to the plot, whether it be in terms of a tenancy, a leasehold or outright ownership, are far more relevant. If these conditions can be met, on the assumption that the plot is of sufficient size to allow some expansion, then the progressive improvement anticipated by Turner and Mangin can be achieved.

Inappropriate standards are, of course, applied to far more areas of housing construction than land alone. Inevitably, if the standards of high-income countries are applied in poor nations the result contributes to the increase in housing costs, placing such shelter out of the reach of the less fortunate in that society. This is true of housing density standards, space per room constraints, occupancy rates and rules on lighting, ventilation and sanitation.

The most serious problems of all are probably caused by the various standards in force with respect to building materials. Mabogunje *et al.*, (1978) given an example of the effect of these constraints upon an ambitious housing project being carried out in Argentina as part of the 1974-1977 Three-Year Development Plan. It was proposed that the Government finance the construction of 510,000 houses. One component of this programme was to be directed to the poor, residents of shanty towns, boarding houses, inadequate dwellings and frontier areas among others. Unfortunately, the National Secretary of Housing and City Planning imposed rigid standards upon the materials which could be used in the construction and the finishes, covering twenty key items ranging from floors (paving tiles) to roof coverings (ceramic, concrete or mixed slabs), including kitchen counters (concrete 0.04 metres thick covered with ceramic tiles) and stoves (to have three burners with oven). It is suggested that these standards were at least in part responsible for the fact that by April 1975, fewer than 11,000 of these low-income houses had been completed.

Standards clearly have some impact upon the idea of cost recovery and in this area, the World Bank approach has had a positive impact. By viewing costs as a variable, the objective becomes one of determining which standards can be cut and of selecting the appropriate technology in order to achieve affordability. Thus, earlier approaches, which involved far more costly construction techniques, and hence resulted in the need for high levels of subsidies, reduced supply and involved undesirable rationing procedures which inevitably discriminated against the poor.

UPGRADING

An important part of this more recent approach to shelter provision within Third World cities concerns not only the allocation of serviced plots for new housing but the *in situ* improvement and upgrading of existing housing. Again, the influence of the early observations expressed by Turner and Mangin can be seen in the design of upgrading projects, with an emphasis, to use World Bank terminology, upon "progressive development".

Upgrading schemes are usually designed for areas of a city which are already built up, such as on the edges of central or commercial areas. The objective here is to transform areas which were frequently developed outside the legal system but which continue to provide residential areas which are convenient to employment opportunities and are popular with their residents. Rather than resort to total clearance, emphasis is directed to the installation of infrastructure — such as water and sewers, possibly to the rearrangement of at least some parts of the layout, to the extension of whatever social services may be available, to the legalisation of tenure and sometimes to the provision of financial and building assistance which could be used to improve houses and business premises.

Martin (1983) identifies four advantages of upgrading. First, it preserves existing economic systems and opportunities for the urban poor. Second, it preserves the low-cost housing stock already in existence at its present location. Third, it preserves the community structure and the safeguards that already exist for the family and the community group. Finally, the alternative, resettlement, is socially disruptive, usually occurs at a less favourable location, involves high commuting costs and reduces access to informal employment.

A very brief look at two such projects will give some idea of the range of components which can be included in this approach. The Kampung Improvement Programme in Indonesia began during the First Five Year Development Plan in 1969-74 as an attempt to improve neighbourhoods in Jakarta. Because of its initial successes, the scope of its content has been increased over time and the methods have also been applied to other cities (USAID, 1981). The programme has succeeded in providing minimum infrastructure to a large number of beneficiaries, including footpaths, secondary roads, surface drainage ditches, water supply systems and public standpipes, individual toilets (mainly pit privies and some community toilets) and rubbish collection facilities. Education and health facilities have also been built. These items have been provided at an investment of U.S. $59 per person in 1976 prices, which represents very good value compared to alternative approaches.

The second project is in Zambia and began in 1974 with partial funding from the World Bank. It aimed at absorbing marginal city population into a coherent urban services system. Beneficiaries received leasehold titles to land, and such services as piped water, paved roads, health clinics and in some cases, water-borne sewerage.

Despite delays in the implementation of certain social services and unexpected increases in costs, by 1981, the World Bank estimated that 19,916 squatter dwellings had been upgraded, exceeding the project target of 16,924 (Bamberger *et al.*, 1982).

Although this type of approach has been increasingly popular in recent years, unfortunately it has received relatively little attention from project evaluators outside the World Bank, particularly compared to the evaluation of somewhat more spectacular site and services projects. As Yeh (1981) has observed, existing case studies are essentially non-comparative, in part because of the diversity of settlement types which exist. The strengths of such an approach, however, appear to be clear-cut and given the potential economic advantage, it would be expected that upgrading should become increasingly popular as a way of improving existing shanty towns.

CAN IT ALL BE LEFT TO SELF-HELP?

Although policy initiatives based on self-help principles — site and services as well as slum up-grading — have become increasingly central to Third World governments' housing policies, certain criticisms of the concepts involved have been made. It would seem that self-help may be more appropriate in some countries than in others, more likely to succeed among higher economic classes than lower ones and more acceptable to certain cultures than to others. Considerable uncertainty, however, surrounds these criticisms, as unfortunately the data necessary to make a comprehensive evaluation of the approach does not exist. As already noted, a limited amount of information is available on World Bank projects and certain case studies of other efforts have appeared in various academic journals. In economic terms, none of these permit one to actually compare the costs involved in either site and services or slum upgrading projects with other progressive housing development that is taking place spontaneously in the informal housing sector in a cross-cultural context. On other grounds, the basis for analysis is even more speculative.

Some analysts suspect that in fact costs may be higher in official self-help schemes than in the unorganised ones. Crooke (1983) suggests that programmes of official agencies impose higher housing standards, and hence higher costs, than poor families would face outside such projects. Rodell (1983) argues that infrastructural standards can bring up the costs. This is because project planners have great difficulties in estimating affordability in projects such as these because the participants are buying incomplete rather than finished houses. The result is that infrastructure can be planned at too high a standard, thus inflating the cost to participants.

In site and services schemes in particular, there is a strong pressure among planners to impose standards of some sort. It is argued that if such development is done completely on a *laissez faire* basis, the result is likely to be little more than the kinds of slums that the planners are trying to replace. Yet obviously if one gives in to such caution, the result is likely to represent an increase, sometimes a significant one, in costs.

The location of site and services projects is another issue which has led to criticism of the concept. It is generally agreed that such projects must be located within easy access to employment opportunities. As most site and services project participants would be expected to find jobs either in the informal sector or the lower-paying parts of the formal sectors, it is important that accessibility to these jobs be maintained. They are usually found in the central areas of cities and if housing is not located near the jobs, increases in commuting cost might be expected to offset any savings from housing that might be planned.

Yet once official agencies become involved in such activities, to justify their effort the planning of large projects seems almost essential. The larger the project, the less the likelihood of finding adequate land near the city centres. Instead, peripheral locations are chosen and the link with the job market is broken. A likely outcome is that the poorer families for which the project may have been designed find it economically impossible to participate and their place is taken up by higher income households.

This problem of assuring that lower income participants can hold their places in such schemes is a particularly serious one. Although it is generally assumed that recipients of such plots will use them in accordance with the objectives of the project and build their own houses, it is frequently found that such plots are quickly sold, often to higher income families who might have been ineligible to buy them initially. Peattie (1982) draws attention to evidence from Kenya suggesting that this is particularly likely to take place if the project is a "successful" one. In the Rangit site and services project in Thailand, 800 of the 1,200 participants sold their plots in the first three years of the project (Rodell, 1983).

The self-help approach, so central to both site and services and slum upgrading projects, is a frequent victim of the progressive development process. Peattie (1982) notes that "to the degree that sites and services projects, 'rationalise' the building process by themselves supplying these skills and materials, a regressive substitution take place, in which project officials or substantial businessmen, normally drawn from the middle class, perform functions which previously provided wages for dozens of marginal entrepreneurs". Given the economic interdependence that exists within shanty town communities — Llyod (1979) cites examples of artisans producing cheap, low-quality goods for others like themselves, a woman laundering for her neighbours so that they can go out to work and a shanty town repairman who owes his status to the ownership of a hammer, spanner and nails. The introduction of outside entrepreneurs acts as a leakage to the internal multiplier which exists. If middle class businessmen gain a first foothold in such a community through the "formalisation" of self-help, it is the residents which suffer the economic loss both through higher costs of housing and infrastructure and lower incomes through lost employment opportunity.

The most serious shortcoming of this approach to project planning is its frequent inability to provide access to the poor for which it was originally designed. As with the other criticisms included here, this seems to most seriously affect site and services rather than slum upgrading because of the size, and hence cost, of projects of that type.

The entire idea of replicability, which has become so central to the more modern approaches to housing provision in the Third World not just in World Bank projects but in others as well, is at least in part to blame for this. To assure the prospect of cost-recovery the poor are excluded from such projects. After reviewing its own shelter projects in El Salvador, the Philippines, Senegal and Zambia, the World Bank concluded that such projects were affordable to families down to the 20th income percentile, and significantly, substantially lower through upgrading projects (Kearne and Pariss, 1982).

In another study (Swan *et al.*, 1983), it was acknowledged that the site and services approach:

> "Does, after all, place quite high demands on the families who are selected. They are called on to make serious long-term financial commitments (including a substantial down payment) and, as well, they must direct money (and often their own labour) into the completion and extension of the house. When a site and services

project is being implemented along with slum upgrading schemes, there is good justification for believing that the latter is more appropriately directed to the very poor whilst the former is addressed to the slightly more advantaged among the low-income groups."

The criteria used to select participants on such schemes use various measures to exclude the poorest members of society. In some cases, it is explicit in that the design of the project is geared to include certain income levels. For example, in the World Bank's El Salvador Sites and Services Project, partially as a result of a designed income range, participation probably extended down to between the 17th and 24th income percenticles although the majority were from the third, fourth and fifth income deciles (Kearne and Pariss, 1982). The Indian project in Kanpur was specifically designed for households with incomes between the 15th and 42nd percentiles (Swan *et al.*, 1983).

In other cases, the constraints which lead to exclusion can be more subtle. In the First Tanzanian National Site and Services Project, again financed by the World Bank, applicants for construction loans needed to build their own accommodation were required to have savings amounting to Tsh. 2,290 in order to qualify for money from the Tanzanian Housing Bank. As the average income of the low-income groups was no more than Tsh. 380 per month, this requirement was an almost insurmountable barrier for the poor (Siebolds and Steinburg, 1982).

To the poor such rigid entry barriers can appear to be even higher when external economic circumstances are taken into account. In the First Lusaka (Zambia) Site and Services Project, it was estimated in 1973 that families with a monthly income of 70 Kwacha could afford the project. As a result of a 10 per cent annual rate of inflation, this income level rose to 85 Kwacha and later to 120 Kwacha. To complicate matters further, the building material index rose from 100 to 135 per cent in the two years after December, 1974 (Bamberger *et al.*, 1982).

The selectivity that results from such financial constraints can be devastating to shanty town economies. Peattie (1982) argues that such projects tend to cream off the more established members of the working class leaving behind in the unorganised system those who are less successful. An advantage of the heterogeneous economic mix in such communities is that demand for goods and services tends to trickle down from the more successful to the less so. If the high income groups are removed from the community to participate in site and services projects, the result may be the creation of what Peattie refers to as a sharply defined underclass.

It is tempting to conclude that site and service-type projects at least might be more appropriate in higher income countries, particularly if full cost recovery is a primary component of such a programme. In nations with lower incomes and where projects are designed to actually reach the poorest members of society, it would seem that some sort of subsidies might be required.

Subsidies are, of course, a sticky issue. The World Bank's argument is a simple one. If a country subsidises a sector such as housing where demand for the sector's output almost always exceeds its supply, then the resources which might have been used to augment supply will instead be diverted to lowering the user's price of the existing supply. As resources are always short in a development situation, such a policy guarantees that demand always exceeds supply.

Part of the problem with subsidies is that almost always the existing subsidy distribution system in a developing country is aimed at assisting not the poor who need it desperately but the better off who need it only marginally. In the Lusaka Site and Services Project, the World bank found this to be the case as a very significant amount was spent by the Zambian Government on housing subsidies but the poorest 30 per cent of the employees in the central government, local government and parastatal sectors received only 1.8 per cent of the total subsidy while the top 10 per cent in terms of income received about 45 per cent of the subsidies (Bamberger *et al.*, 1982).

Within such circumstances, it is apparent that full cost recovery from all income groups is a preferred outcome to one which involves transfers of a regressive nature. And in fact, as a result, the Lusaka project became the first which participants were required to pay the full cost of on-site development and materials loans.

One cannot help but wonder, however, whether the Bank might not have taken a more liberal view had the subsidies worked in a more progressive manner, in effect transferring access to housing from the rich to the needy rather than the reverse? For it would seem that in the poorer nations of the world, such a transfer from one income group to another may continue to be necessary if the poor are to have access to formal sector housing and urban services.

In poor countries, the potential to be gained from transfers is obviously limited and therefore extreme care must be exercised to hold down project costs. From the evidence considered here, it is probable that slum upgrading programmes are more cost-effective than resettlement alternatives.

Greater reliance on self-help principles might be expected to be one such way by which costs can be held down. There is some evidence, however, which suggests that this approach may differ in effectiveness across culture as well as across income levels. Huque (1982) has concluded that in Bangladesh, for example, there is almost no evidence to show that there is a positive relation between duration of residence and self-improvement of housing, nor is there evidence that the absence of building codes and specifications made a difference in the ultimate housing standards which are achieved in low-income communities, nor does legal status of tenureship appear to have any relation with housing improvement. Could it be that what seemed to offer hope in poverty-stricken Bangladesh with a different culture? Why should it not be expected that real income levels, the structure of the local land market, the attitudes of government officials, the vigour with which the planning system is enforced and the influence of various interest groups would affect the receptibility of self-help principles in different ways in different parts of the Third World?

CONCLUSIONS

In this paper, an effort has been made to trace through the major policy influences and instruments which have had an effect upon Third World urban improvement programmes, particularly housing, over recent years. It has been a period of significant change. As noted, in the 1960s, those charged with housing responsibilities interpreted their task as one of building houses for the poor. The houses produced were too frequently inappropriate to the needs of the target population and were, unless generously subsidised, too expensive as well. Under the influence of the writings of Turner and Mangin, by the end of the decade, there began a gradual withdrawal of government involvement in housing provision — although admittedly, some governments never got started in the field — to a greater reliance on self-help principles. In terms of government housing policy, these ideas were translated into site and services schemes and slum-upgrading programmes, frequently with provision for fullcost recovery due to the enormous influence that the World Bank seems to have had in this area. Certain problems associated with the approach have been identified and considered within this paper (Burgess, 1982).

Has government gone too far in opting out of the direct involvement in the housing responsibility for the lower income members of society? What should government's role be?

In attempting to define the boundaries of government involvement in the shelter field, it is difficult not to agree with Payne (1977) who concluded that "the role of the public sector agencies should be conceived as providing those elements which people cannot provide by themselves". Yet this would seem to go considerably further in terms of involvement than many analysts would be prepared to accept. Most importantly, due to the extreme heterogeneity that exists within the Third World, it implies a more active role in some low-income nations than in the more fortunate. It has already been noted that in some countries, self-help simply may not work due to inherent poverty and cultural backgrounds. Certainly if even modest affordability standards are imposed, a large proportion of the population are automatically excluded from any improvement policy. Thus, although in some countries (might Peru have been an exception?), the provision of a secure title to land and basic services may suffice, in others much more may be required in the form of technical and financial assistance if any improvement is to be made at all. There would, however, appear to be a limit beyond which governments should not tread. Professor Koenigsberger has unambiguously summed this up when he said "the government should not be in the business of building houses" (Baross, 1983).

If greater involvement of government in the housing field is advocated, what direction should it take? How is it to be financed? The answer to these questions obviously depends to a large extent upon the income of the nation involved. New towns and elaborate resettlement schemes may be a luxury that the richer Third World nations can afford. Among the poorer countries, however, upgrading is almost certainly preferable to resettlement — including site and services schemes. Existing shanty towns, whether composed of squatters or slums, should be viewed as an asset, part of the existing housing stock, and as far as possible preserved for upgrading and improvement. Pure subsidies may be difficult to afford, yet cross-subsidisation from higher income groups to lower should be incorporated into such schemes. The poorer the country, the lower the costs of making improvements and as a result, the more significant the impact that can be made with modest subsidies.

Yet housing is not an end in itself and should not be considered as such. Upgrading should be just one component part of comprehensive schemes which involve employment generation and an improvement in the access of the poor to whatever social and health services exist within the community. It may not be possible to do everything at once due to financial constraints, but phasing directed towards long-run improvements is possible and should be incorporated into such plans. If project costs can be controlled, by phasing if necessary, while at the same time affordability improves because of increases in household incomes, then the subsidies required — and they may be temporary — should be within the feasible range of the nation involved.

REFERENCES

Abrams, Charles (1964), *Housing in the Modern World: Man's Struggle for Shelter in an Urbanising World*, Cambridge, M.I.T. Press, Ch. 15.

Abu-Lughod, J.L. and Hay, R. (1977), *Third World Urbanisation*, Chicago, Maaroufa Press: 90.

Asian Development Bank (1985), *Malaysia : Urban Sector Profile*, Manila: 96.

Bamberger, Michael *et al.* (1982), *Evaluation of Sites and Services Projects : The Experience from Lusaka, Zambia*, World Bank Staff Working Paper No. 548: 39-40.

Baross, P. (1983), 'Four Experiences with Settlement Improvement Policies in Asia' in R.J. Skinner and M.J. Rodell (eds.) *People, Poverty and Shelter : Problems of Self-Help Housing in the Third World*, London, Methuen Ch. 7.

Burgess, Rod (1982), 'Self-Help Housing Advocacy : A Curious Form of Radicalism. A Critique of the Work of John F.C. Turner' in Peter M. Ward (ed.) *Self-Help Housing A Critique*, London, Mansell, Ch. 3.

Crooke, P. (1983), 'Popular Housing Supports and the Urban Housing Markets' in R.J. Skinner and M.J. Rodell (eds.) *People, Poverty and Shelter: Problems of Self-help Housing in the Third World*, London, Methuen : 178.

Grimes, Orville F. Jr. (1976), *Housing for Low-Income Families*, Baltimore, Johns Hopkins Press.

Huque, Ashraf (1982), *The Myth of Self-Help Housing*, Stockholm, RIT: 101-06.

Kearne, Douglas H. and Pariss, Scott (1982), *Evaluating of Shelter Programmes for the Urban Poor: Principal Findings*, World Bank Staff Working Paper No. 547: vi.

Keare, Douglas H. and Emmanuel, Jimenez (1983), *Progressive Development and Affordability in the Design of Urban Shelter Projects*, World Bank Staff Working Paper No. 560: 4-5.

Lloyd, Peter (1979), *Slums of Hope : Shanty Towns of the Third World*, Harmondsworth, Penguin: 144.

Mabogunje, A.L. *et al.* (1978), *Shelter Provision in Developing Countries: The Influence of Standards and Criteria*, Chichester, John Wiley: 9-15.

Mangin, William (1963), 'Urbanisation Case History Peru', *Architectural Design* 33: 366-70.

—— (1967), 'Latin American Squatter Settlement : A Problem and a Solution' *Latin American Research Review*, 2: 65-90.

—— ed. (1970), *Peasants in Cities : Readings in the Anthropology of Urbanisation*, Boston, Houghton Mifflin.

Martin, R.J. (1983), 'Upgrading' in R.J. Skinner and M.J. Rodell (eds.), *People, Poverty and Shelter: Problems of Self-help Housing in the Third World*, London, Methuen: 52.

McNamara, Robert S. (1975), 'Address to the Board of Governors of the World Bank', Septermber 1.

Lewis, Oscar (1951), *Life in a Mexican Village : Tepoztlan Revisited*, Urbana University, Illinois Press.

—— (1961), *The Children of Sanchez*, New York, Random House.

—— (1966a), *La Vida : A Puerto Rican Family in the Culture of Poverty — San Juan and New York*, New York, Random House.

—— (1966b), 'The Culture of Poverty', *Scientific American* 215 : 4, 5.

Payne, Geoffrey K. (1977), *Urban Housing in the Third World*, London, Leonard Hill: 195.

Peattie, Lisa R. (1982), 'Some Second Thoughts on Sites and Services', *Habitat International*, 6 : 1/2, 136.

Siebold, Peter and Florian, Steinberg (1982), 'Tanzania : Sites and Services', *Habitat International*, 6 : 1/2, 119.

Swan, Peter J. *et al.* (1983), *Management of Sites and Services Housing Schemes : The Asian Experience*, Chichester, John Wiley: 19.

Turner, John C. (1967), 'Barriers and Channels for Housing Development in Modernising Countries', *Journal of the American Institute of Planners*, 33(3): 167-81.

—— (1967), *Housing by People*, London, Marion Boyars.

United Nations (1980), *Patterns of Urban and Rural Population Growth*, ST/ESA/Series A.68, New York.

USAID (1981), *Integrated Improvement Programme for the Urban Poor : An Orientation for Project Design and Implementation*, II, Washington, D.C.: 481-82.

World Bank (1975), *Housing Sector Policy Paper*, Annex. 2, Washington, D.C.

Yeh, Stephen H.K. (1981), 'On Characteristics of Urban Low-Income Settlements and Improvement Strategies: An Asian Perspective', In *UNCHS the Residential Circumstances in the Urban Poor in Developing Countries*, New York, Praeger: 209.

11

REGENERATION OF LOW-INCOME HOUSING AND SQUATTER SETTLEMENT AREAS IN NAIROBI, KENYA:
Partnership Relation Between State and Private Capital

MAKAU KIAMBA

URBAN HOUSING POLICY IN THE 1960s

In the 1960s, the officially acceptable urban house was defined as an urban housing unit of "suitable materials" and having at least two rooms plus its own kitchen and toilet, with a maximum of five occupants. This was the conventional house and practically set minimum standards expected of all housing in urban areas. Anything else that fell below this official standard was regarded as illegal or unauthorised. This definition of conventional housing, therefore, provided the minimum basis on which state institutions provided, and controlled, legal housing in urban areas. The state's official response to unauthorised housing was rejection and in many cases demolition of such housing or settlements.

Kenya's housing policy (1966) was largely based on the recommendations of United Nations Mission on Housing for Kenya (Bloomberg and Abrams, 1965). The United Nations Mission and the Policy Document of the Government saw capital shortage accounting for lack of housing in Kenya's urban areas. In this regard, with limited capital resources in Kenya, emphasis was placed on external sources of private capital. To this end, two institutions, the Housing Finance Company of Kenya (HFCK) and National Housing Corporation (NHC) were set up for the purpose of meeting the challenge. The HFCK, jointly owned by the Government of Kenya (GOK) (the Government, hereafter) and Commonwealth Development Corporation (CDC) was to provide private mortgages with emphasis on middle- and higher-income housing. The HFCK was to presage an approach to providing urban shelter in Kenya's urban areas that was to dominate this area in the 1970s, i.e., the partnership between the Government and private international capital. The NHC, on the other hand, was a reformed colonial Government's Central Housing Authority, and was to co-ordinate and channel funds from the Government to mainly urban authorities with emphasis on the lower end of formal housing. These two institutions, along with the local authorities, thus comprised the main agencies for state intervention in urban housing. As Temple (1973) and Silberman (1972) have observed, publicly provided or funded housing through these institutions up to the early 1970s was biased in favour of middle- and upper-income groups.

The sudden influx of migrants into Nairobi in the 1960s and their acute poverty made it impossible for their land and shelter needs to be met by the existing housing resources based on the "conventional" methods. Lacking access to conventional channels of housing provision, these new urban dwellers sought accommodation in the proliferating squatter and unauthorised housing. By the early 1970s, the housing situation in Nairobi was described as "alarming" (Njau, 1980). During this period Nairobi had an estimate annual growth rate of 1.5 per cent of approved housing as compared to about 7.2 per cent annual rate of population growth. Between 1963 and 1970 it had been estimated that 33,000 housing units were required but only 7,400 were actually built. Between 1969 and 1970, the population of Mathare Valley, the largest squatter settlement in Nairobi, grew form 19,000 to 60,000 inhabitants. By 1972, an estimated 30-40 per cent of Nairobi's population lived in squatter settlements. Of the 124,000 dwelling units existing in Nairobi for a population of 650,000 in 1972, 17 per cent was approved and built by private sector, 53 per cent approved and built by public sector and the remaining 30 per cent was unauthorised (NCC, 1973b; USAID, 1974). Njau (1980) concludes: "The accumulated shortfall by now (1972) reached alarming proportion . . . serious review of policy was required in order to arrest the deteriorating situation".

When the incomes of Nairobi residents are compared to the cost of the conventional housing, the results are even more alarming. A study of housing by-laws, using the definition of "conventional" housing, found out that in the 1970s something like 65-70 per cent of households in Nairobi (about 80 per cent in other Kenya's urban centres) could not afford minimum legal housing (SYA *et al.*, 1980). This was on the assumption that families would be spending 30 per cent of their incomes in housing. The study concluded: "In view of actual incomes and current prices of food and housing, low-income families are presented with the choice of either staying in the self-settled areas or of paying so much for a legal site-and-service house that they cannot afford other essential goods and services. . . . Low cost housing standards are too high for majority sections of the urban population to afford".

The scale of this "alarming" urban housing problem was to play an important role in the shifting of the urban housing provision of low-income groups from the conventional to what was seen as a more "realistic" or "pragmatic" strategy.

THE SHIFT TOWARDS A "REALISTIC" URBAN HOUSING POLICY

Beginning in the early 1970s, there was a clear shift from the above "conventional" housing policy towards what has been referred to as a "realistic" (NCC, 1973a) or "Pragmatic" housing provision strategy (UNCHS, 1983). The evidence of these changes is found in the new urban land and shelter projects and their related community facilities, budgetary allocations for new shelter and in the re-organisation of institutions responsible for planning and implementing the new policy. The new strategy can be summarised as follows: a stronger focus on the urban poor or low-income groups implying those roughly falling below median or the 50th percentile in income distribution; increasing commitment to provide low-cost shelter through reduction in building and planning standards and consequent shifting from completed, contractor-built housing to either housing extendable by owner/self construction or services sites; increasing acceptance and legalisation and consequent improvement of squatter or unauthorised settlements; a shift from subsidisation of land, infrastructure, community, facilities and interest rates to a cost-recovery strategy; an active promotion of the private sector/capital participation in low-income housing; and an increasing re-organisation of institutions to "efficiently" provide and manage urban land and shelter (USAID, 1980a).

The move towards the so-called realistic approach was particularly associated with the strong involvement of international capital in urban development in Nairobi. The International Labour Organisation (ILO) (1972) reported indeed heralded the important prospects for the shift in the perception of unauthorised housing as well as other informal economic activities: "Form the vantage point of central Nairobi, with its gleaming skyscrapers, the dwellings and commercial structures of the informal sector look like hovels . . ., it requires a leap of imagination and considerable openness of mind to perceive informal sector as a sector of thriving economic activity and source of Kenya's wealth".

In the field of urban development, and particularly urban shelter, the new strategy gained more weight in Kenya with the involvement of the World Bank (since 1972). The World Bank was, in this period, involved in a world-wide promotion of "poverty-oriented" provisions of urban shelter by states, especially in the Third World (and was to issue its own urban policy paper in 1975) in the form of site and services schemes and squatter upgrading programmes.

Regarding the important if not dominant involvement of international capital in the new policy direction in the provision of urban shelter, the agencies themselves openly acknowledge this. Indeed the USAID appears most felicitous in this respect: "Apart from USAID projects there are major shelter projects underway financed by the World Bank . . . the CDC and the European Development Fund (EDF) . . . not only have they, collectively, been instrumental in bringing about shift in policy emphasis but also introduced new approaches. . . . Although there was a growing awareness of the need to change the emphasis of prevailing policies, there is no doubt that the magnitude and conditions of USAID and IBRD/IDA projects did influence the speed at which these changes" (USAID, 1979a).

Although the Government gave indications in the mid and late 1960s that it would place emphasis on housing provision to low-income groups, beyond popular rhetoric and exhortation nothing much happened until the mid-1970s. The USAID is therefore quite right in arguing that co-ordinated international capital not only played an important "catalytic role" (1980a) but also that "the Government and Nairobi City Council (NCC) (the Council, hereafter) housing policies in favour of poor seem to be contingent upon donor financing and shaped by donor requirements rather than spontaneous indication of government's direction in the shelter sector" (1980b).

Studies carried out in 1970s and early 1980s by private consultants and funded by international capital, with the Government and the

Council as the main audience, reveal the shifting land and shelter policy for the low-income groups (ILO, 1973; NCC, 1973a; CLAL *et al.*, 1976; WAA *et al.*, 1976; USAID, 1979a, 1979b, 1974; SYA *et al.*, 1980, 1983).

The new policy emphasis that ensued from these studies was that the role of the government and the Council was to provide the land, security of tenure and basic services, leaving the rest of the shelter structure to the private capital, both local and international. To this end, the government was also to regularise and upgrade squatter settlements. A greater degree of co-operation and/or partnership, and indeed clear delineation of roles between public and private sectors was seen as the way to increase the seriously deficient and rapidly deteriorating urban housing for low-income and squatting groups.

INTERNATIONAL CAPITAL AND URBAN LAND AND SHELTER IN NAIROBI

There are many international institutions, or agencies, that have been participating in the urban development in Nairobi, the main ones being the World Bank, USAID, Commonwealth Development Corporation (CDC) and the European Economic Communities (EEC).

Illuminating insight into the nature and roles of these institutions (especially in the developing countries) can be drawn not only from recent debates about these institutions but also from the institutions' own material. Examples of the debate are found in the recent works of Breet (1985), Hayter and Watson (1985), Philips (1982) and Payer (1982). With regard to the urban projects in Nairobi, specific shelter project and review documents by all the parties concerned – the Government and the Council are quite useful in explicating the roles of, and the nature of the relationship between the participants in urban development in Nairobi.

In this paper we examine examples of urban low-income housing and squatter settlement projects in Nairobi in context of the shifting policy emphasis as hinted above. In all these projects there was (and still is) a co-operation between the Kenya State on the one hand, and private capital (especially international capital channelled through international institutions as pointed out above) on the other. More specifically, in the Nairobi's urban projects the World Bank, USAID and EDF have been involved. It is through this approach that the main urban housing projects have been undertaken in Nairobi.

The First World Bank Urban Project: Dandora

The First World Bank Urban Project – the Dandora Community Development Project (hereafter Dandora) in Nairobi – was the first large-scale attempt to provide shelter to low-income groups in Nairobi, in the light of both Kenya's changing housing policy and World Bank's "poverty-oriented" shelter strategy. The project formulation and preparation took almost 6 years, beginning from 1972 to 1975; the loan agreement was signed in 1975. The project site was at Dandora, situated about 10 kilometres east of the city centre and conforming with the Nairobi Metropolitan Growth Strategy (NCC, 1973a).

The project comprised a provision of 6000 serviced plots (including a variety of "wet-core" facilities), materials loans for additional construction, community facilities, trunk sewer infrastructure, and technical assistance. The 6000 serviced plots were of four different sizes ranging form 100 to 160 sq m. This represented a considerable reduction of the 240 sq m minimum plot size previously allowable under Grade II by-laws. They were all provided with a "wet-core" or "shelter unit" around which households were supposed to "consolidate" upon, – build additional rooms in accordance with proto-type plans. In order to accommodate different incomes within the project and yet reach the possible lowest income, in addition to the variety of sizes of serviced plots, three options of wet-core or shelter units were provided; option 'A' of 3900 plots (about 60 per cent of the total plots) each provided with a wet- or sanitary-core only, option 'B' of 1800 plots (30%) each with both a wet-core and one built room and option 'C' of 330 plots (5%) with a completed housing unit. The last option was for demonstration purposes of a completed unit in the project. The project included the financing of materials loans for both options 'A' and 'B' for any additional self-construction (maximum of two rooms). The community facilities provided for the project included schools, health centres, multi-purpose community centres and market stalls.

The technical assistance component of the project included assistance in the creation and operation of an administration unit, assistance in engineering and construction supervision and undertaking of a variety of studies. A special project unit, Site and Services Project Unit, was created in the Council to implement and manage the site and services component of the project. The other project components were to be undertaken by the existing relevant departments in the Council. In 1975, as part of the loan agreement between the World Bank and the Government, the Unit was "promoted" to a full department, – Dandora Community Development Department – within the Council administrative structure. In 1978, the new department was renamed and expanded to the Housing Developing Department to implement not only the Dandora Project but all other similar low-income housing projects in Nairobi. This was the time when the World Bank and the Government signed another loan agreement for the much broader second low-income urban project.

The total project was estimated at January 1975 prices to cost K £10.54 million (approximately US $30.0 million) with a joint World Bank – the Government financing plan consisting of a K £5.0 million World Bank Contribution [comprising International Bank for Reconstruction and Development (IBRD) and International Development Fund (IDA) with equal contributions] and K £5.54 million from the the Government. The council being the project implementing authority was to receive all the money. The World Bank funds were advanced to the Council by the Government at 8.5 per cent per annum and 25-year repayment with a grace period of 4 years. The Government funds were at 6.5 per cent and 25 years, the prevailing NHC terms to local authorities for housing projects.

The above figures excluded the land element for the project. The site for the project measured 350 hectares; about 300 hectares was already owned by the Government, with the remaining 50 hectares acquired by the Commissioner of Lands for the project. The Government made the land available to the Council on a 99-year lease. About 20 per cent of the land was unusable for the project being taken either by quarries, excessive slopes or major city roads. About 6 per cent of the usable land was allocated for the projects' residential purpose; most of this was taken by the 6000 plots with some portion carved out for a "commercial, industrial and middle-income residential" development. That was developed for market sales by the Council and not strictly as part of the main Bank's project. The rest of the land was taken up by circulation and community facilities. The Government was to charge from the Council an annual ground rent of 3 per cent of the unimproved site value for the first 10 years and 5 per cent thereafter for the land used for the residential purposes. The remaining land, used for public purposes charged a nominal fee. This was well in accordance with the new "regularised" strategy, and World

Bank's requirements, in where the Government removes most of the subsidies it had hitherto accorded to the Council's low-income land and housing projects. The Council, however, decided against passing the rental charges to the allottees arguing that this would help in extending the range of eligibility of low-income groups. The land was thus provided "free of charge" for the project. However, the buyers of land developed by the Council for market sale were charged full annual rentals and the Council hoped that this would eventually cover its rental payments to the Government for the residential land.

The plots were assigned or sub-leased by the Council to the eligible allottees for 40 years with a mortgage loan at 8.5 per cent repayable for 20-30 years. The eligible low-income "target population" for the project was the two bottom quartiles of the income distribution of Nairobi population. This was assumed to comprise households earning a monthly income of between Ksh. 280.00 to 650.00. Non-ownership of other residential property and a two-year residence in Nairobi were the other eligibility criteria. The allottees were allowed to sublet their housing units and in fact re-sale was permitted after a minimum of 5 years residence. The World Bank's second project reduces this period to three years. Income from subletting was assumed would help allottees repayment of loans.

The monitoring and evaluation study of the first phase of the project of 100 plots, found over half of the plots were "occupied by people other than allottees" but proceeds on to say cautiously: "It is possible that allottees sublet their plots for a short time on completion of building to recoup the costs of building. It is also possible that allottees intend to completely sublet their plots permanently. . . . This may be because they are higher or lower than income target group, but in either case because they prefer to make profits in Dandora than live there. It is also known that a small proportion of plots have been sold" (SNA, 1979).

It is interesting to note what the Bank itself thought of its first project. The World Bank sees the Dandora project in the context of its broader new strategy:

> "The Bank site and service project would deal with some of the broader urban needs and improve the Council's capacity to implement future low-income shelter projects. The project would address the lack of an effective shelter policy by assisting the Government to implement the first large-scale, low-cost solution to

urban shelter and infrastructure. . . . The project, as a precursor of other site and service projects in Kenya . . . is expected to have substantial influence on Government's approach to urban shelter and infrastructure for low-income groups" (World Bank, 1975).

The Council itself saw the project as a "turning point" in the city's housing policy and says "the World Bank has played a major role in this change of attitude" (Njau, 1980).

The Second World Bank Urban Project: Services and Squatter Upgrading

The second project was intended to "duplicate, reinforce and extend" the first urban project by introducing "significant new components". The project comprised an increased supply of serviced plots, introduction of squatter upgrading as an official Government's policy, specific institutional component aimed at improving the capability of both the Government and the Council for developing and managing urban projects and technical assistance to strengthen financial management of local authority resources. The project included other broader inputs like stimulation and encouragement of employment and income-generating activities for the urban poor and a demonstration pilot health, nutrition and family planning component.

The services plots components of the project included "sites and services plots", "settlement plots" and "low-cost housing plots" for market sale. The plots' sizes ranged from 100 to 200 sq m which averaged 35-40 plots per hectare. Like the first urban project, standards were reduced "to maximise efficiency of land-use". The site and services plots are situated in Mathare North, Kayole and Dandora 6, all located in the Eastland of Nairobi. In order to keep initial costs as low as possible and allow maximum flexibility for self-help, the majority – 86 per cent of the site and services plots were to have no superstructure. Allottees were offered materials loans for consolidation under the project. The sales of low-cost housing sites in the market were seen as part of an effort to promote mixed development, meet housing needs of households immediately above the target population and use the earnings by the Council for providing further low-cost housing.

Originally, the IBRD an IDA were to equally share financing, about 72 per cent (about US $19.4 million) being provided by the

Government (World Bank, 1978). In 1983, however, due to "constrained budget position and high domestic inflation", the World Bank was to increase its contribution to 80 per cent of the total net costs. The terms of financing, both between the Bank, the Government and the Council and the allottees were largely the same as in the first urban project. For eligibility, the target income level was determined between Ksh. 400.00 and Ksh. 1000.00 per month except for Kayole portion which has an income "ceiling" of Ksh. 2000.00. The income ceiling of Ksh. 1000.00 was about the same in real terms as that of the first project. The leases to allottees were for 50 years and re-sale was permitted in the case of site and services plots after 5 years.

The second urban project was started in 1978 and expected to be completed in mid-1980s. Like the first project, it was: "expected to have substantial influence on the Government's approach to urban shelter and infrastructure for lower income groups. Besides directly increasing the supply of low-cost shelter, the project will have impact on urban housing and institutional and financial policies of urban authorities" (World Bank, 1978).

In addition to these expected broader policy issues, the World Bank's participation was made conditional on the understanding that the Government and the Council would institute certain policy reforms acceptable to the Bank. Of significance was the re-organisation of the institutions responsible for urban development in accordance with the recommendation of various World Bank's funded studies. The Government and the Council also, importantly, agreed to a policy on non-demolition of unauthorised settlements within its urban land. Instead, they were to concentrate on squatter improvement strategies as exemplified by the World Bank's project.

USAID Urban Project in Nairobi: Umoja I, Umoja II and the Private Sector Housing Project

The main USAID – Housing Guarantee Programme (HGP) – urban projects undertaken in Nairobi in the light of the new strategy are the Umoja I, Umoja II, (indeed yet to be implemented) and the private sector housing project. Like the World Bank projects, the projects were carried out in the Eastlands, low-income area, of Nairobi. USAID's projects Umoja-I and Umoja II were planned to start in the mid and late seventies respectively with the private sector project following thereafter.

The first Umoja Housing Estate, here referred to as Umoja I, like the World Bank's projects, was targeted for the lowest income level in the regularly employed and in general the income of the families served should be below the median income. This meant household's income ranging from Ksh. 800.00 to Ksh. 1600.00 per month. To reach this income group meant adoption of lower standard of housing provision relative to conventional housing. The Umoja I project was therefore designed for about 3000 "expandable" units. The project component included only the services plot, a kitchen and one room. The allottee would build the rest later on availability of funds. The project involved a US $10 million loan to the Council for on-lending to the tenant-purchasers to repay in 25 years at an interest of 10 per cent per annum. The U.S. private lender was the Federal Home Loan Bank of New York (USAID, 1980). An autonomous unit, Umoja Project Management Unit, under the Council, was created to manage the project. The land was Government owned and was provided for the project at similar terms with the World Bank's projects; it measured approximately 142 hectares.

Initially, unlike the World Bank, Umoja I project forbade subletting in its Tenant Purchase Agreement. A U.S. Audit General's report saw subletting of the housing units by the tenant-purchasers as jeopardising the projects goals, notably those concerning the definition of the target groups (USAID, 1980). Despite this, substantial subletting took place as acknowledged later by USAID itself: "Kenya's urban subletting phenomena is all pervasive among lower income groups. It is now estimated that over 90 per cent of the units in USAID's Umoja I Estate are sublet; 85 per cent of the units in World Bank founded Dandora project are sublet; and 74 per cent in USAID's Secondary Towns' project are also sublet" (USAID, 1983).

In the light of the experience in the Umoja I project and World Bank's projects the USAID allowed subletting, and in fact incorporated it as a factor in the calculation of the eligibility, in the subsequent projects: Hence the argument: "Subletting of a part of a house is common in Nairobi and will be encouraged in Umoja II as a way to maximise the number of beneficiaries and to reduce allottee income floor" (USAID, 1980).

The USAID's Umoja II project, like the second World Bank project, is an extension of Umoja I. Umoja II is physically contiguous and to the east of Umoja I and sandwiched in between Umoja I and the component of World Bank's project in Kayole. Umoja II project, with its implementation delayed until 1985-86, involved 4460 housing units with a HPG loan of US $17 million at 1986 prices. The funds were to be provided by Merrill Lynch Capital Market of New York to the Council for repayment in 30 years with 10 years grace period on repayment of the principal. Umoja II, unlike Umoja I, has five different types of housing units, including courtyard row-houses, maisonnettes and flats. These were meant for low-income household with income ranging from Ksh. 750.00 to 1900.00. The 124 hectares land for the project was Government-owned and similarly provided for the projects as Umoja I. Lower space standards were adopted in the second project. The incorporation of maisonnettes and flats in the second project also meant that the land could be utilised more intensively. The second minor project also economised the land-use for roads giving more emphasis on land for community facilities.

The last USAID project, not yet implemented, involved a US $ 20 million programme to provide financing for low-income housing projects at level sufficient to attract the private institutions, developers and co-operatives. This project would involve entirely the private sector but with the necessary Government's guarantees for HGP loans. The USAID, on the basis of their and the World Bank's experience assured that sufficient project potential exists for housing projection at the lower level to interest private sector and therefore "the primary emphasis will be to demonstrate that provision of low-cost housing is profitable business for developers" (USAID, 1983). Allied with this general rationale, is also the mobilisation of local private capital for low-income housing investment. USAID, thus sees the project clearly "supportive of the Government policy objective of reliance on the private sector". In this regard the project would involve co-operation between all the participants: USAID in providing private international finance capital through the HGP to local private housing financiers and developers; the private developers; in turn, to provide land for the projects; and the Government/Council to undertake the necessary infrastructural and public services provision.

EUROPEAN ECONOMIC COMMUNITIES (EEC) PROJECTS

These projects were financed by European Development Fund (EDF) with a grant of US $ 25 million to the Government and were to be executed by the Council. The projects started in 1975 and were completed in the early 1980s. The projects were: Kawangware

Improvement Scheme in the Dagoretti Area of Nairobi; a site and services scheme in the Mathare Valley and a workshop cluster within Dandora project site, to promote informal manufacturing efforts. Like the other international agencies' projects, the EDF was aimed at financing investments in the field of private housing including utility and social infrastructure with priority to the lower income segments of the population.

CONCLUSIONS

The above brief account of the provision of (or investment in) urban housing for low-income groups and also the overall regeneration of squatter settlement areas in Nairobi indicate a complex if not diverse objectives of this policy area, including the relation of partnership between the state and capital (both international and local); facilitation of capital penetration or expansion into low-income shelter sector, maintenance of social order of cohesion, the introduction of private landed property and consequent commodification or commercialisation of the sector, and some perceivable benefits to the low-income and squatting groups involved. It is worth while pointing out that the issues as identified above are not as clearly distinct and are complex in their interlinked relationship. We nevertheless attempt treating them as identified with the hope that the approach helps us to understand the nature and essence of the relationship of partnership between state and private capital in this area.

An examination of the social basis of international capital (as is represented, for example by the World Bank and USAID) and its changing role in the 1970s followed by its concrete relationship with the Kenya state and local private capital (in Nairobi's urban development in particular) points to the relationship being that of a partnership and co-operation. The relationship appears to be largely based on a coincidence if not complimentarity of interests in their desire for a stable framework for capitalist development. In this regard, the policy emphasis has been towards the provision of urban land and shelter for low-income groups. We started identifying clear and complementing albeit sometimes interlocked, division of roles between the state, international capital and local private capital. We see both the Government and the Council being reduced to the roles of providing the land (including its security of tenure), basic infrastructural and community facilities and legal and international framework for private capital, both local and international. In addition we see the state providing protection through guarantees especially for international capital for venturing to invest in this relatively new and "informal" urban land and shelter sector. As Boyer (1981) observed of such state guarantees, the Government appears to underwrite low-income housing investment by private capital.

The state, in aiding the expansion or penetration of private capital into low-income shelter programmes by sharing the cost of the production of low-income housing can assist the private capital in the social reproduction of labour power through specialisation of the general conditions or at least some aspects of the costs of production in this sector (Preteceille, 1976; Lamarche, 1976; Lojkine, 1976; Gilbert and Ward, 1982, 1985; Jaramillo and Schteingart, 1985). In socialising some of the productive forces which are consequently costless to capital, it is seen as intervening to serve a collective capitalist benefit. Gilbert and Ward (1985) argue "industrial and commercial interests benefit to the extent that labour force is housed cheaply and therefore is less likely to demand higher wages".

Allied with the above state's socialisation of parts of the costs of producing low-income housing, was the promotion of "self-help" or "do it yourself" strategies that come with the World Bank's site and service schemes and USAID's "expandable" housing programme. This is seen as cutting the need for substantial state and private capital expenditure on housing. Capital is, therefore, served by these strategies to the extent that labour power has been partly housed without substantial recourse to either state's or private capital. Referring to similar strategies in New Mexico and Bogota, Jaramillo and Schteingart (1985) observe that "the state had unloaded on to the workers part of the burden of reproducing their own labour force".

It has been argued that states in capitalist societies aid the process of capitalist development and accumulation by laying the basic framework for private enterprise. They also, in order to reproduce the social relation required for the capitalist economic system to survive and prosper, get involved in containing class and social conflict. It is perhaps in this light that the World Bank see lack of housing for the low-income groups, as reflected by urban squatter and slum settlements as "potentially . . . explosive, politically and socially" (USAID, 1980); hence the Bank's "poverty oriented" shelter strategies as typified by its first and second urban projects in Nairobi. In the same vein USAID's concern with "critical urban crises" as "dangerous" and a "threat" to world capitalist development (USS, 1971); hence its policy emphasis on "low-income" families (USAID, 1983) and the basis for its Nairobi's urban projects included Umoja Phase I, Umoja Phase II and the low-cost private sector project.

It is in this context the conclusions by Gilbert and Ward (1985, 1982) and Jaramillo and Schteingart (1985) in their studies of Latin American cities and Amis (1983) and Kiamba (1986) in their study of land and shelter in Nairobi are useful. Amis' (1983) conclusions appear quite appropriate. "At one level the international agencies concern is with political stability. . . . For such agencies this will be synonymous with the preservation of a capitalistic development strategy".

Gilbert and Ward (1985) in their more detailed analysis of three Latin American cities, New Mexico and Valencia, argue similarly: "one of the primary motives for increasing state intervention in low-income settlements in the 1960s was the fear that such areas constituted a major risk to social stability". They even see the mere legislation of illegal and unauthorised squatter settlements as politically important: "Despite poor conditions, illegal settlements act as safety valve to social tension. Through land invasion and illegal sub-division some of the poor receive land on which they can seek work, raise families and usually improve their absolute standards of living . . . to reproduce the labour force".

By the time both the World Bank and USAID started urban projects in Nairobi they already had considerable experience in Latin American cities. It is possible to argue that they could not have been unaware of such benefits as accounted by Gilbert and Ward among others. We have seen the World Bank make its loans for Nairobi's urban projects conditional upon non-eviction and non-demolition of squatter settlements. The Government in turn obliged and stipulated the same as an official policy.

Apart from the mere legalisation of unauthorised low-income housing the much broader and important policy of regularising land tenure and introduction of private land and home ownership (as opposed to public rental housing) can be seen in its wider social context as regards integration, co-operation or incorporation of the low-income groups (along with their land and housing as commodities) into the predominantly Nairobi's capitalist economy. This is very much reminiscent of the "landing the gentry" overall strategy of land reform in the 1950s and 1960s – hence the new strategy's catchwords: "owner occupation", "tenant purchase" and "home ownership". Once private ownership of the land and housing was established, either through allocation of serviced plots and housing units or regularisation of ownership of squatter upgrading, consequent realisation of surpluses was feasible, either through subletting or sale; hence the commodification of land and housing. In all the projects examined, these were permitted; in the case of subletting we saw it being as high as 80 per cent in nearly all the projects. The only project Dandora Phase-I, where detailed monitoring and evaluation has been undertaken, the allottees preferred "to make profits" through subletting rather than living in the houses. The World Bank (1975) itself sees the introduction of private land ownership in squatter settlements having "an element of equity in urban land ownership by giving squatters security of tenure". Gilbert and Ward (1975) too argued by "offering the poor some stake in the property system . . . upheld the property concept throughout the city". In the same vein, Amis (1985) concluded: "In general their (international agencies) aim seem to be to encourage a small-scale private sector integrated into the formal economy . . . the encouragement of small rather than large-scale landlordism is self-legitimating: it helps political stability by increasing the numbers with a vested interest in the system. Similarly by preventing large-scale affluent landlordism with its obvious inequality it removes a potential source of politicisation and conflict from the urban poor."

Once the low-income housing was initially allocated to certain low-income "target population" and squatter settlements legalised, the market was seen as the final arbiter as to who would occupy or own the housing. In Nairobi, as we have seen over three quarters of the occupants in the urban projects were not the original allottees. This appears to be the case of most of World Bank's projects in Third World. After examining the Manila (Philippines) World Bank site and services project, Payer (1982) concluded: "despite absence of bulldozers, the effect of World Bank projects is to realise the potential value of urban property at the expense of really poor, who will almost certainly be driven out new upgraded areas by economic pressure".

White's (1985) study of the Dakar (Senegal) project concluded: "something very different from the planned outcome has occurred". Stren's (1982) study of Dar es Salaam (Tanzania) project revealed similar results. Evaluating the World Bank's urban projects generally, Ayres (1983) admitted that "most of the housing units in Bank financed projects had in fact been occupied by families with incomes higher than originally intended by the Bank". Indeed the World Bank (1975) itself would appear not to have expected otherwise: "As all these communities are improved, it is inevitable that some of those who live in them will be unable to afford even a minimum level of improvements. To insist on cost-recovery in these instances may force the poorest residents out of the communities".

This is not, however, to argue that substantial benefits were not conferred on low-income groups, or some sections of them. As the state responded to broader issues of fostering capitalist development in Nairobi (and in Kenya), well placed sections of low-income groups have mainly benefited from the shelter programmes undertaken in Nairobi.

REFERENCES

Amis, P. (1983), 'The Shanty Town of Tenants: The Commercialisation of Unauthorised Housing in Nairobi', Ph.D. thesis, University Kent at Canterbury : 137, 296-98.

Ayres, R. (1983), *Banking on the Poor: The World Bank and the World Poverty*, Cambridge, Mass., M.I.T. Press: 193.

Bloomberg, I.N. and Abrams, C. (1965), *United Nations Mission to Kenya on Housing*, New York, United Nations.

Boyer, M.C. (1981), 'National Land Use Policy: Instrument and Product of Economic Cycle', in J.I. Neufville (ed.), *The Land Use Policy Debate in the United States*, New York, Plenum Press.

Brett, E.A. (1985), *The World Economy Since the War: The Politics of Uneven Development*, London, Macmillan.

CLAL, *et al.* (1976), *Nairobi's Housing Needs: Meeting the Challenge*, Consultancy Report for NCC/GOK/World Bank.

Gilbert, A. and Ward, P. (1985), *Housing, the State and the Poor: Policy in Three Latin American Cities*, Cambridge, C.U.P.: 15, 273-75, 85.

Government of Kenya (1980), *Report of the Seminar on the Role of the Private Sector in Housing Development*, Nairobi, Ministry of Urban Development and Housing.

Hayter, T. and Watson, C. (1985), *Aid: Rhetoric and Reality*, London, Pluto.

ILO (1972), *Employment, Incomes and Inequality: A Strategy for Increasing Productive Employment in Kenya*, Geneva: 5.

Jaramillo, S. and Schteingert, M. (1985), 'Capital Accumulation and Housing Production in Latin America, 1960-80', in J. Walton (ed.), *Capital and Labour in the Urbanised World*, London, Sage: 185.

Kiamba, M. (1986), 'The Role of the State in the Control of Urban Development: Urban Land Policy for Nairobi, Kenya', Ph.D. dissertation, University of Cambridge.

Lamarche, F. (1976), 'Property Development and the Economic Foundation of the Urban Question', in C.G. Pickvance (ed.), *Urban Sociology, Critical Essays*, London, Tavistock.

Lockine, J. (1976), 'Contribution to Marxist Theory of Capitalist Urbanisation', in C.G. Pickvance (ed.), *Urban Sociology*, Critical Essays, London, Tavistock.

NCC (1973a), *Nairobi Metropolitan Growth Strategy*, Nairobi Urban Study Group.

NCC (1973b), *The Dandora Site and Service Project*, Task Force Report for submission to the World Bank.

Njau, G.J. (1980), 'Nairobi Low-Income Housing: A Challenge to the City', UNCHS Course on Improving Human Habitat, Nairobi: 5, 10-14.

Payer, C. (1982), *The Debt Trap: The IMF and the Third World*, New York: Monthly Review Press: 338.

Philips, R. (1983), 'The Role of the IMF in the Post-Britton Woods Era', *Review of Radical Political Economy*, 15 (2): 59-81.

Preteceille, E. (1976), 'Urban Planning: The Contradictions of Capitalist Urbanization', *Antipode*, 8 (1): 69-76.

Silberman, R.L. (1972), 'The Distributional Impact of Public Housing: A Case Study of Nairobi', Ph.D. thesis, University of Michigan.

SNA (1976 to 1979), *MEDIS Reports*, for GOK/World Bank, Nairobi.

Stren, R. (1982), 'Underdevelopment, Urban Squatting and the Bureaucracy: A Case Study of Tanzania', *Canadian Journal of African Studies*, 16 (1): 67-91.

SYA, *et al.* (1980), *Kenya Low-Cost Housing by-law Study*, for World Bank/GOK, 2: 32-39.

UNCHS (1983), *UN Seminar of Experts on Land for Housing the Poor*, Tallberg: 12.

USAID (1979a), *Kenya: Shelter Sector Study and the AID's Experience*, Washington, D.C, OHUD: 13-14.

——— (1979b), *Kenya: Shelter Sector statement*, Washington, D.C, OHUD.

——— (1980a), *Kenya Project Paper: Nairobi and Community Facilities*, Washington, D.C, OHUD: 5, 6, 12-19.

——— (1980b), *Umoja Estate Housing Guaranty Programme, Nairobi, Kenya*, Audit Report, U.S. Auditor General, Washington, D.C: 20.

USS (1971), *Study of International Housing*, Washington, D.C, Government Printing Office.

WAA, *et al.* (1978), *Low-Cost Housing and Squatter Upgrading Study*, for World Bank/GOK.

White, R.R. (1985), 'The Impact of Policy Conflict in the Implementation of Government Assisted Housing Project in Senegal', *Canadian Journal of African Studies*, 19(1): 507.

World Bank, (1975), *Kenya: Appraisal of a Site and Service Project*, Washington, D.C.: 17, 20, 29.

——— (1978), *Kenya: Second Urban Project*, Washington, D.C.: 15, 48.

12

SOCIAL PARTICIPATION AND HOUSING IN CUBA

KOSTA MATHEY

THE SOCIAL CONTEXT

Many social achievements of the Cuban revolution, like health care, recreational opportunities, education, or the vanishing of open racial or sexual discrimination are remarkable and far superior than any other attempts in social policy in the remaining parts of Latin America. However, housing conditions in Cuba are much less glorious and the deficit is alarming, although the situation is certainly much less severe than in other developing, or even industrialised countries. There are no extended slum areas which were a typical feature before the revolution, no children sleeping in the street and nobody need fear losing a home for one reason or another. Security of tenure is guaranteed with very few exceptions, and "housing eviction" practically is an unknown term. Even in cases where the law would justify an eviction, there is no mechanism to enforce it. However, the current housing problem is mostly felt in terms of overcrowding and poor maintenance of the existing stock. Despite an ambitious mass housing programme, the revolutionary government concentrated its main efforts on agricultural and industrial development. Housing as a very cost intensive and not explicitly productive investment was not given a high priority in the past. Fidel Castro himself once said that a developing country can choose between economic development or housing construction, but it cannot cope with both tasks at the same time.

Housing policies in Cuba underwent different phases with shifting emphasis, and both dogmatic and experimental elements can be identified. During the first decade after the "triumph", a large number of houses were built outside the bigger cities. It was considered a priority task to improve the living conditions of the rural population. In any case, within the capital, Havana, the large number of persons deserting the country had left a considerable number of good dwelling behind which could be redistributed among those people with the greatest housing need, and the worst slums could be cleared without the need for new construction. In addition, the situation remained relatively comfortable compared to other Third World cities, because by activating economic development in other parts of the country, Cuba succeeded in reducing migration into Havana significantly, with the result that the population growth rate of the capital remained below the national average.

MASS HOUSING VERSUS SELF-HELP CONSTRUCTION

In Cuba housing production is organised along three predominant lines: state built houses, individual self-help, and collective self-help construction. Although all three forms coexisted for many years, they were only given a comprehensive legal framework in the general housing law of December 1984, which replaced a greater number of earlier laws and was revised again in parts in December 1988. The total output of houses produced is being laid down, to a certain extent, in the five-year economic plans. But since housing provision relies largely on voluntary initiatives by the users, these figures can obviously not be fixed definitely nor enforced by central government.

Housing built by the state represents nearly half of all dwellings completed, and the majority of these units consist of prefabricated blocks of flats erected by the Ministry of Construction (MICONS). Mass production (large and repetitious concrete panels, parallel orientation of long linear buildings with an uniform number of floors, etc.), of housing has been increasingly criticised — also by Fidel Castro himself — for its monotonous appearance, and for its cultural incompatibility particularly in smaller towns and rural areas (Ortega, 1986; Segre, 1984). However, more recently, some experimental housing projects have been proposed and built which attempt to increase the flexibility of the prefabricated building systems and to improve their aesthetic appearance. One of these projects is part of VAN-VAN redevelopment scheme in Santiago de Cuba.

Housing produced with the direct participation of the Population — or self-help housing as we would call it — can be distinguished in two different forms: individual and collective self-help. *Individual Self-help* ("construccion por esfurzo propio") has always been a major element in Cuban housing production, although for a long period it was not given particular attention within the official programmes and policies (see Table 12.1).

TABLE 12.1: Average Annual Housing Production: 1959-85

Period	Total	Per 1000 inh.	Self-built	Per 1000 inh.
1959-70	34,700	4.5	26,400	3.4
1971-75	42,400	4.7	26,200	2.9
1976-80	49,200	5.1	32,800	3.4
1981-85	68,500	6.9	41,500	4.2

Source: Hamberg (Forthcoming).

In addition to spontaneous, and sometimes illegal, house building efforts by individuals, there also existed isolated state-assisted self-help programmes since the early days of the revolution. These programmes were conceived as temporary measures to overcome the problem of urban slums and, later, to replace the primitive "bohios" (traditional thatch huts) with durable houses built to modern standards. However, self-help was never given large-scale professional attention before the national architects' conference in 1984. By that time the results of the 1981 housing census had become available. The figures revealed that between 1976 and 1980, only 164,000 dwellings had been created through the state and the Microbrigadas. However, the net increase of the housing stock amounted to 246,000 units (Hamberg, 1986). Thus, the striking difference between these figures obviously represented "informal" constructions, most of them built by their occupants in self-help efforts. The census further revealed that, apart from the unexpectedly high percentage of self-built constructions, a large part of these houses exposed serious structural problems — a reflection of the missing access to good standard building materials, and of the lack of professional expertise accessible to these people. In response to this limitation the 1984 housing law foresaw particular provisions in support of self-help housing, namely credit, technical assistance and official outlets for standard quality building materials.

Collective forms of self-help housing include agricultural co-operatives, where house building is one among several other co-operative activities, and regular housing co-operatives. This latter form implied several individual self-builders forming a team which would build their houses together for the period of construction only, by which they could share their own capacities and any external support, too. An additional benefit was seen in the better use of building sites, and a saving of the cost to provide urban services in comparison with individual self-building, because preference was given to multi-family blocks of flats. However, in practice very few housing co-operatives were formed, and from 1986 onwards all political support was directed towards the renewed emerging Microbrigadas, which were considered a much superior form of collective self-help. Eventually within the new housing law of 1988, the previous section dealing with housing co-operatives has been replaced with provisions for different forms of Microbrigadas which had developed over the past few years, and which have become the most dynamic element of Cuban housing provision today, both in terms of new building and for the maintenance and renovation of the existing housing stock. Because the Microbrigadas represent a unique feature in Latin America, or elsewhere in the Third World, the remainder of this paper will deal with them in greater detail.

THE EMERGENCE OF THE MICROBRIGADA MOVEMENT AS A NEW FORM OF HOUSING PRODUCTION

The idea of the Microbrigadas was first put forward in public by Fidel Castro in 1970. The workers within an office, a factory or any other productive unit should be given the possibility to build houses for themselves and for their colleagues. For this purpose, some of them were to be released from their normal work duties and integrated into building brigades, while their colleagues, who stayed behind, guaranteed to maintain the previous level of productivity in the unit. The Microbrigadistas (i.e. the members of a Microbrigada) continue to receive their regular salary from their permanent employer, and therefore their income may exceed the level obtainable by unskilled workers within the building industry. Any houses completed by a Microbrigada team were then to be distributed among all workers of the original work place according to need and work merits, and there was no automatic priority given to the members of a Microbrigada.

Only a few months after the initial public presentation of the idea, the first construction sites were handed over to Microbrigadas on an experimental basis. The model was found to be feasible and good, and more and more Microbrigadas joined in. By 1978, more than 1,100 teams had been formed by some 30,000 brigadistas, having completed 82,000 dwelling. The movement was strongest in the capital Havana, since here the house building activity of the state sector — the established channel for the production of mass housing — was intentionally kept minimal in order to let the historically underserviced provinces catch up with the standards. Satellite cities around the capital were built by the Microbrigadas: typical examples are Altahabana, Reparto Electrico, San Augustin, Cotorro and Alamar — the latter designed to house some 150,000 people.

At that time almost all the houses built by Microbrigadas were 4 or 5 floors walk-up flats following a standard design. To reduce urbanistic monotony, the facades were gaily painted or green areas were cultivated between the blocks. However, what contributed more than everything else to maintain a high social status in these settlements was the fact that the inhabitants were not social outcasts, as tends to be the fate of architecturally similar developments in Europe in these days, but workers selected for their outstanding work and social merits.

Despite recognised achievements of the Microbrigadas, the movement almost came to a standstill by the late 1970s. There was more than one single and evident reason for this halt, and it is evident that the ongoing institutionalisation and restructuring of the national economy played a major influence. More particularly, it was argued that the predominantly artisan building technology applied by the Microbrigadas was not very efficient, and that both the quality of the product and the productivity of the process could be raised by relying more on industrialised systems — which in turn would require a skilled labour force and not the laymen of Microbrigadas. A minor problem associated with the Microbrigadas was the fact that many brigadistas were better paid than regular construction workers on the same site. Another criticism concerns the selective distribution mechanism of the Microbrigada-houses, because it excluded some of the people with the greatest housing need, namely people without regular employment. Also, the work centres themselves became increasingly reluctant to release their workers to join a Microbrigada once the earlier production problems, which had frequently caused overstaffing, had been overcome. Last but not least, a new Economic and Management system, which had been introduced in the second half of the sixties requested the self-financing of these enterprises and called for a more economical and product-oriented use of the labour force.

It was planned that the gap which the dissolved Microbrigadas left behind would be filled by additional, and more efficient, state brigades, which would also incorporate some previous Microbrigadistas who would prefer to remain in the building trade instead of returning to their home base. However, they would be paid directly by the Ministry of Construction.

THE MICROBRIGADAS IN THE PROCESS OF "RECTIFICATION"

The expected increase in the output of houses built directly by the state did not materialise for various reasons. It seemed that the possible productivity gains through industrialisation had been overestimated, an experience also shared by most European countries. In addition to this structural limitation, the newly formed state brigades were not primarily used for housing construction, but for non-residential projects which were granted a higher political priority. Apart from that, construction work is hard and not particular attractive, with the consequence of temporary labour shortages and a high fluctuation rate in the trade.

At the same time as the state sector housing output (which includes the Microbrigadas) dropped, the housing demand increased because the children born in the 1960s baby boom reached marrying age in the 1980s. The increasing housing deficit built up considerable popular pressure in response to which the politicians attributed a much higher priority to housing issues than in the past. The housing law of 1984, marked the first official recognition that it was unrealistic to expect that all the dwellings needed could be provided by the state building sector alone. Now self-help practices obtained explicit recognition and support, along with other novelties like the privatisation of almost all the houses previously rented from the state and the right of the occupants to sell their dwelling freely on the market if they wanted to move.

This policy change was one of the first manifestations of a political reorientation in Cuba in the mid-1980s which has become known under the term "rectification de los errores" (to correct past mistakes). The reform can partly be characterised as a political dedogmatisation in those areas where a gap between state ideology and living experience had become evident, and by the acceptance of certain market mechanisms provided that the practice of this opportunity would not jeopardise the intended basic political and social development. But "rectificacion" also meant restoring vanishing idealism, condemning ascending corruption among officials, and fostering new and more enthusiasm, imagination and voluntary work which had helped to keep the revolution going in its first decade.

In the "rectification" process, many political decisions of the 1970s were revised — revitalisation of the Microbrigadas was one of the affected measures. Fidel Castro himself proposed revitalising the Microbrigadas in another speech in June 1986. He said that it would be absurd to let the Microbrigada movement die considering its past merits, and he added that the Microbrigadas would be particularly useful for those factories or other productive units which suffered temporary work stoppages for one reason or another. He also stressed the idea, that the "Micros" should not just build housing for their own work centre's benefit, but also for the general need (Granma June 9, 1986). Less than 4 months after Castro's speech, some 75 new Microbrigadas with altogether 2,400 workers had been formed in Havana, and most of them has started to work on site by the end of the year. Another four months later, the number of brigadas had even risen to 285, consisting of 6,926 workers, including 781 women. At the end of the year 1987, more than 500 dwellings had been completed, and some 13,000 more were under construction.

By November 1988, the number of Microbrigadistas had risen to almost 38,000 (in 10,000 brigades), exceeding their number at any time before in the 1970s. 3,000 dwellings had already been finished within less than two years, and another 25,000 were under construction. The target for the years 1989 and 1990 was even more ambitious: 15,000 and 20,000 dewelling units respectively. These figures would even be more impressive if non-residential constructions and houses built by the "social Microbrigadas", were included.

Although the old Microbrigada concept of the 1970s was taken up, it was not copied totally. In Havana, which once again was the principal arena of the programme, the explicit goal was to start 'a radical transformation of the capital', a statement hinting at the new urbanistic and architectural emphasis. As in Europe, the euphoria for large housing development in the urban periphery had declined. The need for urban repair and conservation, particularly of historic neighbourhoods, had been recognised, and resulted in various reconstruction and infill projects. It is obvious that industrialised building systems, the domain of the Ministry of Construction in Cuba, are neither a sensible nor economical solution for these tasks. The Microbrigadas, on the other hand, have an obvious advantage in doing such a labour-intensive job with their typical artisan approach. Of course, urban renewal is only one of several areas where Microbrigadas are active today. In the less densely populated peripheral areas of the city they continue to build standard designed blocks of flats, or the finish off high rise buildings of which the basic structure has previously been erected by the ministry's own construction teams.

Since the Microbrigada projects require a close coordination with the local administration, and imply a social responsibility towards the resident population in the neighbourhood, a new organisational set up was chosen. The Microbrigadas are not integrated any more into the hierarchy of the Ministry of Construction, but have their own and independent institutional set up, subdivided in divisions according to the geographic structure of local government units, the "Poder Popular". The decentralised form of organisation also permits a more flexible architectural approach, the use of local materials and the recycling of salvaged building components, a closer co-operation with the neighbourhood, and last but not least a more intensive backing for the individual Microbrigadas through joint technical assistance, supervision, education and catering services.

The biggest difference of today's microbrigadas compared to the previous practice, is their explicit social responsibility: only 60 per cent (50 per cent before 1989) of all the dwellings they produce go to the brigadistas and their colleagues in the unit's work place, the remainder being offered to the "Poder Popular" (local government) for distribution among those members of the community who need a house but are not connected with any Microbrigada. In addition to housing, the Microbrigadas simultaneously provide urgently needed buildings for community facilities. For example, they had completed "circulos infantiles" (child care centres), schools for the handicapped, polyclinics, buildings for neighbourhood doctor's homes and offices, hospital extensions, schools, and a bakery. They even handled bigger projects, like the Zoo, the Botanical Garden, the Aquarium, the pavilions to house the EXPOCUBA and new buildings to accommodate the 1991 Pan-American Games. Several Microbrigadas are grouped together into "contingents", where they co-operate with regular state building enterprises. These figures demonstrate the preponderance of the Microbrigadas particularly in that type of construction which is most visible to the public mind and that it will most likely remain one of the main elements of Cuban housing and construction policy for many years to come.

ORGANISATIONAL PRINCIPLES

Each Microbrigada consists of not less than 33 workers, a "historic" number which was established at the outset of the movement, and has never been changed since. Out of these 33 Microbrigadistas who have been selected by vote among a larger number of volunteers in a union meeting, normally 14 will exclusively work in "social" infrastructure projects as explained above, unless the complete brigade prefers to stay together and build first the houses, and the community facilities thereafter. The weekly work time in a Microbrigada is 60 hours, compared to the 44 in a regular job. This extra labour, in combination with better work morale (i.e., less absenteeism) is reported to result in a productivity level higher than that of a regular building brigade in the Ministry of Construction. In addition, the productivity of the Microbrigadas is improved further by the technical assistance offered by the brigadista's original work centres: for example, any trucks or machinery not in use by the employer over the weekends may be borrowed by the "micros" for free, or certain products and services provided by the centres are not billed to the full amount. Also the Microbrigadas themselves economise by reconditioning machines or trucks already abandoned by other firms.

Due to the fast growth of the Microbrigada movement in 1987, coupled with the still increasing number of building permits for individual self-help housing in the smaller towns, the demand for building materials exceeds the available supply and represents the greatest obstacle to an expansion of the Microbrigada movement at present. Therefore 38 new building materials factories are now being set up, out of which 10 will be exclusively operated by Microbrigadas.

An interesting aspect is the participation of women within the Microbrigada movement. Their share was 12 per cent initially in 1987, which had increased to 22 per cent in 1988; and there were even two Microbrigadas consisting almost completely of female workers. This may be a low figure when compared with other professions in Cuba. But compared to international standards in this trade, the figure is the highest in the world, followed by Czechoslovakia (19%), Hungary (18%), Haiti (16%), Japan (13%), Trinidad and Tobago (12%),

Australia (11%), and India (10%) (ILO, 1984). During various visits to Microbrigadas one gets the impression that the women primarily had the role of helping hands, and the canteen was always under their control. It has also been reported that they specialise in interior finishing jobs (tiles, painting) and operating the lift: occupations that require care but not much physical strength.

FINANCE AND STANDARDS

The building site and all building materials are provided to the Microbrigada by the state, and the salaries of the workers are either paid by their work centre (and refunded by the state since 1986) or paid directly by the state through the Microbrigada (where the workers do not belong to a work centre). In the 1970s the houses then belonged to the state who let it to the tenants. The self-help labour input by the Microbrigada was rewarded by a rent reduction from normally 10 per cent of the family income to only 6 per cent. According to the privatisation policy contained in the housing law of 1984 the houses are sold to the occupants with a credit repayable over 20 years at 2-3 per cent interest. The sale price is subsidised by 25 per cent and not related to the actual cost of a dwelling but is calculated according to a standard formula taking into account the property's amenities, its size and location. Flats built by a Microbrigada are subject to a 10 per cent discount compared to regular state brigade built houses. This means that the price is not related any more to the income of the user, but different incomes are reflected by the variations in the repayment period of the credit, and representing a monthly installment forming 25 per cent of income. However, the cost of housing does not affect access to housing in Cuba. A survey of 180 households done by the author in 1988 revealed that in no case the selection of the dwelling in which the interviewed persons lived had been influenced by it's cost.

Initially, the space standards for houses to be built by the Microbrigadas were the same as for all other houses, ranging from 12 to 15 sq m per person. However, for self-build houses this figure is slightly higher, a regulation which now is also applied to the case of the Microbrigadas — provided that the standard design of the house permits to do so. Where the design is "non-typical" (i.e., non-standard), like in an infill or renovation project in an older neighbourhood, up to 20 sq m may be allowed per person anyway; an another reason explaining most applicant's preference for this type of dwelling. Also in a number of cases participants were able to convince the architects to modify aspects of the initial design, usually resulting in more privacy or greater balconies.

"PURE" MICROBRIGADAS

Following the enthusiastic response by the people to the revival of Microbrigada movement in 1987, additional arrangements departing from the initial set-up have been introduced. One of these options has become known under the name "Microbrigada Pura", which may not be very important numerically but is interesting because it puts an even stronger emphasis on the philosophy of voluntary work — always considered a crucial element in socialist development. The "pure" Microbrigadas only operate during free time (evenings and weekends), and its members continue to work during the day in their regular jobs, for which they are paid. Such an arrangement is typical for certain very specialised professions, which cannot release their employees from their regular duties because their occupation is considered of key importance for the advancement of the society, or other cases where it is not feasible to substitute the workers. Examples are physicians, or the employees of the Academy of Science, who operate a "Pure Microbrigada" in Old Havana.

In other words, whereas in the conventional Microbrigadas the voluntary effort is shared among all workers of a productive unit (because the productivity level must be maintained with less people working), the "extra labour" accrues to the individual worker alone in the "Microbrigada Pura". It results in a working day exceeding the 10 hours of a regular Microbrigada. In respect to the types of houses built, and the amount of the "social" share of the output there is no difference compared to conventional Microbrigadas, but when it comes to the distribution of houses, the "pure" have the guarantee to get allocated a flat after termination of the house(s).

THE SOCIAL MICROBRIGADAS

A significant widening of the Microbrigada concept can be found in the case of the "Social Microbrigadas", which were introduced in different parts of the capital, including "Centro Habana"; and "Marianao" at the end of 1987. In this case, the workers do not belong any more to the same productive unit, but their unifying characteristic is that they all live in the same neighbourhood — the one in which the Microbrigada is operating. The main task for this type of a Microbrigada is the repair or renovation of the existing housing stock and urban infrastructure, whereas new construction remains an exception.

Previously, the maintenance of the housing stock was the responsibility of municipal repair enterprises ("empresas"), which were directed by the Poder Popular. However, the performance of these units was not satisfactory for a number of reasons, and demanded more efficient solutions. In "Centro Habana", where one of the first "Social Microbrigada" was started on an experimental basis, the formal repair enterprise was dissolved, and its previous workers were incorporated into the new brigade. In addition, unemployed people from within the neighbourhood were offered a paying job: youth, adults, housewives, and the elderly. The unemployed youngsters (about an equal share male and female) have the possibility of learning a building trade as a part of the job (two or three hours training per day) while they are receiving a regular income as untrained workers, the same as the housewives (148 Pesos per month). Old-age pensioners, who have worked in the building trades before, function as teachers of the young, and receive their pre-retirement salaries (typically between 203 and 233 Pesos) in addition to their pension. Apart from the paid members, the Social Microbrigadas also incorporate voluntary workers, who are either neighbours joining the unit in their free time, or individuals given paid leave by their regular work centre.

Also in the case of the "Microbrigadas Sociales" the idea of voluntary labour, is — at least nominally — maintained. The regularly paid workers receive a salary for 55 of the 60 hours work per week, the remaining 5 hours are considered their "social" contribution. Unlike the regular Microbrigadas, their 'social' counterparts are not obliged to build an extra 50 per cent dwelling units to be allocated to the "general need" since they themselves represent the "general need", and also because the bulk of the work is renovation of the existing stock, which is already occupied. The underlying assumption is that eventually the entire neighbourhood will be renovated house by house, and the members of the Social Microbrigada will benefit from the works as much as the rest of the neighbours. Because of the specific local conditions, the size of the brigada is not fixed, but varies considerably. This and similar decisions are left to be decided by the neighbourhood of a "circumscription" (election district or ward) — and their elected representative simultaneously acts as the organiser of the Social Microbrigada.

Thus the Social Microbrigada has several functions at a time: apart from addressing the housing problem and maintaining the urban fabric, they also provide a answer to the social problems arising from an apparent lack of attractive employment opportunities. A guaranteed own income, improved housing opportunities, and the social control of the neighbourhood are an incentive to accept the inconveniences of hard physical work and regular working hours. As a supplementary benefit it has also been pointed out that the residents may take greater care of the houses they live in, and that they will be better equipped to carry out future maintenance jobs by themselves, once they have participated in renovating or rebuilding a house.

LIMITATIONS IN PRACTICE

Although the achievements of the new Microbrigadas in the short period are impressive, there are problems, too. As it was mentioned above, the building materials industry was by no means prepared for such a rapid increase in demand, and the shortages in materials delay the completion of many microbrigada projects. Equally, there are not enough talented architects to provide tailored designs for all projects, or experienced engineers and foremen to guarantee a smooth work organisation on site, thus further reducing the progress of the job. Particularly in the social Microbrigadas the resulting frustration contributes to considerable fluctuation among the brigadistas, and in the Van-Van project, in Santiago de Cuba, only 50 per cent of authorised posts are filled. However, these difficulties are not an inherent feature of the concept but can rather be attributed to the premature start of too many Microbrigadas at the same time with too little preparation — a picture that can be corrected by time.

SIGNIFICANCE OF THE CONCEPT

Both the initial introduction and the revival of the Microbrigada concept testify a flexible and imaginative approach to face the acute housing problem in a specific social and economic situation. In both instances there was a sectoral labour shortage affecting the construction industry, with simultaneous overstaffing in other economic sectors (or even open unemployment in the contemporary case of the social Microbrigadas). Some people have argued that the Microbrigadas represent an unscientific approach to solving the housing problem, and that the same manpower could work with a better preparation and less losses if they had been trained for the job and worked in a less spontaneous manner. However this view does not acknowledge the important political, and ideological, impact of the Microbrigadas: First, by stressing the "emergency situation" much more enthusiasm and co-operation can be mobilised from the workers, and the social control by fellow workers and neighbours will be more effective and less harassing than other forms of performance control. Not least of all, the recent social Microbrigadas can — for a few years — absorb (and keep off the streets) a substantial number of those young unemployed which represent the peak of the 1960s baby boom and for which as a temporary problem it would not be opportune to invest enormous sums in new universities and other capital intensive workplaces.

Economically speaking, the more artisan form of production typical for Microbrigadas effectively allows a large number of workplaces and an increase in production in the construction sector immediately, because there is very little fixed capital (installed machinery) required. It is debatable, whether home work units of the conventional Microbrigadas can really maintain their previous level of production while some of the staff are released to work in a Microbrigadas, but — as Fidel Castro pointed out — the solution can increase the GNP in periods where there is not enough work for the employed labour force in a work centre. Again politically speaking the "Microbrigada solution" is also a much more popular alternative to laying off staff in periods of structural or conjunctural work stoppages — which would be the unavoidable answer in a capitalist economy.

However, as a long term solution it might be difficult, if not impossible, to maintain the high level of enthusiasm and voluntary labour which make up the present success to the movement. At least two future developments are possible. One possibility is that the current enthusiasm vanishes and the Microbrigadas are abolished again once they become an economic burden rather than a premium. Another vision is that the introduction of wide spread participation of the population in the provision of housing cannot be reversed easily, but expands further (i.e. by incorporating the users much more in the decision-making process concerning matters of design and standards) and enlarges the platform of grass roots democracy in Cuba.

Assuming that the Microbrigadas were a good idea for Cuba, the question arises whether the concept would also be conceivable in other countries displaying similar problems. In most of Third World states the housing crisis is much worse than in Cuba; and innovative ideas are needed to find a solution. However, if the concept is transferable at all, certain fundamental differences would have to be taken into account.

Critical marxists say that self-help housing policies have an element of double exploitation of the Microbrigadistas. They are exploited by extending the working hours necessary for the labourer's reproduction and demanding unpaid "surplus labour" during "free time". Also the Microbrigada movement involves extra working time (or effort), which is particularly evident in the case of the "pure" Microbrigadas. For this effort — shared between the brigadistas and their colleagues staying behind in the work place — the term "plus trabajo" (extra work) has been introduced in Cuba. Segre (1984) explains:

> "In Cuba, a direct relationship between the production centre and the worker's need for housing is created. The solution lies in the special effort made in the work place and the availability of manpower that this frees up for construction. In the production centre it is called plus-work, and it reflects the workers understanding of the problems inherent in the economic development of a country and the importance of their direct participation in the solution of these problems. This has absolutely nothing to do with the exploitation of workers typical of an underdeveloped capitalist country. There, the worker, after selling eight hours of his labour power, must still take on the construction of his own home. This is a hidden form of appropriation by capitalist entrepreneurs, in that the building loans and materials purchases necessary to carry out the dwelling work are themselves sources of substantial profits."

Towards the end of the first phase of Microbrigada Fidel Castro stressed its importance when he advocated for the revival of the movement. In any case, the amount of voluntary labour invested by the Microbrigadistas and their work colleagues is most remarkable, particularly when one considers that a large proportion of this time is not invested in order to improve the Microbrigadista's personal living conditions. Instead, the benefit goes to the colleagues belonging to the same work place, and the community in general. In fact, there are many Microbrigadistas who do not request to be rehoused. It is difficult to imagine a comparable idealism in a capitalist society. The difference may be that in Cuba this extra work which the Microbrigadistas invest, is not transformed into "surplus value" to be appropriated by a capitalist class, instead the output takes the form of a physical product which can be seen by everybody, and of which the benefit accrues fully to the local community. Hence the concentration of "visible" products, as mentioned above. But also in other "socialist" Third World states, it would be difficult to find a comparably high level of social conscience among such a large proportion of the population. However, few other countries in the Third World have had more than a generation to build a new society. The time span is an important factor when it comes to foster the confidence into the solidarity of the collective.

On crucial aspect of the original Microbrigada programme is the linkage between work place and the place of residence. In capitalist countries, this linkage in the form of "tied accommodation" has been exploited by the employers as a tool to discipline the labour force. In Cuba, however, such a risk does not exist since both the job and the flat are practically guaranteed. Thus the positive and comfortable implications of the linkage can be taken advantage of, primarily by reduction of the journey to work (in Havana commuting times of up to an hour and more each way are common, but the Microbrigada sites are usually located in the vicinity of the original work place today).

The biggest obstacle to implementing the Microbrigada concept in a country with a different social order would be the pressure of competition in capitalist and mixed economies, which forces even the most benevolent employer to exploit his contracted labour force to the extreme. Releasing part of the salaried staff to produce a good that cannot be sold, but will be consumed by the workers directly, would probably ruin the enterprise. Even when one assumes that there are enterprises for which the model is economically sustainable, the workers themselves would probably prefer cash rather than houses to improve their situation, given the average Third World context with deficits in almost all basic needs for the poor, so that they can individually spend it according to their own needs and priorities.

The few situations where the Microbrigada concept might be imported successfully include cases of companies with seasonally changing labour requirements, which could build up a more steady employment pattern. Attractive (and economically affordable) even for more affluent societies in the north remains the idea to temporarily swap one's habitual work place with one in a different occupation (like construction on farming), without having to worry about a loss of income, or giving up the option to return to one's previous job when wanted.

For the model of the Social Microbrigadas, which are not linked to a common work centre from where their members receive an income, the adaptation within a different social context could be more realistic. Particularly in the upgrading of slums, which is a prime task in most Third World cities, the Cuban experience could teach an important lesson. However, a precondition would be that the authorities accept the responsibility to pay an adequate salary to those participants of such a programme who do have any other income, and to depart from the illusion that "full cost recovery", a dogma particularly put forward by the World Bank, can be achieved in all programmes. Lastly, the fundamental problem of transplanting the concept would be that in most other places in the Third World, a sectoral housing project may only achieve a short-term improvement, unless other basic needs (food, health, education) — already guaranteed in Cuban society — are simultaneously provided through an integrated programme.

REFERENCES

Castex, Patrick (1986), *La Politique De Production — Distribution Du Logement A Cuba.* Paris, Groupe de Recherche et d'Echanges Technologiques: 173.

Coyula, Mario (1985), 'Cuba: Housing, Urban Renovation, and Popular Power', *Trialog , 6*, Darmstadt, RFA: 35-39.

Hamberg, Jill (1986), 'Under Construction: Housing Policy in Revolutionary Cuba', New York: Centre for Cuban Studies, 36 Pages; reprint in Rachel G. Brat *et al.* (eds.), *Critical Perspectives on Housing*, Philadelphia, Temple Press: 586-624.

Hamberg, Jill (forthcoming), 'Cuba'. In *The International Handbook of Housing Policies and Practices*, London, Greenwood Press.

Huwer, Reiner *et al.* (1984), 'Cuba: Eine Revolutionare Welt im Bau'. In *Trialog, 4*, Darmstadt: 4-7.

ILO (1984), *ILO Year Book of Labour Statistics*, Geneva.

Lopez, Sicilia (1987), 'Las Microbrigadas: Una Manifestacion Revolucionaria de la Participacion Popular en el Campo de Las Contruccions' paper presented at the "Conferencia Internacional sobre la Vivienda y el Urbanismo", La Habana, Palacio de las Convenciones.

Mace, Rodney (1979), 'Housing', in John Griffiths and Peter, *Cuba: The Second Decade*, London, Writers and Readers Publishing Cooperative: 121-130.

Ortega, Morales Lourdes *et al.* (1987), 'Nuevas Tendencias en La Politica Habitacional la Production de Viviendas en Cuba. Panorama de su Desarrollo' (Band 27). Hamberg: Arbeitsbereich Stadtebau, Objektbezogene Stadtplanung im Forschungs schwerpunkt 6, Technical University Hamburg-Harburg.

Segre, Roberto (1984), 'Microbrigadas and Participation in Cuba', in C. Richard Hatch, *The Scope of Social Architecture*, New York, Van Nostrand Reinhold: 349-360.

13

HOUSING IN NICARAGUA*

ROY DARKE with D. ALEXANDER, J. DARKE and A. MANOGUE

INTRODUCTION

The Sandinista Government in Nicaragua is attempting to rebuild and restructure the economy whilst developing a wide ranging social programme. A main objective is to develop the social infrastructure, associated with improving well-being and the standard of living particularly of the lowest income groups which includes the majority of the rural population. Housing was seen as the third national priority in social development after health and education. The programme of economic development and social provision is being hampered by an unbalanced agro-export economy and recovery from its poor state in the period leading up to the revolution, difficulties with conflicting priorities in changing the focus of agricultural production (between export crops and the production of basic grains principally for national consumption) and by the need for defence against external aggression which has taken an increasing share of public expenditure since the early 1980s.

Housing policies in Nicaragua are outlined with examples of the several types of project being undertaken under the auspices of the state. A shift of emphasis from the primacy of direct state provision towards self-help projects is noticeable in the period from 1980 to 1985, due in part to reductions in resources available for housing and, latterly, to lower national priority being given to the housing programme. In looking to the future it is possible to see a preference on the part of state officials for reinstating priority towards direct state built housing when resources are again available. However, the authors suggest that the conditions for success in self-help housing projects on

---

* This paper was written before the change of Sandinista Government in Nicaragua.

the basis of experience from international examples are amply met in the Nicaraguan context. In part this is due to Sandinista support for popular participation in all aspects of the revolution but also to factors such as the Latin American tradition of self-build and owner occupation of housing.

At a more theoretical level the paper seeks to extend the debate on the merits and demerits of self-help housing which until now has tended to take place largely in the context of market economies and a capitalist ethos. In particular much of the academic discussion on the policy of self-help housing (in English) has given little or no space to examples such as Cuba where there has been a state policy of 'autoconstruccion'. By providing an example of self-help housing from within a proto-socialist context where the state has considerable control over land, the supply of building materials and other resources and where the land market is largely non-existent the authors intend to widen the discussion and show the potential of such schemes not only for housing production but also for political solidarity, community cohesion, education and personal satisfaction of participants.

CONTEXT

In July 1979 the success of the popular revolution signalled the end of the Somoza family dictatorship which had been maintained in power for 43 years through political repression and military force backed by the USA. The uprising was led by the Sandinista Liberation Front (FSLN) which commanded a people's army of several thousand supported by a network of families and households organised on a neighbourhood basis. The Government of National Reconstruction was left with a country in ruins and a financial crisis. The legacy of poverty was such that:

93 per cent of rural housing had no safe drinking water;
50 per cent of the population were illiterate;
60 per cent of the deaths were caused by preventable diseases and
60 per cent of campesinos (peasants) were landless.

The Government was faced with a wide range of urgent priorities for a social programme. However, there was virtually no money for reconstruction as Somoza had fled the country with an estimated $900 million leaving a national debt of $1.6 billion. The cost of the war which had preceded the revolution was estimated at $4 billion; a combination of lack of production, direct damage and capital flight. Nicaragua has a land area of 410,000 sq km (roughly the same size as England and Wales) and a relatively small population of 3 million. Over 70 per cent of export earnings come from agriculture. After 1979 the world price for the 4 main exports; coffee, cotton, sugar, beef has declined sharply. Under Somoza only a small industrial capacity had been built up principally using second-hand North American plant. The industry had been developed not to meet the needs of the people but for the profits that could be made by an elite. Most commodities were imported.

Even before the contra aggression of the 1980s and the economic measures taken against Nicaragua by the USA the economy had been hit by major disasters. In 1972 an earthquake in Managua destroyed 75 per cent of the buildings and an estimated 10,000 people were killed. In 1982 freak floods in Managua caused damage estimated at $365 million — the equivalent of one years export earnings.

The economy is now a mixture of state, cooperative and capitalist enterprise. Contrary to the attempts to portray the government as composed of doctrinaire marxists one of their fundamental principles is to develop a mixed economy, along with political pluralism and international non-alignment. The capitalist sector is important in producing a large proportion of exportable crops and goods vital for earning foreign exchange. Since 1981 the US government has attempted to destabilise the Nicaraguan economy and the country by cancelling existing credit packages and using its influence to block loans and credit from international bodies such as the World Bank and the Inter American Development Bank. In May 1985 an economic embargo was imposed by the USA banning all trade with Nicaragua which had denied an important export market for the country as well as exacerbating difficulties in getting spare parts for vehicles and machinery.

The major current problem for the economy is the drain imposed by external military aggression and terrorism mainly financed by and from the USA. Considerable resources have been diverted from social programmes such as health and housing and re-allocated to defence. Recent estimates indicate that 40-50 per cent of government spending goes on defence. Young people are mobilised in the army and workers and peasants need to maintain constant vigilance in their workplaces and in the fields causing a reduction in production. A further drain on the economy is the informal sector where many people sell goods and services in preference to work in production. Alongside the state system of shops a black market exists where goods can be bought at uncontrolled prices or cheaply for US dollars thus creating a dual exchange rate; the official rate for the cordoba and 'scarcity' rate. During the period since early 1985 the contra war and the economic boycott by the USA have seriously hit production and aggravated the shortage of foreign exchange and pushing up the unofficial rate of exchange.

Within this increasingly difficult context the government has continued to make advances in programmes for education, health, agrarian reform, greater equality for women and in housing. Free elections were held in November 1984 which gave a large majority to the FSLN in the National Assembly. In a 75 per cent turnout 67 per cent of the vote went to the Sandinistas.

INHERITED HOUSING PROBLEM

An estimate from the Ministry of Housing and Human Settlement (MINVAH) is that in 1971, 70 per cent of housing was overcrowded and 54 per cent inadequate — inadequate housing being defined as constructed from scrap materials rather than being without services such as water supply, drainage and electricity which are very widely lacking. The skeletal construction industry based on the capital and only geared to building one-off housing for the bourgeoisie was incapable of repairing the scale of earthquake damage in 1972. In addition there was considerable corruption and squandering of international aid whereby much cash and material support sent to help the population ended up in private hands of those close to the Somozas. In 1979 Managua had 60 per cent of barrios without piped water, sewerage or electricity and in 1984, 20 per cent of households in the capital were without a home of their own, 15 per cent were in inadequate housing and 30 per cent lived in one-room huts.

Typical housing for workers in Nicaragua consists of small single storey units usually self-built from whatever materials are at hand. Internally there is a single room 6 or 7 metres square which may be divided with makeshift partitions. A good deal of family life is spent out of doors under a shaded verandah where hammocks are hung for rest and sleep. Food is cooked over wood fires sometimes in a small kitchen enclosure built on to the house or verandah. The average occupancy rate is 6 to 7 persons per housing unit.

Throughout the 1950s Nicaragua experienced a redistribution in its population with large numbers of peasants moving into the towns and cities. In 1950, 35 per cent of the population was urban; by 1979 this figure had increased to 58 per cent. Almost 2/3 of the population lives in the pacific zone. Urban growth has been disordered and largely uncontrolled creating serious housing problems with much illegal squatting. The attraction of Managua to migrants and past concentration of investment in the capital increased urban problems and created serious regional imbalance.

During the Somoza regime ordinary people had no means of solving their housing problems except by personal effort or self-help. The state did not offer assistance to the poor and only marginal town planning effort was put into plans for the capital. There was a shortage of land for urban migrants with most people being at the mercy of land owners and speculators who divided marginal land within the city into small plots for sale at high rates. Tenure on the urban margins was insecure with owners rarely handing over titles so that households were vulnerable to eviction as land owners took back land for later resale at higher prices to newer migrants. The only alternative for the poor urban family were the illegal shanty towns which developed on waste land or unsuitable plots. At the time of the revolution there were 38 unplanned settlements in Managua supporting about 7,000 households.

SANDINISTA HOUSING POLICY

The post-revolutionary Junta for National Reconstruction gave immediate priority to an ambitious programme of social reform. Housing came next in order of importance to health and education programmes. Responsibility for housing and urban development was given to the newly created Ministry of Housing and Human Settlement (MINVAH). The objectives set for MINVAH can be summarised as follows:

1. To prioritise housing resources on the basis of need
2. To redress inequalities between regions and between urban and rural areas
3. To expand the role of the state in housing provision both directly and indirectly
4. To promote popular participation in the process of housing

provision

5. To reduce technological dependence
6. To change the institutional and financial context within which housing is provided (MINVAH, n.d.; Vigil, 1983; Zunica, 1985).

CONSTRAINTS

The present military situation provides the overriding constraint on the ability of MINVAH to fulfil its objectives. The effects of the war pervade the whole of the life of the country, and the results of the war effort include severely limited availability of finance, labour and materials.

The increasing proportion of national income necessarily spent on defence obviously makes it difficult to fund social welfare provision of any sort. Paradoxically, this increases dependence on goodwill aid from friendly countries and agencies despite the intention to build an independent economy. The unpredictability of the flows of aid makes it extremely difficult to plan and implement a rational housing policy.

The war naturally occupies many people who would otherwise be engaged in productive work including house-building. The armed forces include a regular (though very young) army, conscripts and a part-time volunteer militia. There are attempts to control the numbers of workers from specific sectors of the economy and from anyone workplace serving in the militia at any one time so that work and production are not badly affected by the war. However, the militia attracts the most committed and active members of the community so that work and neighbourhood activities are inevitably influenced.

The war affects the availability of materials directly as well as through the depletion of the public purse and labour power. A potentially abundant building material, timber from the Nicaraguan forests, is difficult to harvest safely as it grows in the more remote and mountainous regions, close to border areas where workers and plant are vulnerable to contra attack and destruction. Furthermore, the US trade embargo means that even basic building materials have to be obtained through indirect and expensive channels. The urban drift of the population also creates added demands such as infrastructure works to expand and extend water supply.

However, many of these constraints would be present in less severe form even without the war. It is characteristic of economies such as pre-revolutionary Nicaragua that they rely on imports and plant obtained from the west, financed by international loans which can be disadvantageous to the developing economy, rather than using indigenous materials and creating appropriate technologies. There is now the will within Nicaragua to develop suitable techniques for an indigenous industrial base but this takes time to create and requires resources including import of some machinery and components. Even the basic infrastructure of Nicaragua is underdeveloped in that large areas of the country are not easily accessible, such as the Atlantic coast region where the principal town has no direct road or rail link to the capital.

Characteristically there are skill shortages at all levels in addition to the labour shortages attributable to the war. There are few who have technological skills, few with more than basic manual skills or experience to run the state apparatus, not enough professionals to help in the development of social programmes. Without an existing body of skilled workers neither is there the basis for education through apprenticeships and passing on know-how. Recent work on self-help housing schemes in other developing countries has brought out the key importance of effective local management and co-ordination but again there is a shortage of people who possess the building skills and management experience to organise, motivate and maintain morale in self-build schemes.

The final constraint to mention is the inherited structure of the building industry. Historically the industry was centred on Managua and many companies and building materials manufacturers were set up by Somocistas. An example was the production of the concrete paviors used for roads in the capital which were built as the main element of Somoza's commissioned town plan for Managua. The paviors were produced in a plant owned by the dictator. Ironically, they were ripped up during the insurrection to form barricades against the National Guard. However, the constraint posed by the underdeveloped building industry is not simply that of ownership but also of size, location and general underdevelopment in the face of the scale of problem and programme needed to significantly improve housing conditions.

POLICIES ADOPTED BY MINVAH

A series of legal measures have been introduced since 1979 to sustain and control housing development. Reforms include expropriation of underused land, particularly waste land in Managua and urban plots where land owners have exploited migrants and tenants in the past. Increasing the extent of state land-holding has been followed by passing land titles to households with priority being given to households with children. Those households that are given title to land or property by the state are unable to sell but can pass on the inheritance to kin thus preventing the commodification of housing. In time a formal system of exchange will need to be introduced to allow household mobility where necessary.

The intervention of the state also extends to housing provision either by direct building or by indirect measures. Three main forms of state housing provision have been introduced to help achieve the national objective of adequate housing for all.

The first of the measures is house building by the government in the form of *housing complexes*. In the complexes the government provides a basic shell serviced where possible with water and electricity while internal arrangements and refinements are left for the occupiers to provide for themselves. In the first years of the revolution direct state provision was the most significant element of the housing programme but its importance has diminished in recent years as the two other elements of the national programme have assumed greater importance. In part this is because they represent cheaper solutions for the government than building complete complexes, as the financial resources for housing are squeezed due to the war.

The second form of state provision, the *materials bank* scheme offers households the basic resources for housing — land, services and building materials. MINVAH provides site plans and technical advice and support for self-builders under this scheme.

The third principal instrument of state housing policy is *progressive urbanisation*. The role of the state is limited in this case to land allocation in the first instance with technical assistance on plot layout and site plans. The recipients have to find the resources to build housing, bring in basic services and develop the social facilities and infrastructure of their neighbourhood. MINVAH's role in these later stages may be advisory and supportive. Resources are either obtained from international sources and aid and/or from self-help within the community.

Under the first of these forms of provision over 35 housing complexes were on site or had been built directly by the state by the end of 1983 using its own construction organisation (COVIN). Direct built schemes accounted for 10,512 dwelling units between 1980 and the end of 1984. Since that time further activity under the scheme has been concentrated in the regions most affected by the war and/or the least developed, most needy areas of the country.

Built forms in the housing complexes range from simple detached single storey timber built dwellings in remote areas such as the Atlantic coast region to 2 and 3 storey flat developments in the urbanised Pacific coast areas around Managua. For example, in a scheme of 118 dwellings that we visited in Leon, construction of the flat blocks is a reinforced concrete frame and solid floor with clay block infill to form external walls and internal partitions. The level of servicing to these flats is relatively high with the provision of shower and flush toilet in a small internal bathroom and a sink in the main body of the dwelling. Upper units have a small balcony. Unit sizes vary but internal partitioning of the unit itself is left to households to provide according to their needs. Flat living is not indigenous in Nicaragua particularly given the high seismic activity and the rural background of most of the population. The multi-storey design has proved to be unpopular with residents who resent not having space to keep livestock or to grow their own vegetables or fruit.

The Leon scheme was completed in 1982; more typical of recent activity is a scheme we visited in the mountainous area near Ocotal close to the northern border. This scheme used a simple concrete block base wall and timber superstructure with sheet roofing to provide single storey, detached housing units for peasant farmers moved from isolated land holdings vulnerable to contra attack. Thirty-nine houses were built or under construction in mid-1985 with a planned settlement size of 100 units. The formation of a producer co-operative linked to the settlement was welcomed by the members that we spoke to. Among the benefits of co-operation and living together were the provision of elementary education, health care and communal dining room for the children.

The form of construction used in this scheme is known as 'minifalda'; literally miniskirt. It is suited both to construction by the direct labour organisation (COVIN) and by self-builders under the materials bank scheme, and is particularly useful in the Pacific zone which is prone to earthquake.

Another system used in direct state provision of housing is the 'Sandino' prefabricated concrete system used extensively in the Pacific region, such as the Sandino Heroico suburb of Esteli. The system was developed in Cuba in the 1960s for use in new towns and agricultural settlements. The main elements of the system are grooved posts which are set into an *in situ* concrete slab at approximately 1 metre centres in order to accept the panels which are assembled 'guillotine fashion' to provide an outer weather proof skin to the dwelling. Roofing is of lightweight timber build *in situ* with zinc sheet or tile covering. The system allows some flexiblility in layout and internal arrangement and has been used in Cuba in two-storey and multi-storey applications but the Nicaraguan schemes have created single storey, standard units laid out on site in grid form. The lack of variety in use of a system which could allow it indicates the resource constraints that obtain in Nicaragua where internal space is built to minima of around 36 sq m floor area and external layout is designed to minimise service runs for water and drainage.

An experimental workshop set up by MINVAH is taking advantage of the availability of pumice, a volcanic by-product, for use as an aggregate to reduce the weight of concrete building elements and thus reduce transport costs and make for easier handling in construction. Thus a Cuban system is being adapted to Nicaraguan conditions. Another example of technological innovation is the attempt to use locally grown sisal in fibre-cement tiles as an alternative to clay tiles, requiring less substantial roofing timbers and offering better safety in the event of earthquake.

Popular participation is a fundamental element of housing policy in Nicaragua today. Much political activity and implementation of social programmes takes place with the help of neighbourhood based groupings linked to the Sandinistan political party. These Sandinistan Defence Committees (CDS) sprang out of the revolution and resistance to the tyranny of the army and National Guard under Somoza. They currently play a role in maintaining vigilance against counter-revolutionary subversion, maintaining good relations within barrios but also spearheading health and social programmes and campaigns associated with improvements and developments in the neighbourhood. Collective house building and improvement of the environment and facilities has become a feature of organised action in the urban barrios with local leaders negotiating with the government and state agencies for land, materials and services. The unit of organisation is very small: a city block consisting of a few dozen or at most a few hundred houses, or a small rural settlement.

An example of the 'materials bank' scheme which is typical of state efforts to improve the quality of housing through self-build is the barrio Edguard Munguia in Managua. The people of the barrio came from a lakeside squatter settlement which was largely destroyed by flooding after heavy tropical rain in 1982. The government offered a new site for the barrier away from the lakeshore and gave support for the construction of new dwellings for those households that were homeless. Other households that were able to save their original dwellings were able to reconstruct them on plots in the new location. At the time of the authors visit 229 households were living in the barrio. Since relocation many households have extended or completely rebuilt their homes and the government has been instrumental, working with the local Sandinista Defence Committee, in identifying dwellings which are inadequate under the official definition by being built of waste materials. These are being brought into a rolling programme of improvement or replacement. The local political committee has also planned and implemented the construction of a large communal building which is used for meetings and social events. Water supply is by standpipes serving a few dozen dwellings each and although main drainage runs under the main distributor road on the edge of the site the dwellings still rely on earth closets. Electricity supply is pirated from the street lights and overhead cables around the site. The local leadership is now campaigning for international aid to help bring water supply to every house and to improve/extend other services. In mid-1985, 40 dwellings were known to need replacement but 95 houses had been built using a standard design and materials purchased from the state. Support for the rebuilding of the barrio and for house improvement had come from the Norwegian Government.

As an example of the third form of provision we mention an extension to the large suburb of Ciudad Sandino that we visited on the outskirts of Managua which was being developed under the 'progressive urbanisation' scheme. Again international aid was a factor in the development of this barrio when residents from the ruins of Central Managua met Swiss volunteers during coffee harvesting. From this contact a fund was negotiated to allow the residents of San Antonio to begin seeking land from the government for resiting and building new homes. The state offered the land at Ciudad Sandino, a site layout and a standard house design. The local leadership organised house construction on a co-operative basis with an expectation that all residents who wished for a house in the new location would work a specific number of hours on construction in anyone month. Houses were built and allocated on a priority basis so that the most needy or deprived households were among the first to move in to completed dwellings. However, another factor in priority allocation was the amount of collective effort that households put into construction. That is, households that were conscientious about the meeting work targets in building homes for others were rewarded by high priority for future allocation. Building materials were not available from the state so that the residents had purchased where they could. For example, roofing sheets came from Panama. Services such as water and electricity were not available on the site and the community had learnt that persistent lobbying of officials and appeal to the highest levels of government were the most effective ways of getting state action to provide services. This example offers a contrast to Edguard Munguia in asmuch that the barrio at Ciudad Sandino was developing as a result of collective effort whereas house building and improvement at Edguard Munguia was being carried out by individual households.

Self-build either on an individual or collective basis would not be capable of meeting all the objectives set for MINVAH, at least in the present circumstances. For example, in the new settlements built in the border areas, agricultural productivity is already diminished by the need for some of the workers to act was armed lookouts while others tend the fields. Self-build in these conditions would be virtually impossible without further help. However, the role of self-build in the developing world has also been the source of considerable debate and some controversy. For that reason we intend to broaden the discussion in order to embrace that issue and draw some international comparisons.

INTERNATIONAL EXPERIENCE

Most states play a role in housing policy and housing production but the specific interventions vary widely from comprehensive policies and actions intended to influence the production, distribution and consumption of housing (including direct state action such as programmes of social housing) to packages of indirect measures affecting financial institutions, land supply, internal space standards and so on which are intended to control and channel producer and consumer behaviour in the context of market provision. Rarely do governments accept the principles of classical economic theory which assumes that a free market regulated by the price mechanism will provide all the dwellings that a society needs. Yet, state policies of direct building are frequently seen as providing only for those who cannot provide for themselves. This residualisation of social housing has again become the main rationale in Britain over the past few years after a broader definition of the role of state housing, particularly under the Labour government of the 1940s. The concomitant of residualisation is a failure to accept the positive need and benefits of state built housing. For many governments in the industrialised and the Third World the principal role for the state in housing still tends to be identified as building special projects for the most needy or 'problem' families. Only in state socialist countries does the state play the major role in housing provision. On the other hand, even where the state plays a dominant role in housing provision, such as in Eastern Europe, a place exists both historically and currently for some private provision of housing especially in rural areas.

In Latin America levels of home ownership are high. In the 1970s no Latin American country had less than 50 per cent owner occupation and many states had levels of between 60 per cent and 70 per cent. Nicaragua was no exception to this general picture with recorded levels of private ownership of dwellings of 64 per cent in 1971 (Boleat, 1985). That proportion has diminished somewhat since 1979 given the development of a state building programme but even within the Sandinistan housing policy it is possible for tenants to buy the homes they are allocated by the government. The statistics on the tenure mix in Nicaragua are not available but about 10 per cent of the stock is now state owned. Gaining a true picture of tenure in Nicaragua is also complicated by the handing on of land titles and rights to dwellings to occupiers by the Sandinistan government (with covenants about retention of the titles within the family which means that the market in property is increasingly restricted).

Self-help housing which plays such a significant role in providing shelter in Latin America may represent a pragmatic response to circumstances in the region. Growing state acceptance of the principle of self-help may also be expedient. The precarious finances of many national economies in Latin America with severe inflation, massive international debts, and volatile markets in key exports limit the potential for large-scale state housing programme. Additionally, the cultural tradition of home ownership even of the most modest dwelling and relatively low per capita personal income (in Nicaragua the latter was $860 in 1980) point toward state support for self-build options in housing. Yet, the pursuit of this form of shelter provision is not without its critics. Firstly, pragmatism dressed up as principle is questioned as a long-term basis for housing provision where the primary rationale of self-build is resource constraint. Secondly, there is considerable ideological disquiet in some quarters where critics believe self-help housing has implications for social control, abrogation of state responsibility and potential reductions in both the social wage and rates for wage labour. Critics, such as Burgess (1982), have pointed to the tendency in commentaries about self-help to over-emphasise user benefits (consumer satisfaction, expenditure linked to means, learning of skills) and a failure to identify other interests which stand to gain. Even the consequent reduction in the size of the state apparatus and the reduction of bureaucratic procedures as a result of self-build policy are seen as benefits to users without identifying the profits and advantage given to land owners, materials suppliers and to governments themselves. The state, can off-load its management and contractual responsibilities by accepting self-help options and by planning and zoning ordinances which may exert considerable social control over the populace and organise political favours and support. Burgess goes even further in his critique and sees self-help housing policy as the ideological means to maintain a capitalistic *status quo* bringing homeless households into the market place, firstly, for building materials and, secondly, by investing their labour power creating a commodity which can be sold on to realise a profit. Self-help housing is seen in his analysis as socialising the poor into the market economy.

The role of the World Bank and other international financial institutions which favour investment in self-help housing (such as the International Finance Corporation and the US based Agency for International Development) has to be evaluated in the light of this radical critique. Since the early 1970s the World Bank has promoted and financed site and services schemes in the Third World. Its advisors have argued that national resource limitations preclude conventional permanent housing and if this were to be provided by the state then supply would be out of step with demand. Financial prudence, the development of free market principles and good economic accounting are essential to this advice.

The main question that is raised for socialist or proto-socialist governments by this broader debate about self-help housing and particularly the view that adopting such policies is an abrogation of the state's responsibilities is whether self-build can be acceptable policy for housing improvement in a revolutionary context. If self-help is accepted even as a temporary expedient another question is whether it can be linked into broader aims for economic and social development and change. The beginnings of an answer to these questions is whether the aims of social justice, redistribution and equality which are elements of a socialist programme can be furthered by self-help policies without the side effects that critics have found so unacceptable. We can only start to indicate that wider issue here but to pursue it effectively requires consideration of the context and action of the state apparatus in all its aspects — judicial, legislative, financial, educational and technical (Ward, 1983) — and how these link to state objectives and to personal well-being and interests. However, we should also beware of losing sight of the potential social, political and ideological benefits of self-help housing policy in a collective and socialist context which may give powers to democratic decision-making and collective responsibility down to the level of the neighbourhood.

In Nicaragua, the growing importance of the materials bank and progressive urbanisation schemes for housing provision (see Fig. 13.1) could be seen as expedient in the face of resource constraints. Certainly, the authors have some evidence from conversations with MINVAH officials that in more favourable circumstances they would wish to expand direct state house-building programmes. Self-help schemes are seen as inefficient and wasteful of materials. Yet socially responsive and socialist states in the developing world continue to turn to self-build options.

Cuba's housing programme since 1959 has passed through a number of phases. In the years immediately after the triumph the principal efforts were directed at state provision of housing using state construction bodies and often putting up multi-storey schemes built from large panel concrete systems originally developed in Eastern Europe. In 1971 Castro introduced the idea of 'microbrigades' with government support (materials and technical aid) whereby workers were 'seconded' from production sectors to build housing units. By the mid-1970s around 50 per cent of new housing in Cuba was being provided by these means. This step towards collective self-help was taken further by the possibility of informal self-build where private individuals and friends have been able to extend or build new with materials bought from the state. Legislation came into effect in mid-1985 which grants home ownership rights to all Cubans, encourages home maintenance and construction by individuals and grants low interest loans through the People's Savings Bank to allow

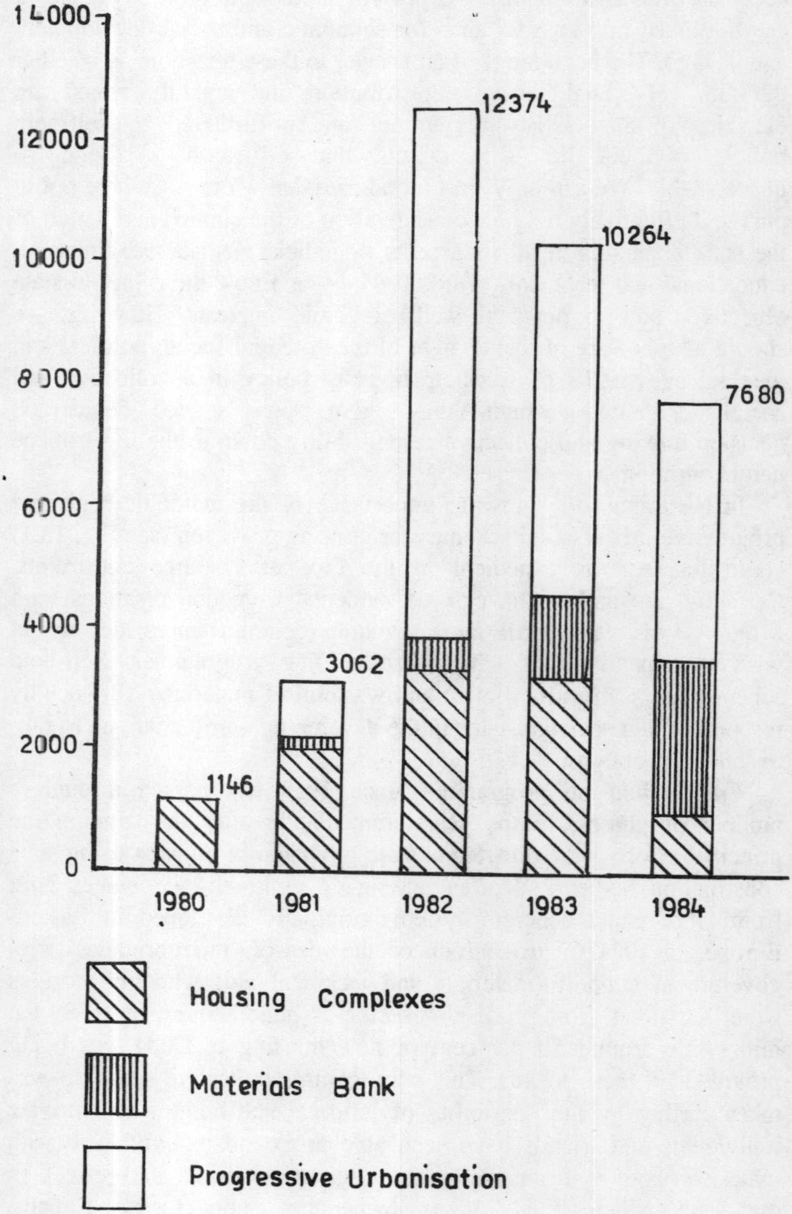

FIG. 13.1: Annual Housing Output (dwellings or plots) Nicaragua — 1980-1984

these improvements to housing by individual effort to occur. Explaining these new measures Castro noted that in a state where capitalism has been abolished and which is advancing towards socialism rents can be set low or homes given away free to users. Cuba was taking the steps to abolish rents and make everyone a home owner with the parallel measure to facilitate home improvement on a self-help basis. The market in land has been eliminated and ownership by individuals of several housing units is obstructed.

The principal lesson from the Cuban experience is therefore that even where the original emphasis on housing policy has been towards heavy state involvement and direct provision in a society which has accepted universal nationalisation in all sectors there has been significant movement to self-help in housing over the past decade. However, self-help policies are being undertaken in a context of social ownership of land and limitations on the property-holding of individuals.

In *Tanzania* the colonial legacy of attempting to develop policy for low-income urbanites has had an effect on policy after Independence. The pre-Independence policy for this sector was direct government provision and the clearance of squatter settlements. In fact lack of resources available to the National Housing Corporation meant that targets for new build were never achieved. Under the Second Five-Year Plan the pursuit of Ujaama and villagisation came to the fore and efforts by the government were directed at use of indigenous building materials and self-help building methods and policy. Direction of the housing programme away from Dar-es-Salaam and the urban centres also allowed development of the rural tradition of self-build. Formation of the Tanzanian Housing Bank by the nationalisation of a private house funding agency helped provide loans for house building by individuals.

Site and services schemes were introduced in 1974 with supplementary funding from the World Bank. A major problem with all these schemes has been the lack of resources available to the government given the poverty of the country and the difficulty of reaching the target population of the lowest income groups. The Third Five-Year Plan has made borrowing easier for the low-income groups by lowering the qualifying criteria and extending loan repayment periods but the problem remains. Additional obstacles are the bureaucratic complexities of the Tanzanian system and a free market in building materials which because of scarcity pushes building costs beyond many people's means. Self-help is seen as a way to bridge the gap between loans raised and costs of construction.

The experience in Tanzania shows that elimination of state provision has left the worst off and the worst housed in an unchanged position with respect to housing.

In *Zambia* resettlement of squatters was government policy into the late 1960s. International consultants such as Doxiadis Associates were proposing wholesale decanting and clearance during this period. The National Housing Authority Act of 1971 had clearance of settlements as its main policy. Yet within the space of 2 or 3 years upgrading became the favoured policy of the government. A limited programme of squatter settlement upgrading had been incorporated into the Second National Development Plan in the early 1970s. By the mid-1970s this was the main thrust of housing effort.

The apparent success of the policy in Zambia has been identified as due to

(a) adopting standards which are affordable by residents
(b) ensuring active participation (made easier by the oral tradition of decision-making in this part of Africa)
(c) careful preplanning
(d) development of a sensitive local administration charged with the implementation and management of specific projects of upgrading and self-build.

A more general conclusion is that user-led policy is most likely to be successful but that involvement of the state is vital and indeed expected by residents in order to give direction and expertise to the projects. A study of a self-help project in Lusaka concluded that the emphasis in such schemes should not be on trying to eliminate the input of public funds but that the state should ensure that money and resources are made available in such a way that the needs and priorities of residents are best served (Martin, 1982). The idea of the state as instigator and partner in self-help efforts is a consequence.

In a broad evaluation of self-help housing schemes in the Third World from the perspective of local organisation and implementation, Skinner (1982) has noted the general factors that have underpinned successful community involvement. These factors include:

1. support for community participation at state level and

complementarity between national objectives and popular participation
2. good relations between the state, its local agencies and the community
3. clarity and clear communication about what the project can offer and participants' role
4. involvement by the community in a comprehensive range of social facilities (job creation, health, education).

Skinner also notes a series of problems and difficulties that have been distilled from international experience such as local antagonism towards government schemes due to

(i) inadequate consultation by the state,
(ii) high costs,
(iii) promotion of unfamiliar or unacceptable construction or materials,
(iv) building work organisation unacceptable to local people,
(v) a socially mixed community and failure by the state to recognise special or differing needs,
(vi) distrust of the project agency (fear of exploitation, state domination, past corruption or poor performance).

EVALUATION

An assessment of housing policy and provision in Nicaragua has to be set in a broader framework: a context of continuing war effort, the immense scale of the problem of improving living conditions, the economic blockade and the physical circumstances of the country which includes natural hazards such as earthquake disturbances on the Pacific coast.

The Nicaraguan experience is unusual insofar as the early priority given to direct state provision of housing built and managed by the state has been quickly subordinated to self-build programmes. The switch between different elements of the housing programme in Nicaragua is to a great extent a pragmatic response to the difficulties facing the country particularly due to the war, lack of resources and changing national priorities for sectoral programmes. However there is also some evidence of a rapid and flexible response to learning from initial mistakes. For example, the flatted developments built by the government in Leon and Managua are now acknowledged as inappropriate, particularly by local MINVAH administrators; mistaken experiments strangely reminiscent of the high rise blocks which formed a major and mainly disastrous part of the British housing policy in the 1950s and 1960s. Given the popularity of the Sandinistan revolution and widespread enthusiasm for development and socially beneficial improvements in the country the interplay between experiment in policy and public response is likely to be productive.

The main points that can be drawn from an, admittedly, limited periods of development of housing policy in Nicaragua fall into comments relating to popular participation, the role of the state and the place of innovation and experiment.

Self-help and popular participation has become a major element of housing policy but it should not be seen as a panacea or the sole basis for improvement in living conditions. The Tanzanian experience warns that there is a role for direct state provision of housing in order to reach those who cannot easily provide for themselves. Equally the self-build approach has to be sustained by a range of other measures particularly with respect to land provision and controls over free exchange if a socialist housing policy is to be sustained. As an aside we might note that those critics of self-build in the West, who see it simply as a form of commodification of housing which trains people for the market economy and socialises an ideology of capitalism, fail to take account of the policy as followed by societies such as Cuba and Nicaragua.

To sustain self-build projects requires a long-term commitment and effort on the part of the people. Nicaragua benefits from the popular commitment to the revolution which crosses classes and groups and is manifested in the grass roots organisations (CDSs) which are built around the Sandinista party. It has been said that the Cuban Committees for the Defence of the Revolution (CDR) have been less successful in sustaining grass roots enthusiasm for the revolution but there are differences between the two countries and the revolutions which may be crucial in the long-term. Whereas the CDRs were introduced at the time of the overthrow of Batista the CDS organisation is built on 20 years of underground neighbourhood organisation by the FSLN directed initially at fighting for freedom. This powerful tradition has laid the strong basis for sustained energy in neighbourhood organisation and action. However it will only remain as a powerful element of social development if the organisations are given space to act and develop themselves and that mean retention of local autonomy and power.

The importance of neighbourhood is not only in terms of implementing policy and carrying through national policy but is also in contributing to the definition and development of those policies. Housing policy and the design of standard dwelling types will benefit from the recognition of peoples' wishes and needs.

Heavy reliance on self-build in national housing policy does not eliminate the need for *state involvement.* Giving priority to the most needy requires a powerful role in direct provision. For example, the resettlement programmes in the North and South of Nicaragua are aimed at groups who are vulnerable to contra attack and the state must continue to take a lead in this policy. Lessons are being learnt in the process and recent schemes have offered not only good quality dwellings but state assistance with agricultural development, communal facilities and collective methods of working which have been additional gains above that of increased security. Equally the state must sustain a direct building programme in the urban areas to cater for those unable to build for themselves.

Other roles for the state include control and supply of building materials and provision of technical support for self-builders. The planning of housing projects will need to be sustained through implementation, overall administration and longer term maintenance and improvement policies and a more localised distribution of these services will ensure that the government acts as a facilitator and agent for the programme without dominating decisions. Provision of land and services remains an essential function of government. The land question is the means by which the aims of greater equality and social justice can be sustained without exploitation and personal profit.

Management and administration of housing areas will remain a long-term state function but deconcentration of these functions is a step towards greater sensitivity and responsiveness to need.

On a more critical note there is scope for the state in Nicaragua to play a larger role in providing further technical support to self-builders perhaps on the lines of the teachers' brigades in the literacy campaign where brigadistas worked alongside people in the local communities giving direct aid, advice and support. The literacy crusade in Nicaragua offers a model of how a social programme can create other benefits including political education and heightened awareness of social issues in the populace. One hundred thousand young people were drafted into the countryside to eradicate illiteracy. In the process the rural population gained the ability to read and write, saw the strength of commitment to improving social conditions on the part of the Sandinista government and the young Nicaraguans who took part gained first hand experience of life and conditions around the country which could only enrich their future approach to political issues in Nicaragua.

The technical work undertaken by MINVAH to provide and improve building elements is a further role for the state in *research and development* which can add variety and innovation to the building programme with important consequences such as use of indigenous materials and savings on import costs.

These are some of the main comments to be made as an initial response and assessment of the housing programme in Nicaragua today. Much more could be added and much more remains to be learnt from this experience. However, it will be obvious to readers that the authors of this paper are enthusiastic about the Sandinistan approach in Nicaragua. The appraisal of any housing policy cannot be a purely technical exercise, but must rest on political beliefs and values. To us, this small beleaguered country shows near ideal blend of grass-roots-based democracy and participation with state intervention aimed both at preserving basic freedoms and at helping the poorest and most vulnerable. Their approach to housing policy is one instance of this. There have been mistakes and difficulties but there is also a powerful will to improve and create a more equitable society. Nicaragua deserves to be given freedom from external aggression to take this bold revolution further.

REFERENCES

Boleat, M. (1985), *National Housing Finance Systems*, London, Croom Helm.

Burgess, R. (1982), 'Self-Help Housing Advocacy: A Curious Form of Radicalism' in P. Ward, (ed) *Self-Help Housing*, London, Mansell.

Martin, R. (1982), 'The Formulation of a Self-Half Project in Lusaka' in P. Ward, (ed.) *Self-Help Housing*, London, Mansell.

MINVAH (n.d.) *Avances del MINVAH* (mimeo), MINVAH.

Skinner, R.J. (1983), 'Community Participation: its Scope and Organisation' in M.J. Rodell and R.J. Skinner (eds.) *People, Poverty and Shelter; Problems of Self-Help Housing in the Third World*, London, Methuen.

Vigil, M.E. (1983), 'MINVAH: Background Notes and Details of Administration', (mimeo), MINVAH.

Zunica, E.H. (1985), 'Research Needs and Priorities in Housing and Construction in Nicaragua', *Habitat International*, 9(2): 73-78.

14

AFFORDABLE DECENT HOUSING:
Expanding the Stock through Assisted Upgrading by Incumbent Residents

NAOMI CARMON

Housing availability has almost ceased being a problem in the developed industrialised countries. In most regions of these states, the number of units in the housing stock is larger than the number of households.[1] In many places, however, a considerable part of the stock is below currently acceptable standards and good housing is very expensive. Hence the focus has shifted from quantity to quality (Burns and Grebler, 1986) and the problematic issue is affordable decent housing that requires affordable housing renovation.

The belief that each household is entitled to decent housing and that the state should take responsibility for providing it was one of the rationales behind state intervention in the field of housing (Milgram, 1978; Schussheim, 1987). Considerable effort was invested in the attempt to define decent or adequate housing. The major conclusion of this enterprise was that unlike adequate nutrition, which can be scientifically determined, decent housing is not an absolute but rather a relative term. Thus, 16 sq m (170 sq ft) per person was considered necessary in order to preserve physical and mental health in Europe, while twice as much, 32.5 sq m (350 sq ft) per person – was considered necessary in the United States (Musil, 1962; American Public Health Assoc., 1950). Even though one can still find researchers and public officials who are searching for the absolute minimum for a person's "housing needs", most of us have recognised the relative character of the term, which changes according to changing conditions in the social and economic environment.

Inadequate housing has three sources: first, there are houses which were originally constructed inadequately; secondly, there are those which have suffered deterioration for lack of appropriate maintenance; thirdly, and most commonly, there are houses which were once considered adequate and have hardly changed for the worse, but are presently considered obsolete and inadequate because housing standards have risen. The aggregation of these three sources has created a large stock of undesirable houses in modern cities.

Several methods have been used in order to deal with the problems of inadequate units and shortage of affordable decent housing. The Urban Renewal approach was to demolish old units and to build standard public housing; this process, which involved forced relocation and resulted in a very small stock of inexpensive dwelling units and in vacant land in the centre of cities unused-for-many-years, was sharply criticised (Anderson, 1965; Gans, 1965). Another method was to ignore the sub-standard and low-standard units and build new dwellings, including subsidised ones on vacant land around the city. Longitudinal analysis of data has shown that constructing surplus lodgings (more than is needed to accommodate the annual addition of households) was a major cause of inner-city housing abandonment and urban decline (Bradnury *et al*., 1982). A third method is encouraging incumbent upgrading: assisting the present population in upgrading their places of residence and bringing them up to a desired level, a level that is in accordance with acceptable standards of living of the time in the relevant social environment (Clay, 1979, 1981). This paper focuses on this last method, which has become especially attractive to low- and moderate-income families in an era of sharply rising costs of new dwellings. The paper describes and analyses an ambitious programme of the Israeli Government to make incumbent upgrading work, and draws some general conclusions from this experience.

PROJECT RENEWAL

Israel's Project Renewal is a national programme for social and physical rehabilitation of distressed neighbourhoods (Carmon and Hill, 1984; Carmon, 1987). Since 1976 it has gradually entered 84 neighbourhoods throughout the country, affecting some 600,000 residents, about 15 per cent of Israel's citizens. The ultimate goal of the Project is social in nature: it aims at reducing disparities between socio-economic groups, but about half of the budget has been invested in physical improvements, mostly in housing and also in physical infrastructure. The Ministry of Housing and Construction, the major governmental partner in the programme, shared the general social goal, but actually aimed at increasing the stock of affordable decent housing.

The current analysis is based on a five-year evaluation study of Project Renewal. The field work was executed in a carefully selected sample of ten neighbourhoods (hereby "the research neighbourhoods") and included: interviewing local informants, from the mayor through officials at all levels to residents; systematic observations; analysis of documents and former surveys; and a general household survey conducted in the homes of 180 families in each of the ten neighbourhoods (Carmon, 1985). The study used the "integrated evaluation" method (Alterman *et al.*, 1984) and was aimed at answering a wide range of evaluation questions related to all the social and physical programmes of the Project. Here, the focus is on the housing programmes alone.

By international standards, the housing situation in the designated distressed neighbourhoods was not very bad even before the Project was started.

With the exception of a very few cases (fewer than one per cent), all residents were living in hard construction (cement) buildings, and in most cases (95 per cent) there was no more than one household per unit. Almost all the dwelling units included at least two living spaces, a kitchen (a kitchenette in a few cases), a toilet and a bathroom inside the unit, and electricity. This was due to the fact that most (90 per cent) of the housing units in Project Renewal neighbourhoods consisted of modern public housing built over the past 40 years. Only one of the ten research neighbourhoods was constructed mainly by private builders, and 50 per cent of its stock were 40+ year-old houses; the other nine neighbourhoods included mainly structures built in the 1950s and 1960s, and an average of about 20 per cent new buildings constructed over the past 15 years.

By Israeli norms of the 1980s, there were too many substandard housing units in these neighbourhoods. About half of the dwelling units had areas of only 28-55 sq m (300-600 sq ft). At a time in which the average size of a new dwelling units is 110 sq m (1200 sq ft), living in units far below this size is considered living in distress, even if the family is small.

Housing density is measured by the number of persons per room (kitchens and bathrooms are not counted as rooms nor as parts of rooms). According to the standards of the Ministry of Construction and Housing, 2.5 persons per room and up is considered overcrowded.

While in 1979 the overall rate of overcrowded housing in Israel was four per cent, the average for the ten research neighbourhoods (before Project Renewal) was 14 per cent.

All of the ten neighbourhoods suffered from deficient maintenance. In five of them for which "before" data on maintenance were available, close to two-thirds of the units were in need of repairs; about half of those required basic repairs (such as replacement of rotten piping) and the other half light repairs (such as repair of shutters and paint). The frontages of most buildings needed renovation.

Abandonment was not a widespread problem: only one of the ten research neighbourhoods had a large number of completely or partly abandoned buildings, accounting for 20 per cent of its stock. Another two had a relatively high rate –10 per cent of vacant dwelling units (in most cases, vacant did not mean abandoned).

The housing programmes of Project Renewal constitute a unique combination of public assistance and public-individual partnership. The following description of the three major programmes will demonstrate their uniqueness.

Selling Public Housing Units to Their Dwellers

One of the special characteristics of public housing in Israel is the mechanism of transfer of ownership of the dwelling units from public housing companies to dwellers, while retaining public ownership of the land. Tenants are encouraged to purchase their apartments at prices far below market value, and at the same time sign a lease renting the land for a period of either 49 or 99 years. The purchase act is personal, resulting in various combinations of renters and owner-occupants in multi-unit buildings managed by public housing companies. These special procedures have caused an uncommon situation whereby in Israel there is a low correlation between private ownership of dwellings and economic resources of households. Even in the poorest neighbourhoods, one may find high percentages of owner-occupants.

Most Project Renewal neighbourhoods, including nine of our ten research neighbourhoods, were public housing projects built on public land by the Ministry of Housing. When construction was completed, the dwelling units were transferred to the management of public companies (mainly Amidar and Amigur), which became responsible for renting them, collecting subsidised rents and ensuring maintenance. When Project Renewal entered these nine neighbourhoods, 46 per cent of the apartments had already been purchased by their dwellers.

Since private ownership of housing is known to be related to better maintenance of property, higher satisfaction with housing, and stability of residence, Project Renewal aimed at increasing the rate of owner-occupancy. However, it was not until October 1981 (about two years after the beginning of actual operation) that somewhat better terms of purchase were offered to residents of Project Renewal neighbourhoods, compared to those offered to residents of buildings owned by public companies in other neighbourhoods, and another year passed before substantially higher incentives were suggested to tenants. Towards the end of 1982, it was announced that 25 per cent of Project Renewal loans for home purchase would not be linked to inflation (a very significant factor under Israel's high inflation), and that the remainder would be linked but interest-free. Residents of other areas of public housing were eligible to receive loans of similar size; these were linked, and interest of 6 per cent per annum was charged on half the loan.

Beginning in late 1982, then, residents of Project neighbourhoods had much to gain by purchasing their dwellings. The price paid for an Amidar apartment during the period when it was most worthwhile, at the end of 1982, was about 10-20 per cent of the market value of the apartment, while two years earlier Amidar tenants had purchased their apartments for 40-60 per cent of the market value. At the end of 1983 the figure rose to 20-40 per cent of the value of the apartment.[2]

When data were collected for the evaluation study towards the end were of 1983, the rate of privately owned apartments in the nine research neighbourhoods was 55 per cent, nine per cent higher than in the pre-Project period. Overall, this can be considered but a modest achievement, since some increase was expected even without the special incentives provided by Project Renewal.

Several reasons can be cited for the fact that the purchase programme met with only limited success. First, the improved terms of purchase came into effect relatively late, some a year and a half and most only a few months before the data collection; in due time, they may show a greater impact. Secondly, tenants renting publicly-owned apartments are allowed to reside in their apartments for their whole lives, paying an extremely low monthly rent, usually US \$13 – \$15 per month, 10 per cent to 25 per cent the cost of private rental in those areas. Moreover, families on welfare pay only part of the sum, and they are often completely exempted from rent. A third and most important reason is that the potential of apartment purchasers in distressed neighbourhoods is far less than 100 per cent, as some of the residents will never be capable of making any significant purchase payments. The properties of very poor households set an upper limit on the potential rate of owner-occupancy. However, according to reliable estimation, this limit is not under three-quarters of the households in most if not all the research sites.[3] Last but not least among the causes of limited success in increasing the rate of private ownership of housing is the general Project Renewal policy which distinguished between owners and renters: the former were required to pay (at least partially) for various improvements, while the latter – who often lived in the same buildings – were given these benefits free or nearly free of charge. This served as a negative incentive for purchase of apartments in Project neighbourhoods.

All these factors were valid for all the neighbourhoods. Nonetheless, considerable differences were found among them. The differential success of the purchase campaign of Project Renewal seemed to depend first and foremost upon the amount of effort invested in it by the local Project manager. A few of the managers considered an increase in private ownership to be the key to neighbourhood rehabilitation, and they therefore invested considerable personal effort in sales promotion. They approached potential purchasers, explained the benefits of purchasing at the right time, and helped them through the formal procedures of attaining subsidised loans. On the other hand, there were local Project managers who publicised the new terms, as required, but did not take any initiative to promote the sale of apartments to their tenants. Another important cause of the variation found among neighbourhoods is related to the possibility of receiving building permits from local authorities. As explained above, security of tenure and low rents served as negative incentives. On the other hand, the knowledge that home ownership meant, eligibility for building permits and subsidised loans for housing enlargements was a positive incentive. In neighbourhoods for which building permits were not difficult to obtain, the programme had a better chance of success.

The interplay of these factors did not prevent Project Renewal from achieving some success in its programme to sell public housing units to their tenants, but it did not enable it to make housing in most of the neighbourhoods predominantly private, as is common in most middle-class neighbourhoods in Israel.

Exterior Renovation of Buildings

Poor maintenance of building exteriors and yards is frequently the most visible problem in distressed residential areas. Forty to eighty per cent of the buildings in each of the ten research neighbourhoods suffered from deterioration and poor appearance. Therefore, improving the facade, i.e., exterior renovation of buildings and yards, was one of the first tasks that Project Renewal took upon itself. In a few cases, this activity was begun even before the local steering committee was formed, in order to demonstrate that the authorities really meant to do something positive for the neighbourhood, and thereby obtain the goodwill and confidence of local residents.

In the course of Project Renewal, the method of renovation changed. In the first three years, all external renovation jobs were carried out by the public companies that managed the rented dwelling units in the neighbourhoods. These companies had been charged with responsibility for maintaining and renovating the buildings since their construction, but Project Renewal enabled them to include additional elements in the renovation activity. The local programmes for exterior renovation included at least a few and in many cases most of the following elements: painting roofs; insulating to prevent dampness in winter and overheating in summer; painting the building frontages, (which sometimes included renewing the plaster coat); adding partitions to conceal clothes lines attached to the walls of buildings (these colourful structures have become landmarks of the Project neighbourhoods); repairing shutters; painting stairways and repairing their lighting systems; adding marble coatings to buildings entrances; installing new mailboxes; installing doors to close off entrances; giving buildings modern address numbering; and developing adjacent grounds, including clean-up, special arrangements for outdoor garbage collection and for fuel (gas) containers, and finally (not in all the cases) – gardening. In fewer places exterior improvements also included repair or even replacement of water and sewage pipes for the building, and installation of solar water heating equipment.

In most neighbourhoods, the greater part of the renovation work was executed in the higher buildings (three- to four-storey walk-ups) in which all or most of the apartments were rented from the public company. Usually, the Project did not undertake renovation unless there was a tenants' organisation in the form of a building committee, the major task of which was to collect renovation fees. The residents' financial participation was minimal – 5 per cent to 10 per cent of the total cost, and even that was sometimes waived for renters who were paying welfare subsidised rent. In a few places, where "luxury improvements" were offered, such as installation of central television antennas or an intercom from the building entrance to all the apartments, all tenants were charged a much higher percentage (about 50 per cent) of the cost. The building committees were hardly ever called upon to participate in the renovation decision-making.

Despite the fact that a lot of work, mostly of reasonable quality (see below, the discussion of sustainability), was accomplished through this method of "institutionalised renovation", both sides seemed dissatisfied. The Ministry of Construction and Housing, which provided most of the resources for the renovation work carried out by the public companies, was unhappy about the high costs of the operation as well as the low level of maintenance by tenants after completion of the work. Tenants, on the other had, complained about long waiting lists and not being able to influence the shape of their buildings.

In 1982, a new method of exterior renovation was introduced, the do-it-yourself method. With this programme, residents were invited to organise in building committees, and to choose among three alternatives, First, they could receive materials from the local Project management and renovate the building themselves (on their own or by hiring skilled workers). Secondly, they could hire a contractor to do the work in accordance with accepted standards – in such cases the Project would pay half of the total expenses and the residents the other half. A third alternative was a combination of the first two.

The do-it-yourself programme of Project Renewal, which was, in effect, a public-individual partnership for the purpose of effecting external renovation of buildings and yards, appeared to have many advantages. It gave the tenants control over the timing, planning and implementation of the renovation work. It also meant significant savings for the Ministry of Construction and Housing because of the residents' participation and because contractors could be dispensed with. Under this arrangement, the financial burden was more equally distributed between owners and renters living in the same building, and there was less likelihood of complaints from residents, as they themselves were responsible for the work done. In addition, there was a reasonable expectation that the strong tenants' organisation required for implementation of the self-help programme would continue to function and that it would take good care of the renovated buildings.

During the first five years of Project Renewal (1979-84), the exteriors of one-third of the apartments in the ten research neighbourhoods were renovated with Project assistance. Out of these 6,000 units, about 4,000 were renovated through the institutionalised method and 2,000 through the do-it-yourself method. The percentage of renovations carried out by the new method is growing rapidly, and local Project directors consider it a major contribution to the present and to the future of the neighbourhoods.

Encouraging Housing Improvements by Owner-occupants

Privately owned apartments, which constituted about half of the housing stock in the research neighbourhoods, were usually better maintained that rented units. Owner-occupants made greater efforts than renters to care for their property and invested money in housing improvements. Even before Project Renewal, eligible households could get small subsidised loans from the Ministry of Housing in order to renovate their apartments. In many neighbourhoods those who could more easily afford it, started a spontaneous process of housing improvement, including very impressive expansions of living spaces, without waiting for public support.

It took some time for the Project to expand its housing operation so as to include the provision of assistance to privately initiated renovation by home owners. Despite the fact that such assistance was in line with the Project's basic principle of extending aid to all types of households in the neighbourhood – the relatively better-off, as well as the poorer sectors of the population – it was not initiated until the decision-making bodies in Jerusalem had been pressured from two directions. Neighbourhoods applied pressure from below through a few local Project managers who were convinced by what they had seen and heard in their own neighbourhoods that encouragement of this spontaneous process would be a key element in rehabilitation. At the same time, the publication and wide diffusion of a research report regarding the relatively low public costs and high individual and collective benefits of this process (Carmon and Oxman, 1981) also served to promote the idea of housing improvement by owner-occupants. The result was a new Project Renewal housing renovation programme for some home owners (1982) which offered small loans for interior "functional changes" and large loans with very good terms of return for housing enlargements.

Compared with past housing assistance programmes, the new one offered three major advantages: firstly, excellent repayment terms, which, under the galloping inflation then rampant in Israel, actually turned part of the loan into a grant; secondly, the maximum area to which an apartment could be enlarged was increased to 114 sq m (1230 sq ft), with optional additions for households of eight or more members; and thirdly, each neighbourhood resident was eligible to join the programme, regardless of his/her age, family status, or economic situation. These changes were designed to attract as many home owners as possible to the new renovation programme, as well as, indirectly, to give tenants the incentive to purchase their units, after which they would be eligible for enlargement loans. The aim was to increase the stock of large dwelling units in order to make them more appealing to their present occupants as well as to future dwellers. For this reason the Project supported enlargements requested by elderly residents, as well as relatively big enlargements for small households. It was hoped that the incentives built into this new housing assistance programme would be strong enough, especially in light of the increased housing prices in Israel, to halt the tendency of relatively better-off households to leave neighbourhoods as soon as they could, contributing to a vicious circle of deterioration.

Home owners did not fail to respond to the opportunities offered by Project Renewal. In 13 per cent of the 12,000 privately owned apartments in the ten neighbourhoods, a few or all of the following interior renovation elements were executed with the help of Project loans: alteration of internal space divisions, changing the location of the kitchen or bathroom, replacement of damaged sewage or water systems, replacement of rotten woodwork, installation of solar water heaters, as well as work required as a direct result of these changes. Routine painting and the like were not considered "functional changes" and were not eligible for the special loans.

In addition, 9 per cent of the home owners utilised the enlargement loans. No official data is available regarding the size of the enlargements, but three studies undertaken in three different neighbourhoods gave us some indication: in the first two, enlargements caused the average size of an apartment to double, so that it reached 90 sq m (about 1000 sq ft) (Carmon and Gavrieli, 1982); the third study also pointed to 90 sq m as the average size of an enlarged unit, but since in that neighbourhood the apartments were larger to begin with, there was an addition of "only" 60 per cent to the original size (Lerman *et al.*, 1985). In almost all cases the enlargers added space to their kitchens and/or bathrooms, and constructed an additional one or two rooms; about half also added balconies.

The Special Merit of Encouraging Self-help Housing Enlargements

Supporting housing enlargements was not the largest programme of Project Renewal either in terms of Project investment or in the number of its beneficiaries. Nevertheless, it may be considered the most important programme from the point of view of the future of the neighbourhoods, and therefore, it deserves special discussion.

Ten per cent of the Project housing enlargements were carried out by the public companies which rented apartments to their tenants. These enlargements were intended for eligible families only, i.e. those who suffered from both high density (usually 3 persons per room and up) and very low income. The other 90 per cent were executed by owner-occupants: they initiated them, paid for them (with the assistance of subsidised loans, not grants), they almost always planned them or participated in the planning process, they supervised the construction, and sometimes, they even did the work themselves. The process was, therefore, termed "self-help housing rehabilitation" or "self-help housing enlargements".

Owner-occupants of very small apartments which had been hastily constructed in the fifties and sixties were the ones who started the rehabilitation process when their needs as well as their economic capabilities grew. Most of the Project neighbourhoods had a considerable stock of one or two-storey buildings inhabited by two to four households, or eight to twelve households. In fact, 20 per cent – 40 per cent of the apartments in these low-rise buildings had been enlarged before Project Renewal entered the scene.

The impact of this spontaneous process was studied and all the major participants in this process were found to have benefited (Carmon and Oxman, 1986; Carmon and Gavrieli, 1987).

The direct beneficiaries were the households carrying out the enlargements. The most immediate benefit, of course, was added living space; the number of rooms was increased, and a better match was attained between the functional needs of tenants and the layout of the apartments. This may explain the high satisfaction enlargers expressed with regard to their housing conditions. Property values increased, often beyond the initial investment; in a carefully designed case study (Carmon and Oxman, 1981), it was found that in an area in which 80 per cent of the apartments had been enlarged, the cost of a 2-room flat was 1.75 times that of an apartment of equivalent size in an area in which only 15 per cent of apartments had been enlarged. This means that present users as well as the next generation – to which the apartment may be transferred – profit. Another benefit stemming from the enlargement effort was increased family income; the undertaking induced men to work longer hours and encouraged women to seek employment outside the home. In another detailed study of such housing enlargements (Carmon and Gavrieli, 1982), 53 per cent reported that men worked longer hours, and 15 per cent reported that women had gone out to work in order to help pay for the enlargements. Finally, the task of enlarging their homes gave residents an important experience in the implementation of an economic project requiring long-term planning as well as negotiation with public and private agencies; this experience may have enhanced their ability to take advantage of future opportunities.

The enlargers' neighbourhoods were improved considerably as a result of the self-help housing enlargements. In addition to adding space and changing the interior of their apartments, most of the enlargers renovated the exterior of their buildings and half made improvements on the grounds as well. There were complaints about the "personalisation" of the building exteriors, but the increased monetary value of the apartments in the immediate area shows that the changes involved positive benefits for their neighbours. The social consequences for the neighbourhood are even more important. The study showed that while self-help housing expansion had a limited impact on the wish to migrate from the neighbourhood, it had a decisive impact on actual mobility, i.e., it stabilised the neighbourhood population. Emigration of "strong" households, such as those who can afford purchasing their apartments and enlarging them, is considered a major cause of neighbourhood deterioration. Halting it by providing residents with the opportunity to improve living conditions within the neighbourhood is thus a crucial component of neighbourhood rehabilitation.

The State of Israel is also a beneficiary of the process of self-help enlargements. For a relatively low cost to the public treasury – as most of the investments were private ones – the housing stock was improved and the lifespan of buildings and neighbourhoods increased. Thus, existing physical infrastructure and social services could be used for a longer period, and the State did not have to erect new services for those who would otherwise have emigrated.

The researchers were very active in presenting these benefits to Project Renewal decision-makers in Jerusalem. Since their pressure was in line with some requests coming from below – from several neighbourhood managers of the Project – it proved very effective. The system reacted, and in 1982 new regulations were issued, resulting in rapid increase in the number of Project-supported enlargements: from 600 in all Project Renewal neighbourhoods in 1981, to 1700 in 1982, and about 3500 in each of the two following years; in 1985 the figure stood at 2250.

Analysis shows that Project Renewal, with its bigger and better loans provided to all interested households in the neighbourhoods and the technical assistance given to enlargers in several places, not only increased the volume and pace of enlargements, but also expanded the potential of implementation and the chances to realise that potential. The contribution of the Project in this area is summarised under the following headings:

Generation of strong motivation for housing improvement and enlargement – In half of the neighbourhoods the Project generated a large amount of housing improvement and expansion among home owners. Data collected by a household survey in 1983 shortly after the special Project programme was announced, revealed that in the course of the previous 25 years (including the first part of the 1980s), 24 per cent of the apartments of the respondents had been expanded, but that during the month of the survey, and additional 20 per cent of householders had already submitted applications for an enlargement loan, or intended to do so in the coming months.

Extension of housing-expansion activity to three- and four-storey buildings – Prior to Project Renewal, almost all housing expansions were carried out in one and two-storey buildings. With the assistance of physical planners and community workers employed by Project Renewal, apartments in taller buildings began to undergo expansion as well, often without requiring all the residents to expand at the same time, and without obliging all those engaged in expansion to construct similar enlargements (Carmon and Vienberg, 1986). Since about half of the apartments in Israeli distressed neighbourhoods are in one and two-storey buildings, and most of the others are in three and four-storey buildings, this extension has made practically the entire stock in potential client of the process of self-help enlargements.

Diversification of the population benefiting from housing expansions in Project neighbourhoods – The Project helped increase not only the number of residents, but also the variety of types of residents who benefited from housing expansions, by including households which could not afford to participate in the past. Previous studies in two of the research neighbourhoods (Carmon and Gavrieli, 1982, 1987) indicated that residents with low-incomes wished to expand their apartments, on the condition that they be provided guidance, and particularly loans, on convenient terms. Since Project Renewal fulfilled these conditions, it is reasonable to assume that the group of expanders not only grew, but also diversified. An indication of the validity of this assumption is to be found in the results of the household survey of June 1983, according to which loans for housing expansion were granted to various income groups; 21 per cent of the interviewees whose reported monthly income was higher than IS 27,000 (this was the average salary of a salaried employee in Israel at that time), received such loans, as did 17 per cent of those whose income was between IS 15,000 and 27,000 per month, and 6 per cent of the low-income group earning less than IS 15,000 per month. Since we know that the phenomenon of apartment expansion by residents spreads as a result of imitation, we estimate that this diversity will have an impact in the future by influencing families of limited income to join the expansion movements.

Encouragement of housing expansions by ensuring legality and improving planning – A central deficiency of housing expansions in the period that preceded Project Renewal was lack of control. Although for the most part expanders were granted building licences, in many cases the licences were given after the fact, and frequently additions did not conform to the conditions stipulated in the licence. Moreover, almost all the expansions were carried out without consulting an architect; the occupants' designs took into consideration the internal requirements of the dwelling, but not the form of the external shell. Surprisingly, in spite of the absence of professional advice, almost no problems developed with the constructions (for the most part, the additions were carried out on ground on which it was easy to build in one to two-storey buildings) and most residents who expanded their dwellings were very satisfied with the results. However, residents and visitors to the neighbourhoods often complained that varying forms and finishing materials made the exteriors of the expansions unaesthetic.

In 1978 Israel's Planning and Building Law was amended to force local planning committees to adhere to existing, approved plans. It placed criminal responsibility on anyone who allowed construction which deviated from the permitted law. The law threatened to reduce self-help expansion activity, but the new framework of Project Renewal contributed to solving both the problems of formal building permission and that of the visual cacophony of the new housing expansions. Project Renewal provided free architectural advice to those households planning to expand their dwellings. In some of the neighbourhoods, dwellers were able to choose an architect from a list provided by the Project. In other cases they could choose one of several alternative architectural designs for expansion. Since architects' designs are prepared in accordance with building and planning laws, it has become relatively easy to obtain approval from the local authority.

Encouragement of housing expansions through improvement of local permit granting procedures – The housing expansion process is greatly dependent on the regulations and goodwill of the local authority involved. As a consequence of Project Renewal successes, the attitude of some of the local authorities towards apartment expansion changed, and regulations and procedures were altered in ways which made it much easier for those who wanted to expand. In Jerusalem, for example, all requests for expansion in the Project neighbourhood are now brought up together in the municipal committee, making the granting of permission faster than if each expander were to present a separate request. In Akko, the committee which grants permits increased the frequency of its meetings and now tends to approve any request within the law, including construction on roofs. In Herzliya, a special sub-committee was established to facilitate permits for expansion in Project neighbourhoods, and the construction fee is subsidised.

Indirect encouragement of housing expansions through investment in neighbourhood infrastructure – In previous studies carried out by researchers of the Neaman Institute (Mayer and Enis, 1981), aerial photographs of one of the ten neighbourhoods taken at five-year intervals were analysed. A direct relationship was found between the paving of roads and the spread of housing expansions in the neighbourhood: most of the expansions were carried out in the five-year period following road pavement. This finding can be explained easily in economic terms: the improvements made by the public authority increased the profitability of investments on the part of the individual. Hence, the heavy investment of Project Renewal in neighbourhood infrastructure – roads, sidewalks, lighting, street furniture ete. – served as an incentive to increase housing enlargements along improved streets.

Summary – Support of housing enlargements may be considered the most important programme of Project Renewal, not only because many households benefited from considerably improved housing conditions, and because the improvement was profitable from the point of view of the public treasury, but mainly because of its current and expected future impact on the neighbourhoods. For the present, the programme has added a considerable number of relatively high standard units to the housing stock of the neighbourhoods, and slowed down the emigration of "stronger" households. For the future, it has given residents incentives for housing improvements, and made the process more profitable for them. It has resulted in an increased enlargement potential, especially by starting the process in taller buildings, and created permanent mechanisms in local government and in the Ministry of Housing and Construction to assist people in taking advantage of these new opportunities.

ACHIEVEMENT EVALUATION

Amount and Distribution of Benefits

During Project Renewal's first five years, the dwellers of about 50 per cent of the 20,000 inhabited dwelling units in the ten research neighbourhoods benefited from at least one programme of housing improvement with Project assistance. The amount of housing benefits derived from different programmes and their distribution among groups of beneficiaries is summarised in Table 14.1.

Table 14.1 shows that the total rate of beneficiaries was very high and that Project Renewal housing programmes reached both the haves and the have-nots in the neighbourhoods. Usually, the more advantageous groups of owner-occupants enjoyed the more significant improvements: enlargements and higher-quality interior renovations, higher not because of larger public subsidies, but owing to the fact that owner-occupants used their own savings and labour in order to achieve the desired results. However, a notable percentage of low-income households were also home-owners, and more than a few of them participated in the programmes which generally reached the better-off. About 15 per cent of those who received loans for enlargements belonged to the bottom third income group in the neighbourhoods. In addition, there were special programmes for the neediest households; those renters with very low-incomes and the worst housing conditions enjoyed housing enlargements fully paid for by the public and/or interior renovation free of charge. The widest and least beneficial programme, exterior renovation, reached people of all socio-economic groups in the neighbourhoods. Quite a number of home-owners were among those who participated in the "do-it-yourself" part of this programme, while most of the beneficiaries of "institutionalised renovation" were renters in buildings belonging to the public companies.

TABLE 14.1: Beneficiaries of Housing Programmes in the Ten Research Neighbourhoods

Programme	Percentage of Total Households*	Major Group of Beneficiaries
Housing Enlargements for Renters	1	The Neediest
Interior Renovation for Renters	6	The Less Needy
Exterior Renovation of Buildings, mostly Rented	34	The Less Needy
Encouraging Private Ownership	9	Intermediate Group
Interior Renovation by Owners	8	Intermediate Group
Housing Enlargements by Owners	6	The Better-off
Total	64	

* There is some overlapping in the above, mainly between 2 and 3 and between 4 and 6. The total rate of beneficiaries, without overlapping, is somewhat above 50 per cent.

Hence, Project Renewal housing programmes did not "fall into the trap" of assisting only those who needed assistance less than others. They combined fully supported improvements of dwellings of households in the greatest need with the provision of incentives (subsidised loans) to better-off households. The latter were encouraged to invest their own savings and labour – to their own benefit, as well as the benefit of their neighbours.

Satisfaction with Housing Conditions

In a survey of households conducted in the research neighbourhood in mid-1983, residents were asked about satisfaction with their housing conditions. It was found that about half of the respondents were satisfied with their apartments (the categories of "very satisfied" and "satisfied" were combined), as shown in Table 14.2.

TABLE 14.2: Satisfaction with the Apartment, by Personal Evaluation of the Contribution Made by Project Renewal to the Improvement of the Apartment of the Respondent (percentages)

	Satisfied	Not so Satisfied	Not Satisfied at All	Total
Contributed a lot	71	20	9	100 (n=170)
Didn't contribute much	54	34	12	100 (n=121)
Didn't contribute at all	51	29	20	100 (n=896)
Total	51	29	20	100 (n=1187)

A common reason for dissatisfaction was that the apartments were too small for their families. Forty-two per cent of the interviewees complained about this. The accepted standard for density still stands at 2.5 persons per room (kitchen, toilet and bathroom are not counted as rooms), and according to this standard, overcrowding in the neighbourhoods decreased from 14 per cent in 1979 (before the Project) to 8 per cent in 1983. What the dissatisfaction finding reveals is that the respondents' level of expectations regarding space in their dwellings is much higher than the Ministry of Construction and Housing standards.

The percentage of respondents in Project Renewal neighbourhoods reporting satisfaction with their apartments – 51 per cent – is considered low for Israel. A general survey of Tel Aviv neighbourhoods found that 68 per cent were satisfied with their living quarters (Harpaz *et al.*, 1978), and a general survey of Jerusalem neighbourhoods found a 70 per cent satisfaction rate (Shuval *et al.*, 1968). However, the satisfaction rate of respondents who reported having benefited from apartment related programmes of Project Renewal, approaches the average for Israel.

Similar findings emerged with regard to the building in which the apartment was located: about half reported satisfaction with the buildings 60 per cent of those whose buildings had been renovated by Project Renewal were satisfied, compared with 42 per cent of those whose buildings had not been renovated.

Thus, the many housing improvements brought about by Project Renewal significantly improved the satisfaction of residents with their apartments and buildings. But the average rate of residents in Project neighbourhoods indicating dissatisfaction with their apartments is still high, compared to other places in Israel.

Sustainability

Sustainability if the extent to which the consequences of an activity will continue to exist in the future. In the field of housing improvements, sustainability depends on two factors: the quality of the improvements made and the organisation for regular maintenance.

We do not have systematic information about the quality of the renovation work executed by home owners. What we know is that people tended to be very satisfied with what they managed to do in their own apartments, and that there were very few complaints about technical defects. We, therefore, assume that the renovations carried out under the self-help part of the programme were of reasonable quality. The only programme for which we have systematic evaluation of quality is the exterior renovation programme. Based mainly on the criterion of using durable materials, the general quality of the external renovations was evaluated as low in one neighbourhood (the first to be completed); low-medium in another, medium in three, medium-high in two and high in the last three.[4] Hence, the quality of the work was at least reasonable in most places, and sustainability seemed to depend mainly on maintenance arrangements.

The interiors of most apartments – some 80 per cent – were evaluated by the interviewers in 1983 as "well maintained", with only 5 per cent as "neglected" and another 16 per cent as "slightly neglected". There was a small difference in favour of owner-occupants.

But the maintenance of common areas of the buildings was evaluated less favourably and was found to be significantly associated with type of tenure. Buildings in which most of the residents were owner-occupants were better maintained than buildings in which all or most of the apartments were rented, as has been the case before Project Renewal. The Project recruited community workers, often assisted by local semi-professionals (women employed as "block organisers") to help organise building committees. They usually managed to keep the committees alive as long as renovation work was in process, but most ceased activity once the major task was completed. In a few cases, the result of neglect had become apparent even before the completion of renovation work. There were only a few examples where building committees in rented buildings maintained a high level of activity over a long period of time. It happened more frequently when the committee was involved not only in maintenance but in other aspects as well, such as organising social activities.

In general, Project Renewal did not succeed in creating a new mechanism for the ongoing maintenance of housing stock in its neighbourhoods. Nevertheless, sustainability of its achievements in the field of housing is quite probable, because in most cases the quality of the renovation work was reasonable, and because home owners form the majority in many neighbourhoods (Project Renewal assistance increased their ranks), and they tend to take better care of their property. There are hopes (yet to be proven) that renters' norms of maintenance will also change for the better, partly as a result of the spread of the do-it-yourself renovation programme, and partly as community workers improve their methods of operation through experience.

RECOMMENDED STRATEGIES FOR HOUSING IMPROVEMENT AT AFFORDABLE PRICES

Our evaluation study of Project Renewal which was based on carefully selected sample of 10 out of 70 Project neighbourhoods, showed that the Project has had significant successes in the field of housing. The most salient were the large number of housing improvements, from which about half of the households in the ten research neighbourhoods benefited, and the distribution of improvements among various groups of beneficiaries, including the poorest residents of the neighbourhoods. The Project has hardly introduced any new programmes; its strength was in identifying especially effective past processes and programmes, developing them and vigorously encouraging their implementation.

Two general conclusions can be drawn from the foregoing: first, that large governmental programmes are not doomed to failure; secondly, that a key to possible success is intellegent use of the existing repertoire of programmes and processes.

Some lessons can be drawn from Project Renewal by looking at its housing programmes in the light of other countries' experience with comparable housing problems.

Selling Public Housing to Their Tenants

Project Renewal programme which encourages tenants to purchase the dwellings they occupy from the public holding companies is in line with programmes of the eighties in the United States and Great Britain. In these countries such programmes are under serious attack by planners, who see their role as defending the interests of low-income citizens. The major argument against this kind of programme is that it reduces the stock of housing for future use by the disadvantaged and pulls the best units out. This claim is less relevant to Israel, because its stock of public housing is still large (about 15 per cent of the country's stock) and because each year new units are added to it, although in smaller quantities than in the past. It is very relevant to Western countries in which governments have ceased supporting new public housing.

In any case, however, we see it as an unfair argument: why should the war on behalf of the future poor be fought at the expense of the present poor? Most citizens seek home ownership; they see it as desirable, both socially and economically. Planners should not prevent the authorities from assisting low- and moderate-income households who reside in public housing and express the desire to purchase their apartments. The justified demand to continue supporting the right to decent housing of every citizen, both in the present and in the future, should be directed by planners to the authorities and coupled with feasible strategies for carrying it out. If the federal government refuses, state governments (like the Government of Massachusetts in recent years) or municipal governments or other local organisations may agree. No matter what, this burden should not be placed on the current residents of public housing. The Israeli experience, and the experience of other countries, in selling public housing to its tenants should be studied in order to enable as many moderate and low-income households as possible to own their homes.

Turning Houses into Responsive Structures

A central message of Project Renewal is that old houses that were not built for change may be made responsive structures, i.e. not only can be renovated but can be dramatically changed, and most importantly, enlarged to fit their tenants' new needs and aspirations. The process started long before the Project, with spontaneous enlargements of small buildings, usually one or two storeys containing two to four tiny dwelling units. The Project demonstrated that technically, economically and socially it is feasible in multi-family houses as well, usually three- or four-storey buildings with eighteen to forty housing units, each owned by its dwellers. The evidence came from low- and moderate-income residential areas which had not been pre-planned for change. The remodelling and enlargements usually took place while the family continued to reside in the apartment.

The lessons of the Project Renewal enlargement programme are relevant to both developed and developing countries, all of which have low- and moderate-income populations in old houses and blocks and all of which are interested in affordable improvement programmes. Major changes, including division of one residential unit into two, combination of two units into one, and additions of living and service spaces, can be made without evacuating the residents, in small as well as in large buildings. They can be economically worthwhile, sometimes depending on whose point of view is being considered and what items are included in the calculations. They can be organised by devoted project managers and/or community workers, even where each building includes a few dozen families all of whom are property owners, and they may be highly desirable as key elements in preventing the decline of urban neighbourhoods and encouraging revitalisation of deteriorated residential areas.

Public-Individual Partnership

The common denominator of the successful housing programmes of Project Renewal was their being public-individual enterprises. The do-it-yourself external renovation programme is an excellent example: half of the resources were contributed by the public (the Project) and the other half by the tenants of the renovated buildings, either in cash or in labour. The programme for selling public housing to their tenants and the programme to encourage renovations and enlargements by owner-occupants assisted the tenants through large loans with convenient terms of return; a large public subsidy was involved in these, but the tenants also had to invest a great deal of their resources throughout the period of loan return. In many cases of housing enlargements, it was reported that the residents investments from their own savings and from private loans were larger than the public loans allocated to them.

What we see does not resemble the public-private partnership which has been much in fashion in Western countries in recent years, that is, the partnership between public authorities and holders of private capital who establish an economic enterprise to provide employment, housing, or any other service to the poor. This is an indirect means of assistance by the government through private entrepreneurs, who oftentimes tend "to cream" it.

In contrast, Project Renewal created public-individual partnerships: partnerships between a public body and a needy individual. The advantage of this method is first, in the direct transfer of the subsidy to the person in need, with no losses to various middlemen, i.e. economic efficiency in resource redistribution. The public-individual partnership has at least two other important advantages: it encourages independence instead of dependence among groups of disadvantaged, and it increases the chances of good maintenance by the tenants, i.e., it increases sustainability of the products. The method appears to be efficient in the short-run as well as the long-run.

Hence, a lesson which can be learned from Project Renewal's experience in the field of housing is that public-individual partnerships can serve as effective and efficient tools in neighbourhood rehabilitation programmes, especially those which are also aimed at reducing disparities among socio-economic groups. Public-individual partnerships appear to be very useful in enhancing housing improvement at affordable prices.

EPILOGUE

When planners aim at goals that contradict spontaneous market forces, they frequently fail. The conclusion is that rather than working against the current, planners should identify and work with those currents which lead in the direction of a positive change. They should recognise spontaneous trends that incorporate desirable attributes and invest deliberate effort in their direction.

A current trend of this nature is the movement of people and business back to the city. Planners may use this historical opportunity to realise their goals, including the improvement of housing conditions for low- and moderate-income households in the cities. They are urged to consider strategies such as the ones suggested above which combine public support with encouragement of individual initiative. In this way they may be above to prevent over-dependence of the individuals assisted, while at the same time enlarging the expected multiplier of public investment.

In our experience, a significant contribution to increasing the stock of affordable decent housing may be achieved, when planners find the "golden path" between government intervention and private enterprise of individual citizens of the lower strata. This golden path, however, is not a constant; it differs from one society to another and from time to time. Therefore, one should start with careful study of the experience of others and then feel free to modify the formula in accordance with the particular conditions and circumstances of one's environment.

NOTES

1. See Hughes and Sternlieb (1987) for American data, Malpass and Murie (1982) for British data and Haber-Fisch (1985) for Israeli data.
2. For additional details regarding programmes and prices, see Lerman *et al.*, (1985). The fluctuations are due to the rate of linkage during this period of inflation; the price in Israeli Shekels often lagged behind the value of the apartment in relation to the American dollar. The average price of an Amidar apartment in 1982-83 was approximately US $10,000.
3. In a detailed test carried out in one of the neighbourhoods it was found that the upper rate of potential owners was 75 per cent of households (of the remainder, 12 per cent were chronic welfare cases, 10 per cent elderly, and 4 per cent involved in family conflicts). See Lerman *et al.*, (1985).
4. This quality evaluation was administered by architect Arie Gonen, who specialises in building maintenance. I would like to thank him for his contribution.

REFERENCES

Alterman, R. *et al.* (1984), 'Integrated Evaluation: A Synthesis of Approaches to the Evaluation of Broad-Aim Social Programmes'. *Socio-Economic Planning Sciences.* 18(6): 381-389.

American Public Health Association, Committee of the Hygiene of Housing (1950). *Planning the Home for Occupancy.* Chicago, Public Administration Service.

Anderson, M. (1965), 'Fiasco of Urban Renewal'. *Harvard Business Review.* 43(1): 6-21.

Bradbury, K.L. *et al.* (1982), *Urban Decline and Future of American Cities.* Washington D.C., The Brookings Institute.

Burns, L.S. and Grebler, L. (1986), *The Future of Housing Markets: A New Appraisal.* New York, Plenum Press.

Carmon, N. (1985), *The Social and Physical Outcomes of Project Renewal.* Haifa: Technion — Israel Institute of Technology (Hebrew).

——— (1987), 'A Neighbourhood Programme that Works: Israel's Project Renewal'. *Policy Studies Journal.*

——— and Oxman, R. (1981), *Self-Help Housing Rehabilitation in Distressed Neighbourhoods.* Haifa, Technion — Israel Institute of Technology (Hebrew).

——— and Gavrieli T. (1982), *Alternatives for Improving Public Housing in Israel — A Comparative Analysis.* Haifa, Technion — Israel Institute of Technology (Hebrew).

——— and Hill, M. (1984), 'Project Renewal: An Israeli Experiment in Neighbourhood Rehabilitation'. *Habitat International.* 8(2): 117-132.

——— and Vienberg, A. (1986), *Participatory Housing Enlargements in Multi-Storey Buildings.* Haifa, Technion — Israel Institute of Technology (Hebrew).

——— and Oxman, R. (1986) 'Responsive Public Housing: An Alternative for Low-Income Families'. *Environment and Behaviour.* 18(2): 258-284.

——— and Gavrieli, T. (1987), 'Improving Housing by Conventional Versus Self-Help Methods: Evidence from Israel'. *Urban Studies,* 24(4): 324-332.

Clay, P. (1979), *Neighbourhood Renewal: Middle-Class Resettlement and Incumbent Upgrading.* Lexington, Mass., D.C. Heath and Company.

——— (1981), *Neighbourhood Partnerships in Action.* Washington, D.C., Neighbourhood Reinvestment Corporation.

Gans, H.J. (1965), 'The Failure of Urban Renewal: A Critique and Some Proposals'. *Commentary.* (April): 29-37.

Haber-Fisch, A. (1985), *Urban Settlements: Housing Stock and Demographic Characteristics.* Jerusalem, The Ministry of Construction and Housing.

Harpaz, H. *et al.* (1978), *Attitudes Towards Living Conditions in Tel Aviv Neighbourhoods.* Tel Aviv, The Centre of Economic and Social Research.

Hughes, J.W. and Sternlieb, G. (1987), *The Dynamics of America's Housing.* New Brunswick, Rutgers, The State University of New Jersey.

Lerman, R. *et al.* (1985), *Project Renewal Housing Initiatives: Their Impact on Housing Conditions and Housing Values.* Jerusalem, Brookdale Institute.

Mayer, R.W. and Enis, R. (1981), *Development of Open Spaces in Givat Olga.* Haifa, Technion — Israel Institute of Technology.

Malpass, P. and Murie, A. (1982), *Housing Policy and Practice.* London, Macmillan.

Milgram, G. (1979), *The Rationale for Assisted Housing: A Review and Discussion.* Washington, D.C., Congressional Research Service, The Library of Congress.

Musil, J. (1962), 'The Sociological Approach in Planning Workers' Housing: The Experience of Czechoslovakia'. *International Labour Review.* 86: 545-86.

Schussheim, M. (1987), *U.S. Housing: Problems and Politics.* Washington, D.C., Congressional Research Service, The Library of Congress.

Shuval, J. *et al.* (1968), *Social Research in Jerusalem Neighbourhoods.* Jerusalem, The Centre for Applied Social Research (Hebrew).

15

LOW-COST HOUSING FINANCE IN DEVELOPING COUNTRIES: With Reference to Egypt

MEDHAT M. HASSAN

INTRODUCTION

Most of existing housing problems can be justifiably considered universal. However, the precise nature and circumstances characterising these problems and their solutions differ between and within countries. It has also become apparent that the best solution to such problems is to define and quantify them as precisely as possible and then to find ways and means of using whatever resources are available to solve them.

While the provision of housing in the more developed countries often presents difficulties, the problems are aggravated on a greater scale in developing countries. This is mainly due to the lack of basic essential resources such as finance, trained manpower at all levels and an adequate management structure. These factors pose a most difficult problem as housing must compete with other forms of development for its share of inadequate or very limited resources.

The first step in any attempt to solve this problem is mainly political, as to the priority of housing and the allocation of the financial and other resources that can be devoted to it. The effective organisation and utilisation of the available investment is the next step.

On the other hand, measures that be taken to increase the volume of capital allocated to housing. Stimulating private savings, the use of housing subsidies, reducing housing cost, and the use of low-cost methods of construction are examples of such measures.

HOUSING AND THE ECONOMY

One of the important reasons for the accumulation of housing problems was that housing has long been considered a subordinate requirement. Urban economists have always viewed housing as consuming rather than producing asset. They argued that a developing country should pay more attention to food production and should concentrate on assets that advance productivity. The United Nations (1961), however, have, for a long time, recommended that a balance expenditure on social and economic development is essential. Housing should be acknowledged as a necessity of life, and should be recognised as an important element of the economic growth of the country.

A well organised housing programme can employ people productively, particularly in cities where there is an influx of migrants. A housing programme can also play an important part in developing savings and in releasing unproductive capital into the economy. Housing construction can be essential to the development of many other industries, such as production of building materials, not only for dwelling but for all types of construction (Abrams, 1964). As regards housing shortages in Egypt, these are largely a result of the descending priority of housing in the economic development over the last 40 years. The percentage of national expenditure on housing has fallen from 32 per cent in 1952-53, at first gradually to 30 per cent in 1957, and then sharply to 11.8 per cent in 1961-62 (Hassan, 1980). Between 1965 and 1975, investment in housing averaged 21 per cent every year. This percentage was slightly reduced to an average of 20 per cent each year during the First Development Plan 1976-81, including the capital allocated for utilities and services (Ministry of Planning *et al.*, 1976).

It is obvious that these levels of investment in housing were small in comparison to the enormous housing deficit figures. This suggests the importance of seeking alternative lower cost solutions for shelter to maximise the number of units actually built with the investment levels available.

Even in the few cases where a large percentage of the gross fixed investment was allocated to housing, it was not benefiting the people in the lower income categories. The high cost of loan services and the required guarantees and securities were among the long list of forbidding obstacles that prevented low-income families from using government capital in building their own houses.

Economic development in Egypt, as in any other developing

country, has suffered for a long time critical problems that have had great effects on housing. However, the government has started, very recently, to take considerable measures to overcome these difficulties. One important measure was the formulation of the Five-Year Development Plans to the year 2000, with a target real growth in the economy of 6.5 per cent.

The first of these plans was the 1976-81, the second 1981-86, and the third 1986-91. These plans concentrated mainly on four basic policies:

(a) the encouragement of foreign investment;
(b) the build-up of the private sector;
(c) the restructuring of the public sector to improve efficiency; and
(d) an increase in labour productivity.

In the First Plan, it was intended to prepare annual plans with detailed programmes and budgets. The first two years, however, have been designated as transitional years with sever budgetary constraints and great obstacles to overcome. By 1981, the end of the First Plan, it was the first time that a surplus had been achieved in the balance of payments and foreign exchange was being made sufficiently available through the flow of foreign investment and through the growing savings of the Egyptians working abroad. Foreign debt charges had been reduced by rescheduling loan payments and by shifting to intermediate and long-term loans to avoid expensive suppliers' facilities. Nevertheless, government investment in housing and related facilities was still far from what has been actually needed to solve the problems of the low-income majority.

Since the First Plan, however, several changes in the economic system have occurred in Egypt that have had important implications on housing policies. One that is worth noting is related to income distribution. The major sources of change in income distribution were mainly Egyptians working abroad, and the rapidly growing foreign and joint investment which paid several multiples of the average salary of government employees. Most of these additional incomes, however, have gone to upper- and upper-middle-income groups. Although not a small portion has filtered down to the lower-income brackets, it has not been felt because of the broad base of the income pyramid.

Another major feature of the changes in the economic system in Egypt was the economic role and resources under direct governmental control. In the past, surpluses of all other sectors used to be transferred to government. The government would then allocate them according to its priorities. According to the changes that have been introduced into the system, non-government sectors are allowed to retain their surpluses. The resources under direct government control as a percentage of total available resources have accordingly declined.

These changes have had direct impact on housing policies. First, the change in income distribution which was skewed towards the higher income groups has required parallel changes in the types of housing produced. The past division of housing units being built according to the formula: 70 per cent to low-income housing, 20 per cent to middle-income and 10 per cent to upper-income could not be strictly maintained. The result was an excessive demand for higher income housing and, consequently, an excessive drain of scarce foreign exchange resources in importing luxurious building materials for new housing types.

Second, the government in the past was responsible for the total supply of low-income housing. Currently with the rise of construction costs over ten times during the last decade, the government could not maintain its past policies. If the decline in the share of government-controlled resources to national available resources was added, an immediate change in government housing policies and role becomes imperative (Montasser, 1978).

SOURCES OF CAPITAL FOR HOUSING

One of the immediate changes required in government housing policies is to establish adequate programmes to increase the flow of capital into the housing market. The importance of such programmes becomes more apparent when comparing the cost of housing currently being produced with what any low-income family can afford to pay for shelter. Although some attempts are being made to overcome the great shortage of housing, the problem is still very serious especially in the large urban centres where construction has not been able to keep up with the flow of rural migrants attracted by the growing new joint investment. The total number of dwelling units being built every year in Cairo, for example, represents only 25 per cent of the housing units actually needed to overcome housing deficiencies in the city.

Nonetheless, government action will still be needed to provide the moving force behind any attempt to increase the total volume of capital required for housing investment. Although, some reallocation of resources may be desirable between sectors, and within the housing sector itself, it is expected that the bulk of additional resources should be made available through more efficient construction and administrative methods, increased savings and as a result of a growing national income.

Any government programmes to solve the problems of housing finance should take into consideration the following actions.

Stimulating Private Savings

This can be accomplished voluntarily by making saving more convenient and attractive, or through compulsory action such as increasing taxes or payroll deductions for special purposes. Public savings programmes may be the only feasible method of getting any popular programmes started. One of the most promising methods of mobilising savings is through the sale of public bonds issued for a special purpose such as housing. However, there would be a net benefit to the economy only if the savings that are invested in these bonds represent additional savings and are not merely siphoned off from some other investment use.

Government, however, can make an important contribution to the promotion of an increased flow of savings into the housing sector by providing the legal, administrative and institutional framework within which private individuals, co-operative groups and special-purpose corporate bodies who are interested in housing and related facilities, can operate at maximum levels of efficiency. The promotional activities that the government can take to increase the flow of private savings into housing would include:

(a) The establishment of a Central Housing Bank with authority to supervise new special-purpose savings and financing institutions. The government has already established such a bank and some time is needed before its benefits can reach the low-income groups and before detailed evaluation can be made on its function.

(b) The creation of a system of ensuring individual savings deposits.

(c) The promotion of mortgage lending on the part of both new and existing financial institutions.

(d) The encouragement of private co-operative savings and building systems.
(e) The establishment of flexible rent control laws.
(f) An interest supplement programme which be initiated by government whereby it makes up the difference between what borrowers can pay and the minimum yield demanded by the private investors. An important element in this operation is the stream of income necessary to provide the differential over the period of the loan or investment. This can be provided through direct appropriations from either central, regional or local governments, earmarked taxes, income from existing or new projects and international aid (United Nations, 1968).

The Use of Subsidies

Subsidies have been used in many countries, developed and developing, in different forms as a tool of public policy to provide housing for low-income households unable to afford housing in the private market. In the United States, for example, various approaches have been introduced. One approach was to allocate direct subsidies to low-income families in the form of mortgage interest and property tax deductions from taxable personal income. Another approach was to provide reduced land costs through purchasing and reselling land at a below market price. A third approach was to lower the cost of capital utilising different mechanisms. Such mechanisms included a below market interest rate loan, insurance and guarantees to the private mortgage lender against access on the loan, and a graduated rate mortgage where the interest rate is very low in the early years and then gradually increases over time along with the family income.

Subsidies have generally been justified as a means of redistributing income. As such, they must compete with subsidies for education, health and other socio-economic developments. The economic significance of housing makes it a prime candidate in many instances for consideration for subsidy. Yet, if care is not taken in their selection and application, housing subsidies can accrue to the higher income families, thereby depriving the poor of needed resources.

In this regard, it may be suggested that, instead of subsidising the building materials for example, subsidies would be given to the finished dwelling units that comply with specified standards for low-income dwellings. Moreover, subsidisation of the rent may be introduced in some cases to help the low-income tenants who cannot afford to pay full rent in the private housing market.

This approach is consistent with the argument that it is far less costly to subsidise the consumer directly than to subsidise the producer. Basically, it is far less expensive, given a limited amount of resources, to give the money directly to people and let them use their own ingenuity, their own intuition, and do their own search, rather than for the government to build new housing for the lowest income people when even people of somewhat higher incomes cannot afford new housing. Nonetheless, there is another argument that there will be always the fear of spending the direct user subsidies on unnecessary goods rather than improving housing standards. However, there are different ways to overcome this problem. In some cases the government would actually pay a percentage of the rent paid by the eligible tenant. Another way is for the government to give the low-income family an earmarked, or a conditional income transfer to be spent only on housing.

The study that had been made in Egypt by the Joint Housing Team of the Ministry of Planning, Ministry of Housing and Reconstruction, and Agency for International Development in 1976, had suggested that the government would provide more housing services through direct housing subsidies than if income transfer had been given to individual households (Ministry of Planning *et al.*, 1976).

Table 15.1 summarises the range of requirements, unit costs and subsidies on different assumptions of unit size and sq m costs for different income groups.

The study assumed that if a low-income household had an annual income of L.E. 600 and on the basis of its needs for food and other necessities, the household should invest 17 per cent of its income in acquiring a housing unit. This household then has the ability to pay L.E. 102 per year for its housing services. This payment will allow the purchase of a unit costing approximately L.E. 1,344 (over a thirty-year period at 6.5 per cent interest). If the government is willing and able to provide this family with a dwelling costing L.E. 2,500 the cost to government in providing the capital for this unit may be approximated as L.E. 191.44 per year. By providing this unit, the government has, theoretically, increased the household's income by 32 per cent and has substantially increased the amount and per cent of income used for housing.

TABLE 15.1: Unit Cost Range and Subsidy Required on Different Assumptions of Unit Size and sq in Costs

Group	Unit Cost	Size	Cost Per sq m	Average Subsidy	Percentage of Subsidy
B	3,900	65	60	423	11
	2,750	55	50	0	0
	2,475 *	55	45	0	0
C	3,025	55	55	1,182	39
	2,025	45	45	182	9
	1,800 *	45	40	0	0
Standard					
D	2,250	45	50	1,307	58
	1,600	40	40	657	41
	1,400 *	40	35	457	33
E	2,250	45	50	2,048	91
	1,600	40	40	1,398	87
	1,400 *	40	35	1,198	86
Core					
D	875	25	35	0	0
	375	15	20	0	0
E	875	25	35	673	77
	375	15	20	173	46

* Costs considered possible through improved design.

If, instead of providing the house, the government provided the family with additional L.E. 191.44 per year, the family would have had a total income of L.E. 791.44 per year. If the household's willingness to invest still stands at 17 per cent of their income, their actual housing expenditure would rise to L.E. 134.55 per year. This would be consistent with a housing unit having a value of L.E. 175.7. Thus, the government has placed the family in a home having a value approximately L.E. 743 greater than that what they would have chosen if they were given an income rather than a housing supplement.

Reducing Housing Cost

It is very important, in order to increase the number of dwelling units offered to low-income families, to reduce the total cost of the dwellings through the use of minimum standards, the use of minimum size required for the basic needs of the household, and the use of local building materials. It is also important to search for an appropriate method of construction in order to reduce the time over which the building is complete.

The research that had been in 1978, jointly, by a team from the Messachusetts Institute of Technology and Cairo University on housing and construction industry developed detailed cost figures for the construction of several prototypical buildings, using various conventional building methods. These include cement skeleton, load bearing brick, and stone wall construction. The research estimated the detailed usage of materials and labour per sq m of construction for each of these building systems. To continue their effort, the research team had developed some tentative estimates for the cost of building identical structures with the large-panel prefabrication system that were then under erection. The comparison of the different systems revealed the following results:

(a) The cement skeleton method of construction cost about 12 per cent more, and large-panel prefabrication about 40 per cent more than the most commonly used method of load bearing brick wall construction.

(b) While prefabricated construction clearly used more capital than other methods, the results have suggested that there was no compensating reduction in labour or materials, as is sometimes alleged to be the conventional rationale for the system. With the Egyptian estimates, labour, capital, and materials costs were all higher under prefabrication.

The results of this study are summarised in Table 15.2. These results, while suggestive, do not necessarily mean that attempts to prefabricate housing should be discontinued. It could be the case that changes in factor prices, for example, would make the system more competitive. It also may be true that with substantial improvement in design, a variant on the system could be developed which would significantly reduce material and labour usage.

The Use of Low-Cost Methods of Construction

The introduction of core housing, as a major variant of the self-help technique, into the developing countries by the United Nations missions, aimed to provide an organised, cheap and practical scheme for the urban and urbanising areas of these countries. The UN missions, have spread the idea which is now becoming an important building device in many developing countries. One advantage of core housing is that it can be mass-produced on the site at a considerable saving. It entails no extensive supervision. It requires a tract of land and the essential utilities, after which the cores can be erected in one mass operation.

TABLE 15.2: Aggregate Costs of Construction Technologies (L.E.*/m²)

	Load bearing brick	Skeleton	Prefabrication
TOTAL COSTS	61.0 (51.0)[1]	67.0 (55.0)	84.0 (60.0)
Materials	45.0 (35.0)	52.4 (40.4)	58.0 (39.0)
Labour	16.0	14.6	17.6
Capital	0.0[2]	0.0	7.8 (3.3)

1. Figures in parentheses use "official-market" prices, all others use "shadow-market" prices.
2. Included in materials and labour cost.

* In 1978 $ 1 = L.E. 0.70

Source: C.U./M.I.T. Joint Research Team, Interim Report Working Papers, 1978.

Some experimental projects, site and services and core housing, have been carried out in different locations in Egypt to demonstrate the feasibility for the development of low-cost housing in adequate quantity to meet the basic requirements of safe and sanitary dwellings.

When applying a core-housing scheme in an urban area, however, there are some measures to be considered carefully:

(a) The core house would not substitute the walk-up apartment building in dense areas. Its greater use is linked to the development of transportation and the opening-up of land areas on the outskirts of cities. It would face major obstacles where land costs are inordinately high.

(b) Unless a house is planned as a core from the beginning, a core-housing project may deteriorate into a slum. Experience in developing countries shows that even families in the lowest income brackets manage to improve and enlarge their homes as the years go by. Hence, the layouts and placement of the houses must be planned for expansion. Provision should be made, in the original plan, for services, public spaces, landscaping, playgrounds, and even car parking.

(c) Loan funds must be made available for interior improvement and future expansion.

(d) Care must be exercised in selecting applicants. Temporary residents are not likely to invest in additions or alterations. Where the house is too far from work, the occupant will hesitate to make improvements. Jobs and security of job status are factors in all housing undertakings, and core housing is no exception. Since people with common interests are more apart to cohere into a community and help one another, the aim of a sound community interest should be kept always in mind.

(e) Initiating training programmes in house building to increase the tenants' ability to build for themselves. Thus, labour cost, as well as the total cost of the completed houses, will be reduced. These programmes would also benefit the un- and under-employed workers to learn new skills and, consequently, improve their income and their living standards.

CONCLUSIONS

It should be recognised that the national context within which housing resources must be increased is greatly constrained. The existing housing deficits are enormous and the economy, although improving, cannot support the level of housing investment which can actually overcome the shortages or even keep up with the new demand.

The main objective of any housing policy, however, should be to achieve the maximum addition to the net existing housing stock. This would require a concerted effort to manage the limited resources in the most efficient way. The current policies and regulations should be revised in order to fulfil certain objectives:

(a) Reduce the average cost of dwelling units in the public and private sectors in order to build more units with the same level of capital investment. This will be possible by reducing the average size of dwelling units, lowering the standards of infrastructure and by improving the building technologies used.

(b) The semi-public and private sectors must be encouraged to play a larger role in housing production. This includes overcoming the problems of mobilisation of finance, shortage in building materials and rent control.

(c) Initiating an emergency programme to concentrate on meeting the needs of the lowest income households who cannot afford to participate in the regular public housing programmes. This programme should seek to conserve the existing housing stock, upgrade the existing levels of services and public facilities, and provide opportunities for expansion to new areas through core housing and site and services projects, to relieve the crisis of overcrowding.

d) Initiating national training programmes in house building to increase the needed skilled labour force.

(e) Finally, all the above objectives should be integrated into an overall comprehensive housing policy which can set a suitable framework within which all various institutions concerned with housing can operate, and which relates housing to the overall national development planning.

REFERENCES

Abrams, C. (1964), *Housing in the Modern World*, London, Faber and Faber :106-110.

Cairo University/M.I.T. (1978), 'An Economic Evaluation of Alternative Technologies for Constructing Housing in Egypt' in *Housing and Construction Industry in Egypt: Interim Report Working Papers*, Section II, Cairo : 29-41.

Cairo University/M.I.T. (1979), 'Project Summaries' in *Proceedings of the Seminar: Core Housing and Site and Services Projects for Low-Income Groups*, Cairo, Ministry of Housing : 15-43.

Hassan, M.M. (1980), 'The Role of Government in Aiding Housing for Low-Income Groups', in *Proceedings of the German-Egyptian Seminar on Housing Problems*, Dec. 13-16: 252-280.

Ministry of Planning *et al.* (1976), *Immediate Action Proposals for Housing in Egypt*, Cairo.

Montasser, E. (1978), 'The Housing Sector as a Component in Egypt's Development Planning', in *Proceedings of the Seminar on Development of New Approaches to Housing Policy and Production in Egypt*, Cairo, Ministry of Housing and Reconstruction : 42-61.

United Nations (1961), *Report of the Economic and Social Council*, 16th Session, New York.

United Nations (1968), *Finance for Housing and Community Facilities in Developing Countries*, New York, ST/SOA/79.

INDEX